Our Place on Campus

Our Place on Campus

Lesbian, Gay, Bisexual, Transgender
Services and Programs in Higher Education

Edited by
Ronni Sanlo, Sue Rankin *and* Robert Schoenberg

The Greenwood Educators' Reference Collection

GREENWOOD PRESS
Westport, Connecticut • London

Library of Congress Cataloging-in-Publication Data

Our place on campus : lesbian, gay, bisexual, transgender services and programs in higher education / edited by Ronni Sanlo, Sue Rankin, and Robert Schoenberg.
    p. cm.—(Greenwood educators' reference collection)
    Includes bibliographical references and index.
    ISBN 0–313–31406–3 (alk. paper)
    1. Gay college students—Services for—United States. 2. Lesbian college students—Services for—United States. 3. Bisexual college students—Services for—United States. 4. Transsexual college students—Services for—United States. 5. Homosexuality and education—United States. I. Sanlo, Ronni L., 1947– II. Rankin, Sue. III. Schoenberg, Robert. IV. Series.
    LC2574.6.O85 2002
    378.1'9826'64—dc21   2001058632

British Library Cataloguing in Publication Data is available.

Library of Congress Catalog Card Number: 2001058632
ISBN: 0–313–31406–3
ISSN: 1056–2192

First published in 2002

Greenwood Press, 88 Post Road West, Westport, CT 06881
An imprint of Greenwood Publishing Group, Inc.
www.greenwood.com

Printed in the United States of America

The paper used in this book complies with the Permanent Paper Standard issued by the National Information Standards Organization (Z39.48–1984).

10 9 8 7 6 5 4 3 2 1

Copyright Acknowledgments

The author and publisher gratefully acknowledge permission for use of the following:

Chapter 16, "The Lavender Leader: An Inqueery into Lesbian, Gay, Bisexual, and Transgender Student Leadership" by Ronni Sanlo appeared in *Case Studies and Best Practices in Higher Education*, edited by Charles L. Outcalt, Shannon K. Faris, and Kathleen McMahon (Greenwood Press, 2000). Reprinted with permission of Greenwood Press.

Appendix M is reprinted with permission of the National Consortium of Directors of LGBT Resources in Higher Education and their website www.lgbtcampus.org.

Portions of Chapter 18, "Lavender Graduation: Acknowledging the Lives and Achievements of LGBT College Students" by Ronni Sanlo appeared in the *Journal of College Student Development* (Vol. 41, number 6, pp. 643–647). Reprinted with permission of the American College Personnel Association.

To our students at UCLA,
the University of Pennsylvania,
and Pennsylvania State University

and in memory of
Matthew Shepard
1977–1998

Contents

Part III. Identifying and Providing Programs and Services

Part IV. Maintaining Your Center

Part V. Appendices

Acknowledgments

As it seems to "take a village to raise a child," so it took a consortium to write this book. We are deeply grateful to our friends and colleagues of the National Consortium of Directors of Lesbian, Gay, Bisexual, and Transgender Resources in Higher Education (Consortium) for their assistance, contributions, ideas, and encouragement for this book. We stand in awe of them as they do this hard and loving work at their institutions. We especially thank our colleagues and friends who submitted the case studies based on their experiences at their campuses that appear in this book: Saralyn Chesnut, Emory; David Barnett, University of Illinois, Chicago; Elizabeth Davenport and Mary Andres, University of Southern California; Shaun Travers, Texas A&M; Therese Eyermann, University of California, Los Angeles (UCLA); Shane Snowdon, University of California, San Francisco; Luke Jensen, University of Maryland, College Park; E. Frederic Dennis, University of Michigan; Pat Walsh and Christine Browning, University of California, Irvine; Sine Anahita, Iowa State University; Janice Austin and Christopher Nguyen, University of Pennsylvania; Carol Fischer, Indiana University; Willa Young, Ohio State University; Brent Bilodeau, Michigan State University; Kristen Renn, Michigan State University; Meylyndah Huskey, Washington State University; Heather Lockridge and Leily Saadat, University of Pennsylvania; Brett Beemyn, University of Iowa; Pat Alford-Keating, UCLA; Steven Leider and Charles Harless, UCLA; Erin Cross, University of Pennsylvania; Bev Tuel, Colorado; Margie Cook, Northern Illinois University; Belmont Freeman, Yale; Richard Johnson, UCLA; Beth Harrison-Prado, University of Michigan; Shane Windmeyer, Indiana University; Christine Browning, University of California, Irvine; Jonathan Winters, University of California, Berkeley; Becky Ross, University of Pennsylvania; and Angela Nichols, University of Minnesota.

We thank Greenwood Press, especially Jane Garry, for giving us the opportunity to present our profession in a way that makes it accessible to any college or university. Marcia Goldstein provided both the guidance and the prodding as this book was in a variety of iterations. Nina Duprey and her production team maintained patience and a sense of calm regardless of how frantic we became. We are grateful to these women who guided us every step of the way.

Three national student affairs organizations have worked in eager collaboration with us and with the consortium as we attempted to raise the position of center director for lesbian, gay, bisexual, transgender (LGBT) issues to a professional standing in higher education. The National Association of Student Personnel Administrators (NASPA), the Council for the Advancement of Standards in Higher Education (CAS), and the American College Personnel Association (ACPA) provide ongoing active, visible support for LGBT people in higher education. We are especially grateful to the national board of CAS for the development and publication of standards and guidelines for LGBT services and programs.

The National Gay and Lesbian Task Force continues to provided a wealth of assistance to the consortium and to the three of us individually. We thank them for their continued teamwork. We are especially grateful to them for putting their indispensable *Campus Organizing Manual* on the Web where it is free for the downloading.

Bret Beemyn extends his deepest appreciation to David Barnett, Mindy Michels, Beverly Tuel, and Harold Wechsler for their assistance in designing the survey instrument he used in his chapter. He also thanks the center/office directors who participated in his study and the designers of the National Consortium of Directors of LGBT Resources in Higher Education's Web site (www.lgbtcampus.org), where he obtained his initial information.

Ronni acknowledges her supervisor, Dr. Robert Naples, assistant vice chancellor for student and campus life at UCLA, for his encouragement and support of the LGBT Campus Resource Center and of Ronni's work. Ronni understands that she occasionally challenges Bob's sensibilities and appreciates his being such a great sport. She thanks her parents, Lois and Sandy Lebman, her greatest cheerleaders, for their constant faith and pride in her. She offers deep gratitude to Steven Leider for his excellent coffee, and is indebted to her colleague and friend Beth Zemsky for the vital heart-to-heart discussions about our work throughout the years. With abiding friendship, Ronni is grateful to Robyn Punch for the "balance" breaks and excellent adventures to tropical places, and to Sarah Hodell for bringing a special grounding and the excitement of "aloha" into her life as this work was being completed. Finally, Ronni thanks her LGBT students at UCLA, who continue to remind her with their grace and their courage why she does this work.

Sue thanks all who have gone before her who paved the way for her to do this work. She offers a special thanks to her mom and the rest of her family for their unconditional love. They provided Sue with the strength of soul to carry on when she wanted to run and supported her in all of her life choices. Sue is also grateful to her teachers Mary Romeo and Ree Arnold for offering their guidance and encouragement and to her friends, colleagues, and students who helped her to realize that while this work is often hard, we are never alone.

Bob thanks his family and friends for their love and support, his colleagues at the University of Pennsylvania and throughout the country for their wisdom and dedication, and the many students with whom he has worked over the years for their commitment and inspiration. Together they changed the world.

As a team, we acknowledge the courage and strength of soul of our students at UCLA, the University of Pennsylvania, and Pennsylvania State University, who serve as our inspiration for doing this work. We lovingly and sadly acknowledge Matthew Shepard and countless others who lost their lives because of ignorance and hatred. Most profoundly, we acknowledge and feel the loss of those students who took their own lives because they thought that they had no one with whom to talk.

Finally, we are deeply, deeply grateful to our best cheerleader and pal, Dr. Curt Shepard, for his vision, his courage, and his loving friendship.

Introduction

The death of Matthew Shepard profoundly saddened and shocked campus lesbian, gay, bisexual, and transgender communities and their allies around the nation. For campus administrators who serve LGBT students, Matthew's story is our worst nightmare—an innocent young man murdered, his family, friends, and community devastated, simply because he was himself, because he courageously chose to tell the truth about his sexual orientation. We offer our deepest condolences to all who knew and loved Matthew during his short life, and we share the pain felt by campuses across the nation.

Matthew's tragic, unnecessary death reminds us of the climate of fear in which LGBT students must live. Sadly, his story is an extreme version of what many LGBT students face each day: discrimination, harassment, verbal abuse, and, all too often, physical violence. Every day, students are targeted merely because of who they are. We cannot permit this climate of intimidation to prevail. All students, LGBT or not, deserve access to safe and respectful educational environments where they can reach their full potential.

The homophobic tone of recent public discourse must bear its share of responsibility as well. When powerful people—politicians, ministers, civic leaders, and editorialists—use their positions to spread ill-informed, hateful opinions, they create a climate in which others feel justified in using violence.

As people who care about the safety and well-being of LGBT college students, we urgently call on every community to take a stand against homophobic violence. It's too late to save Matthew Shepard, but we can and must take steps to create a safe environment for all youth, both on and off campus.

LGBT students are arriving on campuses every year with the expectations that their voices will be heard, their concerns acknowledged, their needs met, and their educational environments welcoming. Institutions with LGBT campus resource centers or offices are prepared not only to provide services for LGBT students but also to help the campus move toward becoming a welcoming community and to serve the entire campus community in the areas of diversity and social justice.

As Smith (1998) noted LGBT students are demanding their own resource centers. Increasingly, institutions are adding them. These centers—similar to women's, Latino, and African American centers common to many campuses today—are important places for LGBT students to feel safe and to have access to needed materials as well as to meet others like themselves.

Demands for LGBT resource centers and curriculum change tend to be the central issues for much of the agenda of LGBT student activism on campuses. However, basic issues such as coming out are still critical for most LGBT students. To respond, many colleges and universities are developing diversity and sensitivity training programs for campus units such as their police departments, the Greek system, health care providers, faculty, staff, and others. Some campuses are also employing "safe space" programs.

Coming out at a campus with an acknowledged inclusive environment complete with an LGBT center or office is much different from coming out at institutions that have a history for being intolerant. Smith (1998) described the climate, for example, at Brigham Young University (BYU):

As recently as the late 1970s and early 1980s, coming out had life-and-death consequences for students. Reports of BYU gay students being subjected to electroshock and other forms of therapy and a high rate of gay student suicide helped prompt the formation of Affirmation, an organization of gay and lesbian Mormons. Progress has been made, however. Sam Clayton, a BYU senior and one of a small number of openly gay students, says the university marked a milestone in 1997 when the administration made a statement that regardless of sexual orientation, students were welcome as long as they stick to the campus' honor code which requires all students to be celibate unless married. Clayton says it is ironic that it is the honor code which allows him and other students to be openly gay. At the same time, the administration has turned down a request for formation of a student club on sexuality, saying it would be too controversial, according to Clayton. And the BYU Men's Issues Group still attempts to convince gay students to become heterosexual, he says. Nevertheless, Clayton believes the university is open to dialogue on the issue. And he sees signs of hope that change will occur. For example, he conducted a survey a year ago that found that 56 percent of BYU students agreed that homosexuals should be able to attend the university as long as they stick to the honor code. And he is encouraged that his department, sociology, agreed to let him do a study for his senior thesis of how gay and lesbian students have been treated at BYU.

In high schools around the country lesbian and gay students are winning cases against school districts because their schools failed to provide a safe environment for them. Puch (2000) wrote:

When school administrators think school safety, they should be thinking about policies to keep gay and lesbian students safe from harassment. If they don't, they could face legal troubles. Lambda Legal Defense helped win a verdict against Ashland, Wis., school officials who failed to take action when former student Jamie Nabozny was harassed and beaten. Nabozny received a nearly $1 million settlement. Gene Amberg, superintendent of the Urbana school district, said school officials need to be aware they can be held liable for failing to protect their students.

It is important that administrators in higher education take note of these types of litigation. It may be only a matter of time before a college student also files—and wins—a similar suit against a college or university. At the 1998 National Association for Student Affairs professionals (NASPA) Annual Convention in Philadelphia, a workshop on creating a welcoming campus environment for LGBT people was facilitated by Dick McKaig, vice president for student affairs at the University of Indiana, David Ambler, the vice chancellor for student affairs at the University of Kansas, and Mary Rouse, then dean of students at the University of Wisconsin Madison. While Ambler, Rouse, and McKaig acknowledged that there might be ethical dilemmas for some people, they emphasized the responsibility of senior student affairs officers (SSAO) to be true to the principles of student affairs: bigotry of any sort must not be tolerated on our campuses.

Rouse, Ambler, and McKaig offered a list of things that SSAOs might do to create a safe campus environment for LGBT people (Sanlo 1998a).

- Be aware of harassment and threats of violence
- Develop a good harassment reporting mechanism
- Know that LGBT people – including staff and faculty – are the most at-risk population on campus, at home, and even in their faith communities
- Know that this population has a huge suicide rate among young people
- Know the history of the LGBT civil rights movement
- Understand current politics
- Use inclusive language
- Give grants
- Go to events and programs
- Develop allies. Don't try to do this work alone
- Set up committees or task forces to address LGBT issues and as an instructional voice
- Interview potential staff for positive attitudes
- Talk about these issues, stir the pot, encourage folks to think and to act
- Conduct an audit of university materials and printed matter for inclusive and welcoming language
- Have good working relationships with student leaders for effective conflict mediation
- Services available for any student must be available for all students including LGBT students
- Work on these issues everyday, not just when there is a crisis
- Create an LGBT Campus Resource Center and hire a full-time professional director

Given the typically heterosexist values underlying higher education, the work involved in proactively addressing LGBT students and building a campus community inclusive and welcoming of LGBT faculty, students, and staff is often controversial and demanding. Advocates do not have an easy task. Systematically examining and publicizing the extent of the problems of violence, invisibility, and even inclusion and thoughtfully developing comprehensive intervention strategies are necessary steps to building support for change. One of the strategies employed by university and college administrators is the creation of LGBT resource centers or offices on campuses to provide for the needs of the LGBT members of the academic community.

This book is about the transformation of college and university campuses into places of welcome and respect, where social justice prevails. The purpose of this book is to provide suggested guidelines for people who are investigating the idea of establishing and operating LGBT centers or program offices on their own campuses. We present ideas for change in a myriad of ways and present in case-study format the ways in which some campuses have responded to the needs of their LGBT community.

Part I presents an overview of the history of LGBT centers in higher education. It discusses needs assessments, proposal development, and models of types of centers as well as issues related to documentation of the LGBT campus population. Part II provides information about starting an LGBT center or office. It discusses general information about hiring center directors and presents strategic development for successful action planning. Finally, it examines the importance of advisory boards for LGBT centers. Part III offers the selection and implementation of basic services and programs for centers or offices, while Part IV explores visibility, funding, and staffing issues in the context of an incredibly busy and active unit on campus.

A word about authorship and format: This book is a collaborative effort among three colleagues who have spent their years as friends building the profession of the LGBT campus resource center director. Unless a chapter or a case study author is specifically cited, the chapter or case study was written collectively by the team.

We hope that decision makers on campuses will allow their support of LGBT students, faculty, and staff to be made visible through their day-to-day actions, and that they will model the behaviors of change and inclusion, support programs, become knowledgeable, and make the hard decisions about serving this invisible population. We hope decision makers will do these things because they are true to their professional principles and because they know it's right. As Gandhi said, "Be the change you wish to see in the world." Our students and our institutions deserve nothing less.

Part I

LGBT Centers on Campus: What Are They and Why Do You Need Them?

Care more than others think is wise
Risk more than others think is safe
Dream more than others think is practical
Expect more than others think is possible

Leadershape

Chapter 1

An Overview of This New Profession in Higher Education

Matthew was a 21-year-old gay man. He was slight of frame, had been educated abroad, had studied German and Arabic, and had a particular interest in the Middle East. He was a political science major who wanted to be a diplomat and went to the University of Wyoming to further his studies. He found friends and joined a queer organization. According to his friends, Matthew was happy and, for the most part, felt safe. On October 8, following a queer organization meeting, Matthew met two men in a local bar. In his usual trusting manner, Matthew came out to them. Allegedly, they told him that they, too, were gay. Then they lured him from the meeting place, drove him out of town, beat him mercilessly, and hung him on a fence post, leaving him to die.

Gwen is a 20-year-old junior at Penn State. She grew up in a rural part of Pennsylvania and is an active member of her local church, teaching Sunday school and singing in the church choir. Gwen is also a lesbian who went to great lengths to keep her sexual identity a secret throughout her high school years. When she entered the university, she joined a queer group and decided to finally share her secret with her family. How did she tell them? When was the right time? On November 24, over the Thanksgiving holiday, Gwen told her family. Her mother said she was "deviant" and was "going to hell," and pleaded with Gwen to talk to their minister. Gwen's father insisted that either she get therapy or he was taking her out of Penn State.

Twenty-six-year-old Masen was questioned by a financial aid officer as to why he was not registered for selective service, a required item on financial aid applications. Masen tried to explain that when he turned 18, the age at which he would have registered for selective service, he was still female. It was humiliating for him to have this conversation at the financial aid office "cage" with a line of students behind him.

Matthew's death dramatically demonstrates how unsafe it is to be lesbian, gay, bisexual, or transgender (LGBT) in America. Gwen's dilemma illustrates just one of the challenges facing LGBT youth that their heterosexual peers do not encounter. Masen's issue raises an entire new set of challenges for an underserved population. In all of these cases, the young people were students on college campuses.

THE CREATION OF LGBT CENTERS AND OFFICES ON COLLEGE AND UNIVERSITY CAMPUSES: WHY NOW?

Matthew's bashing was so brutal, so coldhearted, and so grotesque that it captured national media attention. But the truth is that gay-bashings—perhaps not as dramatic as Mathew's—are happening on college campuses every day. Gwen's quandary is also one that is not unique, and Masen's situation is just coming to light. Unfortunately, both the lesbian, gay, bisexual, and transgender students and the professionals who provide services for them clearly understand that these incidents could just have easily happened on any one of our campuses.

Just as unfortunately, attacks on our campuses often go unreported. It is not unusual for students to feel afraid of the system of helping providers on campus, unaware of how they will be treated, wondering if they will be revictimized by their own university system. Students also may feel that by reporting an attack, they will be outing themselves, that is, revealing their sexual orientation or gender identity, perhaps for the first time. Perhaps they are not yet ready for their families to learn their true identities. Recently, a first-year track athlete was working out in the weight room of his campus when a group of older student-athletes surrounded him, accused him of being a "faggot," then beat him so badly that he needed many stitches on his face. Many young LGBT college students simply cannot handle the added stress with which they must deal.

Early in my career at Michigan I was called to the hospital because a young man had attempted suicide. He was an elite athlete, an outstanding student, and active in his fraternity. He had been dealing with his sexual orientation and felt too ashamed to talk with anyone about it. Now, with a failed suicide attempt and his Catholic Republican parents on their way to see him, he was mortified. I spoke with his parents as they arrived. The young man told them quite directly why he had attempted suicide. I remember his father, with tears streaming down his face, looking lovingly at his son as he scooped him up in his arms. He said, "If you're gay, then get out of this bed and be the best gay man you can be." That young man who nearly died that day is now an attorney with a bright and brilliant career ahead of him. (Submitted by Dr. Ronni Sanlo, UCLA)

Federal law does not prohibit discrimination on the basis of sexual orientation or gender identity. Civil rights legislation to protect lesbian and gay citizens has languished in the Congress since 1974 and has no immediate prospects for passage. Consequently, discrimination based on sexual orientation and gender identity remains legal in the United States. Twenty-eight states have enhanced penalties for hate crimes that include sexual orientation (see Table 1). There are still 19 states that do not include hate crimes based on sexual orientation and 10 states with no hate crime laws at all (NGLTF 1997). In fact, only 12 states have sexual orientation in their non-discrimination laws (see Table 2). Laura Markowitz, a prominent family psychologist and editor of *In the Family,* notes that "with no federal equal rights protection and few states taking seriously this issue, victims of gay-bashings often feel they are losers in a war that no will acknowledge is being waged" (Markowitz 1998, p. 18).

Table 1
States with Sexual Orientation in Their Hate Crimes Laws

Arizona	California
Connecticut	Delaware
District of Columbia	Florida
Hawaii	Illinois
Iowa	Kansas
Kentucky	Louisiana
Maine	Massachusetts
Minnesota	Missouri
Nebraska	Nevada
New Hampshire	New Jersey
New York	Oregon
Rhode Island	Tennessee
Texas	Vermont
Washington	Wisconsin

(Source: HRC web site, www.hrc.org, July 1, 2001)

Table 2
States with Sexual Orientation in Their Non-Discrimination Laws

California	Nevada
Connecticut	New Hampshire
Hawaii	New Jersey
Maryland	New York
Massachusetts	Rhode Island
Minnesota	Wisconsin

(Source: HRC web site, www.hrc.org, July 1, 2001)

Regardless of the legal system's response, hate crimes carry a message not only to the victim but also to the entire stigmatized minority community that victimization is the punishment for stepping outside culturally accepted boundaries. We, as LGBT people, are increasing our visibility and organization, which, in turn, have triggered a backlash. The backlash is fueled by heterosexism—the assumption of the inherent superiority of heterosexuality, an obliviousness to the lives and experiences of LGBT people, and the presumption that everyone is, or should be, heterosexual. Based on the ideology of heterosexism—or what Rich (1980) calls "compulsory heterosexuality"—a systematic set of institutional and cultural arrangements exists that rewards and privileges people for being or appearing to be heterosexual while establishing potential punishments or lack of privilege for being or appearing to be lesbian, gay, bisexual, or transgender. Like racism, sexism, and other ideologies of oppression, heterosexism is manifested both in societal customs and institutions and in individual attitudes and behaviors. Heterosexism is preserved through the routine operation of major social institutions such as employment, where discrimination on the basis of sexual orientation remains legal in many states; marriage, where same-sex couples generally are denied the community recognition, legal protection, and economic benefits accorded to married heterosexual partners; the law, where sexual intimacy between same-sex partners remains illegal in one-half of the states and the constitutionality of such laws is upheld by the U.S. Supreme Court; and religion, where most mainline churches condemn homosexuality as incompatible with Christian teaching.

The theology and subsequent social actions of many religious and political leaders are predicated on the devaluation of LGBT people. For example, Louis Farrakhan, Nation of Islam minister and 2000 candidate for the U.S. presidency, said that homosexuality is a threat to Islam's perfect order and is an abominable, perverse product of a sick society. Similarly, Jerry Falwell, right-wing Baptist evangelist, referred to homosexuals coming out of the gutter instead of the closet. Recently, the U.S. Senate refused to consider the nomination of gay businessman James Hormel to become ambassador to Luxembourg because of his sexual orientation. In the U.S. House, Representative Joel Hefle of Colorado spearheaded efforts to overturn President Clinton's executive order banning discrimination against LGBT persons in federal hiring. U.S. Senate Majority leader Trent Lott touched off a storm in June 1998, when he called homosexuality a sin and compared it to alcoholism, kleptomania, and sexual addiction.

When leaders foster a climate of prejudice, as in the days of Jim Crow, they give cultural permission to less scrupulous followers to inflict violence and spew hatred upon their targets. This is evident on college campuses and in public schools around the country, where LGBT students, faculty, and staff are frequent targets of harassment and discrimination. Anti-LGBT violence is a logical, albeit extreme, consequence of heterosexism. In part, to respond to the societal context and subsequent heterosexist campus environment, administrators at a small number of colleges and universities around the country created LGBT offices or centers to provide for the needs of LGBT students, faculty, and staff. While this was happening in the early 1990s, the National Gay and Lesbian Task Force (NGLTF) created the Campus Organizing Project. Several of the professional staff from the campus LGBT offices (including the authors of this book), whose job responsibilities included providing LGBT resources on their respective campuses, met with Curtis Shepard of the NGLTF Campus Organizing Project to discuss LGBT campus issues and concerns in higher education. Due to the rapid increase in the number of LGBT centers and offices springing up around the country, the group initiated the idea of creating a national organization of campus center directors. Building coalitions across colleges and universities would provide a means of sharing information and ideas, obtaining encouragement and support, and organizing.

HISTORY OF THE CONSORTIUM: THE CAMPUS PROJECT

Kevin Berrill launched the Campus Project at NGLTF in 1987 and served as a liaison with LGBT campus leaders until his retirement from NGLTF in 1991. During the initial years, limited resources prevented NGLTF from fully funding or fully staffing the project. A large part of Berrill's work revolved around examining the campus climate for LGBT individuals. During his tenure at NGLTF, Berrill issued several reports regarding anti-LGBT violence, including violence on college campuses (Berrill 1989, 1990). Between 1991 and 1993, the project was maintained by volunteers, but by 1993, NGLTF rededicated itself to addressing the needs of LGBT students, faculty, and staff on college and university campuses. Meanwhile, the NGLTF Board of Directors agreed to explore ways of fully funding the Campus Project.

Realizing that the demand for support and assistance from campus activists was overwhelming the capacity of NGLTF to respond, and recognizing the organization's responsibility to young people within the LGBT movement, as well as the historical role of campus activism in social change movements, the NGLTF Board of Directors agreed to explore ways of fully funding the Campus Project in 1993. As part of this exploration, the Board authorized a study to determine how NGLTF could be of assistance to organizing efforts on college and university campuses. Telephone interviews and campus visits with LGBT students, faculty, and staff from dozens of institutions across the country revealed a consistently low level of functioning on the part of most LGBT campus organizations. This research revealed that student groups in particular were rarely engaged in efforts to bring LGBT subject matter into the curriculum. They were not strategizing for domestic partner health benefits. They were not marshaling resources to end ROTC[Reserve Officers' Training Corp] discrimination. Nor were they participating effectively in efforts to defend LGBT communities from attacks from the radical right. In 1993, Curt Shepard was selected to direct the Campus Project from a NGLTF field office in Los Angeles. Based on the exploratory investigation, he identified the Campus Project's primary goal: To foster the growth of campus organizations that are healthy, effective, and equipped to participate meaningfully in improving the quality of life for LGBT people in academe. (Shepard, Yeskel, & Outcalt 1995, i-ii)

Shepard traveled around the country visiting college campuses and meeting with LGBT professionals. He assisted us in strategizing and organizing around LGBT campus issues and concerns. In collaboration with Felice Yeskel at the University of Massachusetts and Charles Outcalt at UCLA, Shepard and NGLTF published a campus organizing manual (Shepard et al. 1995). The manual—which is available at no cost at www.ngltf.org—has been instrumental in assisting LGBT campus professionals in addressing the challenges at our institutions.

In November 1995, at the NGLTF Creating Change leadership conference in Detroit, several LGBT campus directors met to discuss the need for a formal organization of LGBT professionals on college campuses. This dialogue continued at the March 1996 American College Personnel (ACPA) annual meeting in Baltimore, where LGBT campus professionals met again, this time to begin to create the framework for a new national organization. The first part of this meeting was spent discussing the successful programs and initiatives on our own campuses, an exercise that was both energizing and empowering. The collaboration had begun.

On November 7, 1996, 25 LGBT campus professionals met at the NGLTF Creating Change Conference in Washington, D.C. Melinda Paras, the outgoing executive director of NGLTF, met with the campus directors. She described the NGLTF restructuring that eliminated the Campus Project.

In 1994, NGLTF eliminated *Special Projects*, which included the Campus Project (headed by Curt Shepard) and created *Field Organizers*. The Field Organizers dealt with all of the issues in their areas (i.e., campus concerns, anti-gay prejudice and discrimination, health care needs, etc.). According to Ms. Paras, NGLTF could not financially sustain the previous structure. She noted that in addition to the Field Organizers, a new Policy Institute was created for research and development of tools to use in the field. Ms. Paras further indicated that due to the limited resources, NGLTF would not fund a full-time person at NGLTF to work with Campus Directors. However, she suggested that "there is a commitment to the campus project" and that she as well as the new board, "have a commitment to assist the campus directors." "I see you, the campus directors, as a source of consistent leadership on campus in comparison to the constant student leadership turnover." The question that lay before the group was how NGLTF and the Campus Directors might collaborate knowing that NGLTF was not going to fund a full-time person. (Consortium minutes, November 17, 1996, www.lgbtcampus.org).

Paras further indicated that due to the limited resources, NGLTF would not fund a full-time person to work with the campus directors. The question that now lay before the group was how NGLTF and the campus directors might collaborate.

During that same meeting, Kerry Lobel, the incoming NGLTF executive director, also met with the campus directors and reiterated NGLTF's commitment to college campuses. In fact, Lobel wanted to strengthen NGLTF's relationship with us. The directors decided to draft a position statement regarding their future relationship with NGLTF. It was discussed at the next meeting that was held in connection with the annual NASPA/ACPA joint meeting in Chicago in March 1997, was a turning point for the LGBT campus directors. We debated who we were and where we were going as an organization. The discourse revolved around our organizational structure and function, our autonomy, and our mission. The concept of professionally aligning with other national LGBT organizations was a focal point. We decided that we needed to be connected to both NGLTF as well as the professional student affairs associations.

We decided to conduct biannual group meetings at the annual NGLTF Creating Change Conference and at the annual conferences of either the ACPA or NASPA. Because of our past history with NGLTF we invited Kerry Lobel to meet again with us. Together we examined the relationship between NGLTF and the campus directors. We also realized in this meeting that we needed to create a more formal structure to provide us with a visible identity and a vision to share with other national groups. A task force was created and charged with developing a draft of a constitution and bylaws for the new organization to be presented for a vote at our November 1997 meeting.

The Pocono Parents—the affectionately named task force that consisted of the authors of this book—met in July, 1997 and presented a draft of an organizational structure to the LGBT campus directors at the November NGLTF Creating Change Conference in San Diego. The proposal was accepted, and the National Consortium of Directors of Lesbian, Gay, Bisexual, and Transgender Resources in Higher Education was created. The combined vision and mission of the consortium is to achieve higher education environments in which lesbian, gay, bisexual, and transgender students, faculty, staff, administrators, and alumni have equity in every respect. The goals are to support colleagues and develop curricula to professionally enhance this work; to seek climate improvement on campuses; and to advocate for policy change, program development, and establishment of LGBT office/centers. The consortium offers information of use to those who work with college and university students. The consortium continues to meet twice a year and communicates extensively via the Internet. For up-to-date information, the reader is directed to the consortium's award-winning Web site at http://www.lgbtcampus.org.

THE POCONO PARENTS: A VISION AND AN IDENTITY

Three campus directors—Robert Schoenberg, University of Pennsylvania; Ronni Sanlo, University of California Los Angeles; and Sue Rankin, Pennsylvania State University—met at Schoenberg's bungalow in the Poconos in July 1997 and created a structure, a mission, and an identity for the campus directors. The new name—the National Consortium of Directors of Lesbian, Gay, Bisexual, and Transgender Resources in Higher Education—reflected the degree of diversity of services among all the directors. On some campuses LGBT issues and concerns were addressed with part-time persons—generally graduate students—while on other campuses, one or more full-time staff coordinated a full-service center whose mission was to serve students, faculty, and staff. The purpose of the consortium was to:

- provide support to colleagues serving lesbian, gay, bisexual, and transgender communities in higher education;
- consult with higher education administrators in the interest of improving campus climate and services for lesbian, gay, bisexual, and transgender students, faculty, staff, administrators, and alumni/ae; and
- advocate for institutional policy changes and program development that recognize the needs of lesbian, gay, bisexual, and transgender people

The new consortium's structure consisted of a Board of Directors whose members included the chair, the chair-elect, the scribe, the treasurer, and the chairs of the specific work groups. These work groups included Strategic Response, Education/Training, Conferences, Publications/Communications, and Research.

THE CONSORTIUM TODAY: ANSWERING THE CHALLENGE

The consortium provides a forum for LGBT professionals in higher education to address the challenges facing LGBT students, faculty, and staff on university and college campuses. Further, the consortium provides national visibility for LGBT members of the academic community and provides a vehicle for institutionalizing LGBT issues and concerns in academe, similar to what is currently afforded to other underrepresented groups.

In 1996, Gose indicated that "thirty institutions [of higher education] have full-time administrators whose sole responsibility is coordinating gay and lesbian activities—twice the number counted in 1992." Today, there are over seventy institutions that employ a paid professional who has at least part of her/his job responsibility coordinating programs and/or services for LGBT students, faculty, and staff (see Appendix A).

As more institutions acknowledge the demand and the need to serve this growing population on campus, more LGBT centers will be established. As a result, the need for trained professionals in this field will also grow. The consortium is available to provide higher education with guidance in the development of new centers, and to provide necessary support to LGBT center directors and others on campus who do this work.

Chapter 2

Assessing the Needs and Proposing Solutions

[We] challenge higher education institutions to affirm and enact a commitment to equality, fairness, and inclusion. [We] propose that colleges and universities commit to the task of creating inclusive educational environments in which all participants are equally welcome, equally valued, and equally heard. For in order to provide a framework within which a vital community of learning can be built, a primary mission of the academy must be to create an environment which ideally cultivates diversity and celebrates difference. Association of American Colleges and Universities, 1995

In order to build a vital community of learning a college or university must provide an environment where: intellectual life is central and where faculty and students work together to strengthen teaching and learning, where freedom of expression is uncompromisingly protected and where civility is powerfully affirmed, where the dignity of all individuals is affirmed and where equality of opportunity is vigorously pursued, and where the well-being of each member is sensitively supported. Boyer, American Council on Education, 1990

The number of lesbian, gay, bisexual, and transgender (LGBT) offices and resource centers is growing rapidly on college and university campuses throughout the country. The recent surge in the growth of these centers and offices is the focus of this chapter. The initial section of the chapter reviews the various means by which proposals for offices or centers originated. In most cases these proposals were created reactively, that is, in reaction to antigay incidents on campus. In a fewer number of cases the proposals were written proactively, that is, in response to LGBT student, faculty, and/or staff advocacy. Following is a description of the program at Emory University.

Case Study 2.1
Emory University

Emory University's Office of Lesbian/Gay/Bisexual/Transgender Life began operations in the fall semester 1991 as the Office of Lesbian/Gay/Bisexual Student Life. The impetus for starting the office came from a group of undergraduate and graduate students who approached the dean of the Division of Campus Life and asked him to give them space and funds. He agreed to do so, offering them a room in the student center, several pieces of used equipment, and a small start-up budget. Two graduate students were hired as coordinators of the Office of LGB Student Life; each worked 20 hours per week for the 1991-1992 academic year. In December 1991, an incident occurred that led to the expansion of the office: two male students were seen kissing one another in their residence hall and were subsequently taunted and harassed. The two students filed a formal grievance, but the administration's response was deemed inadequate, and in March 1992, a campuswide protest demonstration drew several hundred participants. In response, Emory's president appointed a committee to assess the situation. This group submitted a report recommending, among other things, that a full-time professional be hired to direct the Office of LGB Student Life and that the constituency served by the office should include not only students but faculty and staff as well. In keeping with the committee's recommendations, Saralyn Chesnut was hired as the first full-time director of the renamed Office of Lesbian/Gay/Bisexual Life in the fall of 1992. The office was still located administratively within the Division of Campus Life, and Chesnut reported to the director of the Office of Student Activities. Her staff initially included part-time graduate students and work-study students; an additional part-time program administrative assistant/office manager position was funded in the fall of 1996, and this position finally became a full-time one in the fall of 1998. Also in the fall of 1998, the dean for Campus Life approved the expansion of the office's constituency to include transgender people, and the name of the office was changed again, to the Office of Lesbian/Gay/ Bisexual/Transgender Life. Currently, the staff of the Office of LGBT Life includes a full-time director, a full-time administrative assistant/office manager, and, during the academic year, part-time graduate student and work-study student positions. The director reports to the dean of students within the Division of Campus Life and holds an adjunct faculty position in addition to her administrative appointment. The office provides services and programs to students, faculty, and staff of Emory University. (Submitted by Saralyn Chestnut, director of the Office of LGBT Life, Emory University)

WHY CREATE AN LGBT CENTER/OFFICE?

Based on a review of the histories of current LGBT centers or offices, most were created for one of three reasons. The first—and by far the most prevalent—was a university or college administration's response to incidents of homophobic harassment. The second most often cited was the administration's response to faculty, staff, and/or students' insistence that the campus provide a "safe place" and/or a means for educating the university/college community regarding LGBT issues and concerns. Finally, the third—and unfortunately the most rare—was an administration's recognition that an LGBT resource center was an important step toward fostering diversity and providing a welcoming campus climate.

Regardless of the primary motivation, in nearly all of the histories a committee or task force was created and charged with providing recommendations to the administration as to how to address the LGBT communities' needs, issues, and concerns on campus. These committees/task forces usually comprised students and faculty and were commissioned with providing reports and recommendations to the central administration. For example, the LGBT Center at the University of Minnesota was founded in 1992 after incidents of homophobic harassment led to the creation of a task force. The five recommendations from the task force report included:

1. the establishment of an LGBT center
2. same-sex spousal equivalency benefits
3. educational training
4. updating all publications to reflect the university's policy on diversity and the inclusion of sexual orientation in its antidiscrimination statement
5. establishment of an LGBT studies program—the only recommendation not yet implemented

The first step taken by many of the task forces was to provide an assessment of the campus climate for LGBT students, staff, and faculty. The data collected served to support the recommendations that they provided. The rationale to conduct an assessment was that one of the primary missions of higher education institutions is unearthing and disseminating knowledge. Further, recent research suggests that the climate on college campuses not only affects the creation of knowledge but also has a significant impact on members of the academic community, who, in turn, contribute to the creation of the campus climate (Kuh & Whitt 1988; Peterson 1990; Rankin 1994, 1998; Tierney 1990). Therefore, preserving a climate that offers equal learning opportunities for all students and academic freedom for all faculty—an environment free from oppression—is suggested as one of the primary responsibilities of educational institutions.

A meta-analysis of over 30 campus reports that focused specifically on the climate for LGBT members of the academic community was conducted by Rankin in 1998. Due, in part, to the results of the campus reports, several institutions created LGBT resource offices or centers. Further, the recommendations from the reports often served as the initial goals and actions for the office or center.

Meta-Analysis Summary

Each institution's purpose for assessing the campus climate was unique, prompted by a particular set of circumstances occurring on that campus (e.g., efforts to include sexual orientation in the university or college's nondiscrimination policy or the campus administration's response to homophobic incidents). The campuses surveyed included public and private institutions and varied in both size and geographic location. The methodologies used to examine the campus climate also varied. Of the 30 college and university reports reviewed, 13 conducted surveys, 6 conducted focus groups or interviews, and 5 opted for a combination of both quantitative and qualitative methodology (6 reports did not indicate their method of assessment). Just as there were a variety of stimuli for writing the reports and various methods employed to complete the assessment, the population samples also differed. For example, the University of Arizona queried 600 faculty and staff regarding their perceptions of the campus climate for lesbian, gay, and bisexual people. In contrast, the University of Massachusetts conducted three surveys purposefully sampling lesbian, gay, and bisexual students, resident assistants, and student service personnel. Open forums and public hearings where all members of the academic community were encouraged to share their views were held at Vanderbilt University, Rutgers University, and the University of Wisconsin, Madison. Pennsylvania State University and the University of California, Davis conducted in-depth interviews with LGBT faculty and staff.

While it is difficult to compare the investigations due to differences in research methodologies, instruments, and samples, it is clear that LGBT prejudice is prevalent in higher education institutions. For example, in studies where surveys were used as the primary tool, the data indicated that LGBT students were the victims of prejudice ranging from verbal abuse (2%–86%), to physical violence (6%–59%), to sexual harassment (1%–21%).

In those investigations that utilized qualitative data, analogous findings were reported indicating the invisibility, isolation, and fear of LGBT members of the academic community. For the professor, counselor, staff assistant, and student who is lesbian, gay, bisexual, or transgender, there is the constant fear that, should they "be found out," they would be ostracized, their careers would be destroyed, or they would lose their positions. While the reports indicated differences among the experiences of these individuals, their comments suggested that regardless of how "out" or how "closeted" they were, all expressed fears that prevented them from acting freely. Three themes emerged from the interviews, focus group comments, and open forum statements presented in several of the reports. (see Appendix B)

The pervasive heterosexism in higher education institutions not only inhibits the acknowledgment and expression of queer perspectives but also affects curricular and research efforts. Further, the contributions and concerns of LGBT people are often unrecognized and unaddressed, to the detriment of the education not only of LGBT students but of heterosexuals as well. In summary, the results of the campus climate review reveal two important themes. First, institutions of higher education do not provide an empowering atmosphere for LGBT students, faculty, and staff—an atmosphere where their voices are heard, appreciated, and valued. Second, and perhaps more significant, the results suggest that the climate on college campuses acts to silence the voices of its LGBT members with both subtle and overt oppression.

The findings of the campus climate review also indicate that 50% to 90% of those who responded stated that they did not report at least one incident of anti-LGBT discrimination. D'Augelli (1989) wondered, "Why hasn't this problem made its way through the usual streams of anointment as a campus problem?" The answer is "locked in the closet of lesbian and gay life on campus. It is a closet inhabited not only by self-identified LGBT students, faculty, and staff, although they constitute most of the inhabitants, but is shared by heterosexual people on campus who know the needs of lesbians and gay men but do not speak out on their behalf" (D'Augelli 1989, p. 129).

Given the results of the climate assessments, the establishment of some type of formalized LGBT presence on campus was recommended by nearly all of the campus task forces or committees. In most cases, the professional whose job responsibilities would now include LGBT needs, issues, and concerns was also charged with ensuring that the other committee/task force recommendations were implemented. Administrations' responses to creating an LGBT presence on campus were as varied as the reasons for the creation of the task forces and committees.

THE ADMINISTRATION'S RESPONSE: CREATING AN LGBT PRESENCE ON CAMPUS

As Dr. Doug Bauder, the coordinator of Indiana University's Gay, Lesbian, and Bisexual Office, said, "It seems to me that our [GLB office's] single most important function is simply being. It's being visible [and] providing a presence on campus" (Bauder, 1998). If nothing else, creating an LGBT presence on campus provides visibility and a context for meaningful discourse. In a community where invisibility has been the norm, this presence speaks volumes. How this visibility comes to be is the focus of this section.

One of the earliest LGBT student centers was the Lesbian-Gay Male Programs Office (now the Office of LGBT Affairs) at the University of Michigan, founded in 1971. This was the first time that a major university offered supportive services to lesbian and gay students.

Case Study 2.2
The University of Michigan's History of the Office of LGBT Affairs

On March 17, 1970, the University of Michigan (UM) chapter of the Gay Liberation Front (GLF) was initiated with the purposes of battling stereotypes of gay people, of fighting homophobic prejudice, and of invalidating the mental illness model of homosexuality. By 1971, GLF was formally recognized by the Student Government Council as a student organization. With pressure from the Black Action Movement, which was active on campus, and from GLF, in September 1971, two co-coordinators, known as human sexuality advocates, were hired on a quarter-time basis to staff an ad hoc committee to deal with lesbian and gay issues on campus. This was the first time that a major university offered supportive services to lesbian and gay students. By January 1977, the advocacy positions were upgraded to half-time status. By the late 1970s the office offered speakers bureau "raps" in classes and residence halls. By 1982, the Office of Human Sexuality became part of Counseling Services. In March 1984, UM President Harold Shapiro issued a presidential policy statement prohibiting discrimination based on sexual orientation and created a Task Force on Sexual Orientation (TFSO). In 1991, a Study Committee on the status of Lesbians and Gay Men published *From Invisibility to Inclusion: The Status of Lesbian and Gay Men at the University of Michigan*—better known as the Lavender Report—which issued recommendations for University-wide implementation of non-discrimination based on sexual orientation. In September 1993, Regental Bylaw 14.06 was revised by the Board of Regents to add the words "sexual orientation," which officially prohibited discrimination based on sexual orientation. A "14.06 Task Force," appointed in October by President Duderstadt, recommended that in order for equal status and opportunity to be actualized by the bylaw revision, such status must include health benefits to domestic same-sex partners of faculty and staff, and same-sex couples in domestic partnerships must be eligible for family housing. In May 1994, these recommendations were approved by the Board of Regents and implemented by President Duderstadt. The first gay male couple officially moved into family housing in August

1994, and enrollment for health benefits for domestic partners began in November 1994. In January 1994, the office's structure and leadership were changed by the Division of Student Affairs to bring them into line with those of other programs offered under the division, moving from a co-coordinator situation to a single professional directorship. Dr. Ronni Sanlo was hired and assumed leadership in May 1994. In September 1994, the name of the office was changed to the "Lesbian Gay Bisexual Programs Office," then changed again in 1997 to include transgender people. The new name became the Office of Lesbian, Gay, Bisexual, and Transgender Affairs (OLGBTA). The OLGBTA functions proactively, providing programming, educational services, leadership training and development, and campus coalition building with non-LGBT organizations. It also acts as a coordinating body for the many LGBT student, faculty, and staff groups that exist at the University of Michigan while being an advocate for students in need. (Submitted by Ronni Sanlo, former director, University of Michigan OLGBTA)

It was another eleven years, in 1982, before the University of Pennsylvania center was established. The Stonewall Center was created in 1984 at the University of Massachusetts at Amherst, and a third at Grinnell College was established in 1986.

There is no packaged, step-by-step process to creating an LGBT presence on your campus. However, this section provides several suggestions and examples that may assist you in the process. Due to the diversity among colleges and universities, LGBT presence on campus is created within the parameters of the campus culture, economic influences, geographical location, and benchmarks, both within and outside the institution. An office or center may be staffed by a half-time professional with little to no facilities or resources or two or more full-time staff, a large operating budget, and a suite of offices. The offices may be housed within student affairs, academic affairs, or both. The centers may be stand-alone units or be a part of a multicultural center, a gender studies program, or an office of institutional equity. The options are as numerous as the offices currently operating.

Case Study 2.3
University Illinois, Chicago

The roots of the Office of Gay, Lesbian, Bisexual & Transgender Concerns (OGLBTC) lie in the work of members of the Chancellor's Committee on the Status of Lesbian, Gay and Bisexual Issues (CCSLGBI), which was formed in the fall of 1991 by Chancellor James Stukel. During the first years of its existence, the CCSLGBI identified the creation of an office to serve the lesbian, gay, and bisexual (LGB) populations of University of Illinois, Chicago (UIC) as a key goal. In tandem, the LGBT student organization PRIDE evaluated needs of the LGBT student body. They saw an office as a key requirement to adequately serve students. In 1993, CCSLGBI submitted a proposal to the associate chancellor for affirmative action programs for an office to serve not only students but also faculty and staff. She reviewed and forwarded it to the chancellor. In 1994, PRIDE held a petition drive demanding that an office be created to serve LGB students and gathered several thousand names. They received support from several student groups, including undergraduate student government. At a media event held by PRIDE, the associate vice chancellor for student affairs and enrollment management announced that the university would create such an office. In July 1994, Dr. David Barnett was invited to serve on a one-third-time basis as interim director for the Office of Gay, Lesbian and Bisexual

Concerns. Barnett was a staff psychologist at the UIC Counseling Center, and his director agreed to release his time for this assignment. The office was allocated funds for a full-time clerical worker and a small operating budget. It was assigned to report to the associate executive vice chancellor for academic affairs. The OGLBC was assigned to temporary quarters in a distant building owned by the university in space requiring extensive cosmetic repairs. The remodeling was completed in November 1994, and the office opened to the public, but the building was too far away to attract visitors. A second proposal was submitted to expand time for the director to work on a full-time basis the next academic year. The proposal reiterated the need for a more central, accessible location on the east campus of the university for the office. Barnett was invited to continue his work with the Office as acting director on a three-quarters time basis for the next academic year. In December 1995, the office moved to new temporary quarters on the fourth floor of a more centrally located building. While smaller in total space, the new location was much more accessible to students, faculty, and staff. A dramatic increase in visitors proved this point. In the late fall of 1995, a search was begun for a full-time director of the office. A search committee was formed and eventually made its recommendation to the vice-provost. He offered the director position on a full-time permanent basis to Barnett, starting September 1, 1996. The name of the office was expanded to include "Transgender" in the summer of 1998 at the request of the director with the approval of the vice-provost. The office moved once again, in 1998, to what is hoped to be a more permanent—and visible—location on the first floor of the same building. The OGLBTC is part of Academic Affairs and reports to the executive associate vice chancellor for academic affairs/vice-provost's office. Parallel units, Office of Women's Affairs, Latino Cultural Center, and African-American Cultural Center, also report here. The office primarily serves students, but significant time and energy are devoted to concerns of staff and faculty. Most OGLBTC programming does target student audiences. (Submitted by David Barnett, former director, Office of GLBT Concerns, UIC)

To those administrators who are considering creating an LGBT presence on campus, it may be helpful to consider the aforementioned parameters as well as the following questions:

What is our mission?
What are we trying to achieve?
Who are we serving?
Who is our primary customer?
Who are our supporting customers?
What are our resources?
Where is the funding coming from?
Who are our allies?
Where will the challenges come from?
How ready is the campus for this visible LGBT presence?

There are potential challenges as well as potential benefits inherent in the myriad of possibilities from which to choose. For example, if your response to "Who are we serving?" is "Students," what are the potential challenges? The answer, in a word, is "students." Counseling, creative conflict resolutions, and last-minute directives are part of a director's daily tasks. On the other hand, the potential benefits are a passion, energy, creativity, and pushing the boundaries, all of which, though exhausting, can bring about rapid transformation on a college or university campus.

Case Study 2.4
Pennsylvania State University

In 1990, a Gay and Lesbian Task Force was appointed by then President Joab Thomas in response to the LGBTA community effort to add sexual orientation to the university's nondiscrimination policy. By late 1991, the task force released a report that presented a number of recommendations to improve the campus climate for LGBT individuals. One of these recommendations was to create an LGBT student center. This recommendation was not acted on until 1994, when the Student Issues subcommittee of the Committee on LGB Equity presented a proposal to "develop and create a full-time standing position to address the specific needs of LGB students as well as the educational needs of the University Community in this regard" (minutes from the Committee on LGB Equity Meeting, October 31, 1994). Two years later, in April, 1996 a meeting was held with university administrators to review a proposal for an LGBT Student Center. In 1997, at the committee's annual meeting with the president, several students expressed their concerns over the lack of a "safe space" for LGBT students and made their case for the "institutionalization of LGB programming and educational efforts at Penn State." In January, 1998, a position was created to address the students' concerns. The coordinator of LGBT equity position was created and supported by both the vice provost for educational equity and the vice president for student affairs. The position was 50% of a current staff member's position, and some of the responsibilities included coordinating the LGBTA Resource Room, providing visibility for the LGBT community, collaborating with existing LGBT groups regarding educational programming and events, and providing a safe place for students, faculty, and staff. The current vision for the coordinator is that "lesbian, gay, bisexual, and transgender people and allies will be fully included and affirmed as valued participants in every area of the Pennsylvania State University community." (Submitted by Sue Rankin, educational equity, Pennsylvania State University)

Case Study 2.5
University of South California

At the University of Southern California (USC), the Center for Gay, Lesbian, Bi Student Support is located within the Center for Women and Men. The Center for Women and Men (founded as the Office for Women's Issues in 1989) provides crisis intervention, student support, and programming around issues of gender-based abuse and harm: sexual assault, dating violence, sexism, discrimination, harassment, battery, and so forth. It offers innovative preventive education in such areas as preventing rape and addressing gendered violence. The connections between such issues as related to gender and to sexual identity have been well chronicled by scholars of feminist theory and queer theory in recent years. Links between homophobia and misogyny are well documented. The needs of gay, lesbian, bisexual, and transgender students with regard to the provision of support services are not dissimilar to the needs of women, needs to which campuses have responded with the provision of women's centers over the past two decades. Women's experience of discrimination, harassment, assault, sexism, and so on, provides a lens through which campus homophobia and heterosexism may be interpreted and addressed. It was with this realization that USC's Center for Women and Men began providing support services to gay, lesbian, and bi students from 1993 (we added transgender later, as did others). The GLBT community on campus learned by word of mouth that the

CWM was a safe and confidential reporting place and a place from which advocacy could and did proceed. The formal creation of an office to address the needs of GLBT students followed in 1995. While the addition of a "center within a center" was, in part, the accidental consequence of a lack of new funding (and of the presence of a director who enthusiastically embraced both constituencies—gender and sexual identity), it is a model of which we are now very proud. Students are coming to understand that oppression of various kinds is intertwined. Peer educators who present rape awareness programs never omit their understanding of the fact that rape is not always "heterosexual." The senior administration of the university has been warmly supportive of the approach and services offered. (Submitted by Elizabeth Davenport, assistant dean for student affairs, director, Gay, Lesbian, Bi Student Support, University of Southern California)

Case Study 2.6
Texas A&M

Gender Issues Education Services has three equal missions, including women's development resources, advocacy for victims of sexual violence, and GLBT education and support. Our services can be divided into four distinct units: support and advocacy, educational programming, services and referrals, and information and resources. Gender Issues Education Services exists to bring to the attention of Texas A&M University the conditions and issues that limit the personal and academic success of women students, survivors of sexual violence, and lesbian, gay, and bisexual students. Some of the existing barriers include, but are not limited to, sexual harassment, institutional sexism, sex-based discrimination, sexual assault, relationship violence, and homophobia/heterosexism. Gender Issues staff recognize the impact that these barriers, as well as others, can have in terms of impeding a student's personal and/or academic development. Staff members are available to students for support or advocacy in person or over the phone. Staff members help students define their experience and become aware of services and resources available to them on campus and in the community. Gender Issues Education staff include a full-time professional staff coordinator, a full-time support staff office manager, two graduate assistants, one student assistant, and three to five volunteers each semester. The coordinator and office manager are responsible for overseeing the day-to-day operations and provision of services. The graduate staff assist with a variety of functions, including programming, newsletter production, student organization contact, and event planning. The student assistant serves on special projects and as further support staff. Volunteers either commit to set hours or work on an as needed basis, depending on their preference. The entire program operates on a budget of approximately $90,000, including salaries, fringe benefits, advertising, supplies, materials, and all other expenses. The office is funded through the student service fee allocated by a student service fee advisory board on an annual basis. (Submitted by former Texas A&M coordinator, Gender Issues Education Services, Shaun Traverse, University of California, San Diego)

Case Study 2.7
University of California, San Francisco

The University of California San Francisco (UCSF) Chancellor's Advisory Committee on Gay, Lesbian, Bisexual, and Trans-gender Issues was created in 1994. That committee's annual reports for 1994-1995, 1995-1996, and 1996-1997 called for the hiring of an LGBT "resources coordinator" for the campus, but the chancellor's responses to those reports did not make mention of the committee's recommendation. In late 1996, the city and county of San Francisco passed legislation requiring city contractors to offer domestic partner (DP) benefits to employees. In meetings between UCSF (a city contractor) and

San Francisco officials, UCSF administrators indicated that extension of DP benefits to UCSF employees was not a decision that the UCSF campus itself could make. The UCSF administrators explained that, while the campus chancellor supported DP benefits, UCSF employees could receive them only if the regents of the statewide University of California system voted to extend them to all UC employees. It was highly uncertain, however, when such a vote might occur. To demonstrate UCSF's commitment to LGBT concerns in the period before the regents' ultimate approval of DP benefits (in November 1997), UCSF officials prepared a number of recommendations to the campus chancellor. Among them was creation of an LGBT resources coordinator position at 60% of full-time, for a one-year period. (The job's temporary status reflected the fact that the then-chancellor was serving for one year, on an interim basis.) In winter 1997, the chancellor approved the position as a one-year "pilot," funded by UCSF's Division of Advancement and Planning and housed within the division's Center for Gender Equity. UCSF's first LGBT resources coordinator, Michael Scarce, served from June 1998 until his resignation in June 1999. In July 1999, the coordinator position was approved by the chancellor as a permanent, full-time job (again, with funding from Advancement and Planning and placement within the Center for Gender Equity), and Shane Snowdon was hired. The LGBT coordinator reports to the director of the Center for Gender Equity, does not supervise any staff, and provides programs and services to UCSF students, staff, and faculty. (Submitted by Shane Snowdon, coordinator, Lesbian, Gay, Bisexual, Transgender Resources, UCSF Center for Gender Equity)

Case Study 2.8
The University of Pennsylvania

What is now the Lesbian Gay Bisexual Center at the University of Pennsylvania began its life in a carrel within the Student Activities office in the fall of 1982. Actually, it was first discussed in the preceding school year following a few very disturbing homophobic incidents on campus. The worst of these was the beating of a gay sophomore at the hands of a fellow student for no apparent reason other than that the victim conformed to certain stereotypes of how gay men behave. As a result of expressions of concern by student leaders, some of whom happened to be lesbian or gay, and a couple of enlightened administrators who championed student causes, I was hired to work three days a week in both Student Activities and the Counseling Service as a point person for lesbian and gay concerns (there was no mention of bisexual or transgender people at that time). Since the generation of my position had been among a small number of individuals, and I was presented with no job description when I began, I focused initially on those activities that seemed most vital to students who had lobbied for the position, or colleagues whose opinions I respected, and on my own knowledge and intuition. Fortunately, I found a significant segment of the campus receptive to my efforts, and I met with some success. I wish that I could say that I had an intentional strategy about the development of the program, some kind of strategic plan. In fact, almost every moment of my hours on campus was taken up with doing the work, not reflecting about it or planning for the future. About three years after the work began, my supervisor and I engaged an organization development consultant, who, not coincidentally, was directing (and still directs) an LGBT program that began at about the same time as ours. As a result, I was able to achieve some clarity about direction for the program. One matter became clear: we needed to establish a programmatic identity for the work, this identity needed to be distinct from me. This was achieved by choosing a cumbersome, but precise, name for the program (which has, long since, been abandoned). Cumbersome though it may have been, the work having a name other than mine was a significant step. I lobbied for more hours of employment. Over the next few years my time expanded from three days a week to five, from 9 months to 12. Simultaneously, I stressed the need for more help. I had had a work-study student or two from the outset. I argued for a second half-time staff person, not only to assist with the volume of work but also to make available to students a female counterpart, who, I assumed, would encourage greater participation of women in our activities. The request was granted, and, in the 12 subsequent years, that position evolved from one part-time staff position to two half-time staff positions, then to one temporary full-time position, hopefully soon to a permanent second full-time position and perhaps before too long, a third. A restructuring of the Student Activities office resulted in my being required to move to new space, a move that I resisted, as it meant leaving the student union building. As it turns out, the two small rooms assigned to us were four times larger than what we had before, and, within a year, the third and final room on our floor was assigned to us. We now had (and still have) three rooms in a former fraternity house in the center of campus. We now need much more space, and our offices are not handicapped-accessible, which troubles us. But a rainbow flag flies outside our third-story window overlooking the central campus green, and it is remarkable how many spontaneous visitors it brings us. Another reorganization a few years later resulted in my reporting lines being shifted directly to the office of the senior student affairs person. By this time, I was employed full-time and had reasonable staff support. Because of my new reporting line, I was now expected to undertake some of the tasks typical of more mature nonprofit organizations. These included annual planning, annual reports, budget proposal, and management. All required a definitive mission statement and organizational goals and measurable objectives—a far cry from the planning by intuition of several years before. Five years ago, we created an advisory board made up of students, faculty, staff, and alumni. This step was a result of some tension about the program's priorities and practices and part of a continuing effort to make decisions based on real information provided by consumers and colleagues. Now what has come to be called the Lesbian Gay Bisexual Transgender Center has two full-time staff, four work-study students, and two graduate interns. Our budget is over $100,000, not including costs associated with our space on campus, or computer equipment that is purchased centrally. The advisory board is highly effective and helpful. We work with 10 active LGBT organizations—undergraduate student; graduate/professional student; faculty/staff; and alumni. We offer a wide range of services and programs. We have begun working with the university's Development and Alumni Relations department to cultivate relationships with potential donors. Still, even at age 17 and with all the advantages that we have managed to accrue, we cannot be all things to all people. Though we probably come as close as any center in the country to being "full-service," there are services that we would like to provide and programs that we would like to sponsor that time and resources do not allow. With the generous support of two alumni, we are, as of this writing, undertaking a full-scale strategic planning process. We have engaged a consultant who is an expert in strategic planning and in nonprofit organization management in general. This endeavor represents another step in our growth and development. It will help us to know what we are doing now that we might be able to let go, what we are not doing that should become a priority, and what sources we might be able to tap for support of future operations. The results will provide the foundation for a capital campaign that might yield much bigger and better space on campus and, ideally, an endowment to fund the center's services and programs in perpetuity. (Submitted by Robert Schoenberg, director, LGBT Center, University of Pennsylvania)

STRATEGIES FOR CHANGE

To successfully address a problem as endemic as institutionalized hetero-sexism, a comprehensive program of intervention is needed. The recommendations provided in the campus reports suggest several implications for policy-makers and program planners in higher education. In order for institutions of higher education to welcome the complexity and richness of the world of the Twenty-First century, there is a need to shift basic assumptions, premises, and beliefs in all areas of the institution—only then can behavior and structures be changed. In the transformed institution, heterosexist assumptions are replaced by assumptions of diverse sexualities and relationships. These new assumptions govern the design and implementation of any activity, program, or service of the institution. This sort of transformative change demands committed leadership in both policy and goal articulation. New approaches to learning, teaching, deci-sion making, and working in the institution are implemented. They will demand the forming of relationships between individuals who are radically "other" to each other. These transformed assumptions, premises, and beliefs provide the environment with the catalyst for change.

A synthesis of the recommendations suggested in the 30 campus reports reveals four areas where change may occur: structural transformation, policy inclusion, curricular integration, and educational efforts. (See Appendix C). Appendix D offers an example of what might be considered in the process of de-veloping a structure.

It is important to note a number of challenges that may occur when trying to implement the recommendations. The implementation phase is the most cru-cial phase in transforming the campus climate. Is the administration supportive? Is there fiscal support? Change demands committed leadership in both policy and goal articulation. Are those administrators who have the power and author-ity to make decisions making public and affirming statements? Are the resources available to implement the recommendations? Are the recommendations pre-sented in the university's strategic plan? The other key players in transforming the campus climate are faculty and students. Are they involved in the planning and writing of the recommendations? Tierney and Dilley (1999, p. 22) argued that rather than focusing exclusively on surface-level issues—faculty appoint-ments, an inclusive curriculum, a gay-friendly environment—that structures need to be "disrupted." "If one assumes that the structures of knowledge in part have defined normalized relations that have excluded homosexuals, then one needs to break those structures rather than merely reinvent them." As Audre Lorde (1984, p. 112) so eloquently stated, "The master's tools will never dis-mantle the master's house."

One wonders if the implementation of policy changes, more inclusive cur-riculum and service programs, and the creation of an LGBT presence on campus will indeed deinstitutionalize heterosexism or if, as Tierney and Dilley suggest, we need to "disrupt" the existing structures. These are the challenges facing LGBT professionals on college campuses. Strategies for addressing these chal-lenges are presented in the following chapters.

Chapter 3

The Development and Administration of Campus LGBT Centers and Offices

Brett Beemyn

On October 11, 2000—National Coming Out Day—a gay male couple who had met as undergraduates at the University of Pennsylvania (Penn) announced a $2 million donation to their alma mater to fund an expanded Lesbian Gay Bisexual Transgender (LGBT) Center on campus. While the gift to Penn's LGBT Center is, to date, the largest donation of its kind, it is demonstrative of the rise and phenomenal growth of LGBT centers/offices on college and university campuses in the last decade. Prior to 1990, there were only five such centers/offices with paid staff. In addition to the University of Pennsylvania, support services for LGBT students were provided by the University of Michigan, the University of Massachusetts, Amherst, Grinnell College, and Princeton University. During the 1990s, more than 50 colleges and universities established LGBT centers/offices with at least a half-time paid director (see Appendix A). Contributing to the development of many of these centers/offices has been the National Consortium of Directors of Lesbian, Gay, Bisexual, and Transgender Resources in Higher Education, an organization for LGBT center/office administrators that was founded in 1997 to offer mutual support and advice, seek improvements in the campus climate for LGBT people, and advocate for the establishment of LGBT centers/offices at other institutions.

The dramatic increase in campus LGBT centers and offices represents an important change in higher education today, but this trend has largely not been reflected in studies of LGBT people or the literature on colleges and college student development, where the establishment of LGBT centers and offices has received scant attention. The one notable exception is Sanlo's (2000) recent article in which she examines the backgrounds, qualifications, and salaries of LGBT center/office administrators, their motivations for doing this work, and the administrative location and operating budgets of their centers/offices. Through E-mailing surveys to members of the consortium in 1997 and 1998, Sanlo was able to gather data on 23 of the then 26 LGBT centers/offices with a full-time professional director.

Recognizing the tremendous growth in the number of LGBT centers/offices in just the last few years (e.g., at the start of 2001, there were 44 with full-time directors) and wanting to learn more about their development and administration, I wanted to update and expand upon the findings of Sanlo's study. In February and March 2001, I sought to determine centers' constituencies and target audiences, to whom directors reported and with whom they consulted, their centers' staffing patterns, the amount and sources of their funding, and how space was utilized. Like Sanlo, I sent a brief survey to the LGBT centers/offices listed with the consortium, but in contrast to Sanlo's study, I included centers/offices with at least a half-time director in my research, because many of these administrators are as actively engaged in this work as their full-time colleagues. In addition, the creation of their positions represents a significant commitment to LGBT services on the part of the institution. I found that 56 LGBT campus centers/offices are staffed at least half-time by a paid professional, and of these, 54 (96%) responded to my survey, including all 35 centers/offices that have more than one paid staff member and all 19 that label themselves "centers."

I begin by discussing the characteristics of the institutions that have created LGBT centers/offices and conclude by identifying current trends in the establishment and administration of centers/offices that are likely to continue, at least in the immediate future.

CHARACTERISTICS OF THE INSTITUTIONS WITH LGBT CENTERS/OFFICES

Today, LGBT centers/offices are found at colleges and universities in almost half of the states and the District of Columbia, but they seem to be concentrated in the Midwest (18, or 32%), West (17, or 30%); and Northeast (15, or 27%). Only 6 centers/offices have been established at institutions in the South (11%), and there are no colleges or universities with centers/offices in the Southwest, Great Plains, or mountain states, except in Colorado. Not surprisingly, the largest number of centers/offices are found in states that have historically had more liberal political climates and educational policies, including California (12), Minnesota (4), and Michigan (4). Centers/offices are also concentrated on campuses in urban areas. Twenty-two of the institutions with centers/offices are in cities with populations of more than 100,000, including six institutions that are located in cities with more than 1 million people. Only seven schools with centers/offices are in cities of fewer than 10,000 people, and most of these institutions are private liberal arts colleges known for being more progressive than the small communities around them (U.S. Census 2000). Similarly, all but 6 campus LGBT centers/offices have been established at universities, and most of these are large research institutions. For example, 14 of the schools have more than 30,000 students, and the combined enrollment of the 56 institutions with LGBT centers/offices exceeds 1 million, with an average of nearly 21,000 students (U.S. Department of Education Web site). Under the 2000 Carnegie Classification of Institutions of Higher Education, close to three-fourths of the schools with centers/offices are listed as "Doctoral/Research Universities—Extensive," constituting about 40% of all schools in this category (Carnegie Foundation 1994). Again, there is tremendous regional variation. Only 2 of the 38 public doctoral/research universities in the South have centers or offices, whereas 10 of the 12 West Coast institutions of this type do so (and of the two without centers/offices, one is in the process of creating a center and the other has a student-run office).

In addition to regional location and the size of the student body and the surrounding community, another important variable affecting which institutions have LGBT centers/offices is the size of a school's endowment. As might be expected, the institutions with centers/offices tend to be among those with the largest endowments, indicating that having greater financial assets makes a college or university more likely to be willing to fund services for LGBT students. Of the 20 most highly endowed schools (excluding statewide systems), half have LGBT centers/offices (Chronicle 2001). Also not surprising is the fact that few religiously affiliated institution have established such centers/offices, only Emory University and DePauw University, both of which are associated with the Methodist Church, have done so.

THE CREATION OF LGBT CENTERS/OFFICES

The first university known to have provided support services specifically for its lesbian, gay, and bisexual students was the University of Michigan, which hired two human sexuality advocates in 1971 in response to pressure from students, including members of the campus Gay Liberation Front. Although other institutions did not follow Michigan's lead for more than a decade, the process of center/office formation was often similar at other colleges and universities. More than one-third of centers/offices were established largely as a result of student initiative, and in another third, students served as a secondary catalyst. Slightly less important factors were the recommendation of a committee examining LGBT issues on the campus and the involvement of faculty and staff (the primary force in the creation of 31% and 26% of the centers/offices, respectively).

While a number of colleges and universities have undertaken surveys of the climate on their campuses for LGBT students, staff, and faculty in the last 15 years, few LGBT centers/offices were established directly as a result of this research. Rather, by calling attention to the prevalence of hostility and discrimination against LGBT people, many of these studies seem to have galvanized students, staff, and faculty to begin developing LGBT support services, leading ultimately to the creation of a center/office. More than half of the 49 institutions that Robin Miller (www.lgbtcampus.org) identified as having conducted campus climate surveys subsequently established centers/offices, but on average the centers/offices opened more than three years after the studies were released.

Events such as hate crimes or hate incidences were also not a major, direct cause for the creation of centers/offices. Only one institution ranked on-campus events as the most important factor, and just six others listed it as a secondary reason. Two schools, though, mentioned the significance of an event that happened beyond their campuses—the murder of gay University of Wyoming student Matthew Shepard in 1998.

THE CONSTITUENCIES OF LGBT CENTERS/OFFICES

In just the relatively few years that they have existed on most college campuses, centers/offices have undergone a dramatic change in how they see themselves and their missions. Initially, centers/offices almost exclusively focused on sexual identity issues, and their primary responsibilities were to provide support services to lesbian, gay, and bisexual students and to educate the campus community about their experiences. But in the last few years, many centers/offices have begun to make connections between sexual identity and gender identity, as transgender people, including many transgender students, have become more visible and have sought to be formally recognized by lesbian, gay, and bisexual programs and organizations. As a result, in the late 1990s, many centers/offices modified their names and mission statements to incorporate transgender individuals. The extent and speed of the change are striking: of the 23 centers/offices established before 1995 that specified constituency groups in their names, only the University of Minnesota included the word "transgender" since then, all but two have added it (Ochs 1995). In the meantime, every center/office established in the last five years has been trans-inclusive, most from the outset, so that today, 46 centers/offices refer to themselves as "LGBT" (or "GLBT") and 6 others use alternate encompassing language ("queer," "rainbow," "Stonewall," or "pride").

Although only four centers/offices specifically include LGBT allies in their names, most also do extensive outreach to heterosexuals, from providing encouragement and a safe space for those who are LGBT-supportive, to trying to educate those who have less positive attitudes. My survey asked centers/offices to estimate the percent of time they spend working with LGBT people, heterosexuals, and both groups together. None of the 45 centers/offices that answered this question indicated that they serve only LGBT people. In fact, 9 devote less than 50% of their time to working with members of the LGBT community, and only 5 do almost no outreach to heterosexuals on campus.

One of the ways that some centers/offices involve "straight but not narrow" people in their work is through a safe zone, SAFE (Students, Administrators, and Faculty for Equality) on Campus, or Allies program, which enables students, staff, and faculty to identify themselves, in the words of Allies at Texas A&M University, "as individuals who are willing to provide a safe haven, a listening ear, and support for lesbian, gay, bisexual, and transgendered people or anyone dealing with sexual orientation issues" (Texas A&M Allies, http://allies.tamu.edu 2001). At most institutions, individuals who are interested in participating in the program attend a training session, after which they receive a logo or placard to display outside their office or residence hall room to indicate their involvement. While safe zone programs have traditionally been developed and facilitated by students—and the majority exist at institutions without LGBT centers/offices—many centers/offices help support and administer the program on their campuses.

CENTER/OFFICE OVERSIGHT

The extent to which centers/offices do outreach to the entire campus community through safe zone programs and other educational activities is demonstrated by the fact that the majority of survey respondents indicated that their target audience consists not only of students but also of staff, faculty, and administrators. Only four centers/offices (7%) stated that they exclusively focus on students, and three of these are located at selective private institutions: Carleton, Oberlin, and Stanford.

Reflecting the different constituency groups that they serve, the centers/offices that consult with an advisory board generally include representation from a broad cross-section of the campus community. More than a third of centers/offices have advisory boards, and, on average, these boards include students, staff, faculty, administrators, and, in some cases, also local community members and alumni. While students in general make up the largest single group (with an average of five members), they rarely constitute a majority on advisory boards and do not substantially outnumber staff (an average of four members) or faculty (an average of three members).

Still, for most centers/offices, students remain the primary constituency, which is evident in another aspect of their oversight—where centers/offices are housed administratively. The greatest number are freestanding units within a student affairs division (18) or part of a dean of students office (13) and directly report to an administrator at the level of vice provost/vice chancellor/vice president for student affairs or dean of students. A smaller number are situated within a multicultural center/office of multicultural affairs (10) or a women's center (3) and report to the director of that center/office. Only two centers/offices are located exclusively within a division of academic affairs, and, as Sanlo (2000a) concluded from her research, their day-to-day operation is very similar to the functioning of the centers/offices housed in student affairs.

FUNDING AND STAFFING

In her 1997–1998 study, Sanlo found that the operating budgets of LGBT centers/offices—the money that they spend on programming, support services, general office expenses, and the salaries of work-study students and other part-time personnel—varied widely, from $5,000 to $38,545, with an average of $16,720. Adding the salaries of full-time staff members, their total funding on average exceeded $62,000 (Sanlo 2000a). In the last two years, this figure has risen to nearly $84,000 for the centers/offices with at least one full-time staff member, with eight centers/offices having annual budgets of at least $100,000.

Most of the additional funding has been used to increase staff size, continuing a trend for centers/offices to grow over time. Of the 54 centers/offices in this study, only 17 began with a full-time director, and 10 were run by part-time students and volunteers. Today, 42 have full-time professional staffs, including 14 that have two full-time staff members and two that have three full-time staff members. The growth of centers/offices over time is also demonstrated by the fact that all but one of the 16 centers/offices with two or more full-time professional staff people were created before 1996. Moreover, only 11 centers/offices have not increased the size of their staffs since being established, and six of these have been founded in the last two years, so presumably they have not existed long enough to justify expansion.

The vast majority of LGBT centers/offices receive most of their funding through the college or university's general budget. More than one-fourth also rely on student fees for part of their operating expenses. But five state universities completely avoid using public funds for their centers/offices because of opposition from conservative state legislators and the threat of a backlash. For example, when Indiana University announced plans to open its GLBT Student Support Services office in 1994, a state legislator "tried to hold the university hostage," threatening to withhold much of the institution's funding until administrators abandoned the proposal. The university president was able to defuse the crisis through using private donations to establish the office, and since then, school officials have continued to finance the office this way rather than risk another controversy (Doug Bauder, personal communication, February 21, 2001).

Aside from seeking to avoid public financing, some centers/offices have solicited private donations in the last few years as a means to supplement their institutional funding, and the success of alumni outreach at the University of Pennsylvania and a number of other colleges and universities will likely lead to more such efforts. Currently, though, only 12 centers/offices actively encourage alumni giving. Few have also sought and obtained grant money: just 7 LGBT centers/offices were making use of grants at the time of the survey.

CENTERS VERSUS OFFICES

To this point, I have not distinguished between LGBT centers and offices, because they are similar in many aspects of their development and operation, such as their constituencies, funding sources, and how they were created, but centers and offices do differ in some significant ways. In terms of administrative oversight, centers are more likely than offices to be freestanding units, to report to a higher-level administrator (typically a vice provost, vice-chancellor, or vice president), and to consult with an advisory board. Not surprisingly, centers also tend to have bigger staffs, more space, and larger operating budgets. Seventeen of the 19 centers have at least one full-time professional staff member, and nearly half have more than two full-time staff members, as compared to 18% of offices. Reflecting their greater staff size, centers on average have four rooms, while offices have two—one for the director and another that serves multiple functions, such as a work space for part-time staff, a lounge or meeting room, and a library. Centers generally have separate spaces for at least some of these purposes, and several have other amenities like a kitchen or a computer/study room.

It naturally follows that centers would have larger overall budgets on average than offices. However, the two largest budgets belong to offices, and, as with staff size, a more important factor in budget size seems to be the age of the program. Ten of the 12 centers/offices with the largest budgets were established in or before 1995, and the 3 oldest centers/offices are among the best funded.

THE FUTURE OF LGBT CENTERS/OFFICES

Most LGBT centers/offices have been able to increase their operating budgets and the size of their staffs over time, as they have shown the tremendous need for support services for LGBT students. This trend is likely to continue, especially among the newest centers/offices, which are only beginning to demonstrate their importance. The impact of the recent economic downturn on institutions of higher education may mean that centers/offices will grow more slowly, but it is unlikely that future expansion will halt, given the overall effectiveness of centers/offices, which has led in part to LGBT students, staff, and faculty becoming a visible and significant constituency on many college campuses. Moreover, in the absence of greater institutional support, some centers/offices would still be able to increase their budgets through alumni donations.

Even though only three centers/offices were established in 2000 (the lowest number for a single year since 1997), there is little evidence to suggest that the growth of LGBT student services is at or approaching a standstill. With more students coming out in college or already open about their sexual identities when they enter higher education, schools will be increasingly hard-pressed to ignore their needs and to pretend, as many did for years, that LGBT students do not exist at their institutions or do not have any concerns different from those of their heterosexual peers. Even such religiously conservative schools as Brigham Young University (BYU) and Oral Roberts University (ORU) have had to recognize the presence of LGBT people on their campuses this year, even if, in the case of BYU, it was to expel two students for violating the school's ban on "homosexual conduct." At ORU, the reception was more tolerant: gay alumni made their presence known at the school's homecoming without incident.

Clearly, though, an institution like Oral Roberts is not about to offer any formal recognition to its LGBT students, much less establish an LGBT center/office, in the foreseeable future, and it is unlikely that many other religiously affiliated institutions, especially those in the South or West, will do so either. As in the past, the creation of new LGBT centers/offices is more likely to occur at large state universities or small, progressive liberal arts colleges in the Northeast, Midwest, or California. Efforts to develop a center/office also face a greater chance of success at institutions that have relatively large endowments and where wealthy LGBT alumni can be identified and successfully courted.

Perhaps the most important factor in the development of LGBT centers/offices is one that is not so easily quantifiable, and that is the personal and political landscape of a particular campus. For example, do LGBT students feel that there is a need for a center/office at their college or university, and do they have the means to advocate for one? Given the principal role of students in the creation of most centers/offices, these questions are critical. Moreover, to what extent are staff and faculty willing to support a center/office, and how open are key administrators to such a proposal? What is the attitude of regents or trustees or, at state universities, of legislators? Examining these campus-specific factors might help explain, for instance, why Harvard and Yale have not established centers/offices, despite being the two wealthiest institutions in higher education and being located in politically liberal cities and states, and why centers/offices exist at all nine University of California schools, but none are found among the four university centers in the State University of New York system. Researchers thus need to consider both the general characteristics of the institution and its individual qualities in order to understand the likelihood that a specific college or university will establish an LGBT center/office.

Chapter 4

Documenting Their Existence: Lesbian, Gay, Bisexual, and Transgender Students on Campus

Therese Eyermann and Ronni Sanlo

On many campuses around the country, lesbian, gay, bisexual, and transgender (LGBT) students are unwilling to share their sexual or gender identities (Sanlo 1998b) either verbally or on forms and surveys. As a result, institutions are un-aware of the number and presence of LGBT students and their needs. Since the Kinsey studies in the late 1940s, researchers have attempted to determine the number of gay and lesbian people in the general population with little empirical success. Kinsey, Pomeroy, and Martin (1948) and , Kinsey, Pomeroy, Martin and Gebhardt (1953) reported that 37% of adult men and 13% of adult women had at least one sexual experience to orgasm with another person of the same sex and that 4% of men and 2% of women were exclusively homosexual in prac-tice. Other studies, conducted both by gay rights proponents and antigay groups, have documented varying figures, but there is still no concrete evidence of the number of lesbian, gay, bisexual, or transgender people in the U.S.

There are several reasons that these data are so elusive. First, some surveys regarding sexual behavior rely on people to self-disclose same-sex interactions, thoughts, or feelings. It is unlikely that people would answer such questions honestly or at all if they do not explicitly trust the anonymity of the process. Second, some surveys rely on people to identity themselves through labels such as *homosexual, lesbian, gay,* and/or *bisexual.* While some LGBT people may use these labels, many others may not. They have decided not to attach a label to their non-heterosexual identity or they have not yet come out enough to identify with a label or they use different terminology, all of which are the experiences of LGBT college students (Manago 1999). Finally, while some people may have strong feelings of same-sex attraction, it is likely that they remain in heterosex-ual relationships or become non-sexual and never act on their feelings of such same-sex attraction.

Two factors may affect data related to college students. First, while sur-veys may ask opinions about views on issues related to LGBT people, few insti-tutions or national databases ask respondents to identify their sexual orientation or gender identity or ask about it on a regular basis. For example, the Annual Freshman Survey conducted by the Higher Education Research Institute (HERI) does not include sexual orientation or gender identity in its demographic information, so the numbers of LGBT students remain unknown.

Primary academic missions generally state that institutions champion an environment that fosters the academic and personal development of all students. Some institutions include LGBT students in their equity statements, yet few, if any, institutions are aware of the actual number of LGBT students on their campuses. Administrators and others often ask how many LGBT students are on their campuses. When they want to know how many African American students, for example, are at an institution, they simply refer to institutional admissions data. But when they want to know how many LGBT students are on campus, officials likely find themselves resorting to asking the one or two openly gay students or staff.

The second factor that limits ability to know the number of LGBT students on campuses is that students may not use the labels that researchers suggest or impose. Of the few campuses that do ask this question on their various surveys or forms, most use traditional terminology of *homosexual, gay, lesbian,* and/or *bisexual.* This type of labeling may offend some LGBT students or may seem too explicit for their stage of sexual awareness.

This study investigates whether terminology used to document the sexual identity of college students affects the response rate, specifically, the number of non-respondents. It is hypothesized that traditional labeling may inhibit some LGBT students from self-identification. It is important to determine beyond anecdotal evidence that LGBT students are on our campuses, regardless of how they choose to label themselves, and that they must be included in appropriate programming and services. Their presence must be acknowledged, documented, and included in campus offerings from services to curriculum.

Researchers have examined marginalized students to determine if their college experience and outcomes differ significantly from the experiences and outcomes of majority students. Astin (1982), Allen (1986), Astin, Tsui, and Avalos (1996), Nora and Cabrera (1996), and Sax, Astin, Korn, and Mahoney (1998) noted that some minority students might experience lower satisfaction with college, perhaps leading to lower retention and persistence rates than those of majority students. Although many institutions have traditionally thought of marginalized students in terms of ethnicity or gender, LGBT students have only recently been seriously considered in the higher education arena.

The difficulty with identifying LGBT students begins with the problems of how to define the meaning of sexuality. Kinsey et al. (1948, 1953) defined sexual orientation based on exclusively same-sex practice as well as on sexual experience at any time in one's life. The General Social Survey, which uses the rule of exclusively homosexual activity in the previous year, found 2% of men and .7% of women would be considered homosexual (Smith 1994). These data do not take into account those who consider themselves non-heterosexual but who have not engaged in same-sex sexual activity.

The most recent comprehensive research in this area to date used a combination of labeling and feelings of attraction (Michael, Gagnon, Laumann, & Kolata 1994). Michael et al. (1994) reported that 1.4% of women and 2.8% of men identified themselves as "homosexual," although a larger proportion of respondents (5.5% of women and 6% of men) reported erotic attraction to persons of the same sex. These two examples illustrate the methodological problem of defining sexual orientation in terms of labeling versus behavior. Since these data were based on the national population, it is unclear how applicable these figures are to those in the 18-to-22 age range. That is, there may be differences in percentages of LGBT adults in the population at large (from which the preceding studies took their samples) and those found on college campuses.

Few studies empirically look at sexual orientation on college campuses, and fewer still that include gender identity. The American College Health Association (ACHA) conducts periodic surveys of college students on health issues. In the 1997–1998 survey, students were asked to identify their sexual orientation by traditional labels as well as by behaviors during the past academic year. The National Consortium of Directors of LGBT Centers in Higher Education (2001) revealed that only a handful of institutions sought to identify the number of LGBT students. Of these institutions the majority used traditional labeling terminology in their surveys. The percentage of students who identified themselves as gay, lesbian, or bisexual was typically 4% or less. Very few institutions asked the question based on to whom the student is most attracted, men or women. For these institutions the percentage of students identifying as attracted to someone of the same sex was around 7%. While regional and institutional climate may well contribute to the percentage of students identifying as homosexual or bisexual, the wording of the question may also be a factor.

The Klein Sexual Grid suggests that sexuality is fluid and that attraction is often the first step in the process of identifying one's sexual orientation (Klein, Sepekoff, & Wolf 1985). Klein et al. (1985) proposed an alternative way of looking at sexual orientation, using a combination of time and behavioral scales. The seven behavioral scales begin with feelings of sexual attraction and continued through a straight/gay lifestyle. Timescales represent the past, present, and ideal preferences. Since Klein identified feelings of sexual attraction as the prebehavior stage, and since the process of sexual orientation awareness may culminate in the college years, the wording of sexual self-identification questions may be important. This study compared the response rates of self-identified LGB (but not transgender) students through traditional labeling versus feelings of attraction, an early identifier of sexual orientation.

METHODOLOGY

The residential life office of a large public research university on the West Coast conducted an annual student consumer satisfaction and quality of life survey among its residence hall population. This anonymous survey queried students on a variety of issues related to community, programming, academics, and noise issues in the residence hall. The survey also collected student-reported demographic information concerning gender, ethnicity, and class level.

This research study analyzed survey results from the years 1996 through 1999. Response rates during those years were between 50–60% of the total residence hall population of approximately 6,200 students. The characteristics of the residents who responded to the satisfaction and quality survey were similar to the characteristics of all residence hall students in terms of gender, ethnicity, and class level.

During the years 1996, 1997, and 1998, the survey asked students to identify themselves as heterosexual, gay, lesbian, or bisexual. This question had the single largest non-response rate of any question on the survey, about 10% annually. Additionally, this question elicited the largest response effect and the largest number of write-in comments, most of which were either frivolous or abusive in nature. For example, several respondents who identified as male wrote that they were lesbians; several respondents indicated preference for bestiality; but most write-in comments were homophobic.

Discussion with an LGBT residence hall rap group revealed that LGBT students disliked labels. Further, the younger the age of the student when she or he came out, the less comfortable she or he seemed to feel with the use of labels. In addition, some students of color, especially Latinos/as and African Americans (Cimons 2000), articulated that the labels "lesbian" and "gay" were not part of their cultural language and had no meaning for them (group interview, July 1999). As a result, the text of the survey was changed in 1999 from the previous labels to "To whom are you most attracted?" with options being men, women, and both men and women.

FINDINGS

The surveys in the years between 1996 and 1998 employed traditional labeling methods. The general responses of heterosexuals, bisexuals, and those choosing not to answer were fairly constant over time, while the percentages of gays and lesbians decreased during that time. Since the surveys are completed anonymously, respondents are not linked together across years. Combining the yearly samples into one large data set, utilizing the typical procedure for nominal data, the chi-square test would tend to overestimate any effect. Therefore, it was determined more appropriate to convert each sexual orientation category into dichotomous variables utilizing the more stringent analysis of means t-test. Converting variables of this type into "dummy variables" is a common procedure used to deal with categorical variables statistically.

The left half of Table 3 identifies the years between 1996 and 1998. These were the years that traditional labeling methods were employed. In general, the responses of heterosexuals, bisexuals, and those choosing not to answer were fairly consistent over time. The percentages of gays and lesbians decreased over time. The right half of the table shows the computed responses of students in 1999, when the sexual identity question was asked in terms of attraction.

A comparison of these two sets of wording shows that: the percent of students identifying as heterosexual was fairly consistent over time; and t tests for the heterosexual samples showed no significant difference in heterosexual response for the years 1996, 1998, and 1999 (p<.01). Similarly, there is no significant different in heterosexual response for 1997 and 1999.

However, there appeared to be larger percentages of students in 1999 who could be identified as lesbian, gay, or bisexual than in previous years. Specifically, the overall percentage for non-heterosexual students increased from less than 4% in the years 1996 through 1998, to 8.3% in 1999.

T-tests for presumably gay students showed that while there was no difference in their responses in 1997 and 1998, there was a significant difference between those two years and 1999. Likewise, the means analysis for presumably lesbian students showed that there was a significant difference between the 1999 responses and those given between 1996 through 1998. Additionally, there were no significant differences in the bisexual response between 1996 and 1998; however, there was a significant difference between the responses for those years and the responses for 1999.

The non-response rate was much lower in 1999 than in 1996, 1997 or 1998, decreasing from roughly 10% to 3.7%. There was no statistical difference between non-response in years 1996 to 1998 using a 99% confidence interval. However, there are significantly fewer non-responses in 1999 than there are in the previous years. Figure 4 graphically represents the constancy of the heterosexual response over time, combined with the simultaneous increase in presumed LGB responses along with decreases in non-response from 1998 to 1999. This lends itself to the supposition that those who previously did not answer the question now chose to respond. One theoretical explanation for these phenomena could be that those who chose not to respond in previous years felt uncomfortable with the labeling terminology, while the attraction wording was less threatening or felt more accurate. However, there could also have been more LBG students residing in the residence hall in 1999 than in previous years.

Another difference between the two sets of surveys, 1996–1998 and 1999, was the number of written comments in the margins of the surveys. Whereas the number of write-in comments in previous years typically numbered around 150, in 1999 the number of write-in comments dropped to 54. In addition, the tone and quality of the comments were less hostile than in previous years. Although it is impossible to determine the sexual orientation of the authors of the write-in comments, they do call into question the effects that labeling may have on all students regardless of sexual orientation.

Once LGB students were identified, further data analysis using other survey questions revealed that these students have significantly different perceptions concerning their satisfaction and sense of community in living on campus than do heterosexual students. For example, LGB students were more likely to report witnessing acts of racism, sexism, and homophobia than were heterosexual students.

While this new format for obtaining information regarding sexual orientation appears to provide more complete data, it is limited by several factors. First, when students were asked to whom they were most attracted, the addition of the word "sexually" to the word "attracted" was deliberately avoided in order to limit negatively charged reactions. However, it is likely that the term "attracted" may have specific nonsexual connotations to some students, especially those of different cultures or international students. Therefore, the terminology may still be inadequate.

Second, a stronger comparison of the response rates to each of the two questions (i.e., labeling versus attraction) could have been made had both questions been asked on the 1999 survey. Respondent awareness of this test of terminology could elicit bias, thus creating two samples, each with its own version of terminology. Combined with other information on the survey, it could have provided a likely composite of the type of student who prefers one terminology to the other.

Further research is needed to determine how labeling affects response rates on similar surveys. Additionally, transgender students' presence, views, and needs must eventually be included in these types of surveys to determine service provision for this population.

IMPLICATIONS FOR PRACTICE

In order to determine which programs and services best fit the needs of lesbian, gay, and bisexual students, their existence must be documented, their issues and opinions understood and made known, and their persistence to graduation facilitated. However, it is difficult to determine the presence and needs of lesbian, gay, bisexual, and transgender students if they feel that terminology does not always apply and thus inhibits their responses.

Based on this study, the recommendations for practice in higher education are:

1. On campus surveys, ask students to identify themselves not only by the traditional labels of heterosexual, lesbian, gay, and bisexual but also by to whom they are sexually attracted.

2. Do not assume that just because a student does not identify with the terms "lesbian," "gay," or "bisexual" she or he is heterosexual.

3. Do not assume that just because a student does identify with the terms "lesbian," "gay," or "bisexual," she or he exclusively acts on that terminology.

Careful consideration of the impact of how lesbian, gay, and bisexual students identify themselves, how researchers identity them, and how their behaviors and labels may not be congruent may assist institutions to move away from labels per se and toward definitions that include a broader range of experiences of sexual and gender identity.

Table 3
Sexual Orientation Trends

* "What is your sexual orientation?" Response Options: "Heterosexual," "Gay," "Lesbian," or "Bisexual."
** "To whom are you most attracted?" Response Options: "Men," "Women," "Both Men and Women."

Percent Responding in Each Category					
Labeling Wording*	1996	1997	1998	1999	Attraction Wording**
1. Heterosexual	85.58	90.30	87.23	87.9	1. Men Attracted to Women and Women Attracted to Men
2. Gay	1.67	0.73	0.83	2.1	2. Men Attracted to Men
3. Lesbian	1.01	0.27	0.17	2.7	3. Women Attracted to Women
4. Bisexual	1.36	0.96	1.32	3.5	4. Men/Women Attracted to Both
5. Missing	10.39	7.7	10.4	3.7	5. Missing
n	2,580	2,598	3,485	3,800	

Table 4
Homosexual and Bisexual Responses*

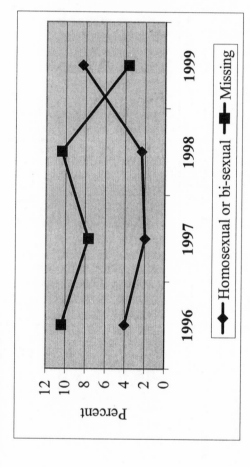

*Labeling ('96-98) vs. Feelings of Attraction ('99)

(Missing Values: 4.04% in 1996, 1.96% in 1997, and 2.32% in 1998 rising to 8.3% in 1999)

Part II

Starting Your Program or Center

Chapter 5

Matching Directors and Centers or Offices: Hiring for Success

LGBT campus resource centers are the newest service units in student affairs on college and university campuses (Sanlo 2000). While the first LGBT office opened at the University of Michigan in 1991, others did not begin to appear until the late 1980s. By 1994 there were new centers at the University of Pennsylvania; the University of Massachusetts, Amherst; the University of Minnesota; Ohio State University; Duke; and the University of Illinois, Champaign-Urbana and Chicago. One year later, UCLA; the University of California, Irvine; Cal Poly Pomona; and others opened their doors. By January 2000, there were nearly 40 LGBT centers on college campuses with full time professional staff; another 30 campuses had offices with part-time coordinators—usually graduate student interns. (see Appendix A).

Because there are no courses of study in higher education to train professionals to become LGBT center directors, most of the first generation of directors have come from the ranks of LGBT community activists. However, over half of the full-time directors earned doctoral degrees primarily in higher education administration, educational leadership, student services, or counseling. Second-generation directors are now coming to the profession directly from student affairs units after spending either an internship at an LGBT center or establishing a mentoring relationship with an LGBT center director.

There are a growing number of opportunities for people to become LGBT center directors as institutions add such centers to their student affairs or academic affairs divisions to meet the demands of LGBT students, faculty, and staff. A director from within an institution—that is, employed elsewhere in the institution—or from the outside may be hired to initiate a center; a director from within or outside may be hired to replace a director in an existing center; or an institution may hire a part-time professional or a graduate student intern as director rather than expend funds for a full-time professional. This chapter looks at each of these possibilities and presents case studies from people who have experienced these areas.

NEW CENTER/NEW OUTSIDE DIRECTOR

The best scenario is, of course, to be the first director in an institution's new center. The director has the freedom to develop the center and to create a service agency that is both unique and challenging. With the National Consortium of Directors of LGBT Resources in Higher Education as a support network—and with professional organizations in higher education such as the National Association for Student Personnel Administrators (NASPA), the American College Personnel Association (ACPA), the American College Health Association (ACHA), the American College and University Housing Organization (ACUHO), and others supporting inclusion of LGBT people and issues—a foundation already exists for a new director to hit the ground running as she or he hires staff, conducts needs assessments, develops programs, and reaches out to the campus LGBT community.

There are problems that some new directors—whether hired from within the institution or new to the institution—at new centers have faced: institutional politics among the stakeholders who developed the center; supervisors who are unsure of the role of the director and the center; and students who are unclear about the center's role in their lives and activities. Centers are often developed after a long process by many people on campus, especially those involved in the LGBT campus community. At some institutions, those stakeholders have expressed the need to retain control of the LGBT community by not allowing the new director to fully do his or her job. At an institution in California, the LGBT center advisory board, which has control of the center, will not allow the new director to see or participate in the budget process. At an institution in the Midwest, the LGBT commission continues to exclude the center director from related LGBT politics.

Since LGBT centers and services are new on many campuses, there is a lack of clarity regarding the supervisory process of the center. Indeed, few supervisors are aware of the needs of LGBT students and of the service that the center actually provides. At one institution, the new director received mixed messages from her supervisor regarding her work because the supervisor was unsure of what actually was needed and what was being provided. Finally, LGBT students who have worked hard to prepare and present programs and some services on campus are now unsure of how they fit into the process of a new center and sometimes become resentful that someone is now being paid to do the nearly impossible things that they were attempting to accomplish. In all of these scenarios, the center director must be absolutely sure about her or his strategic plan and must be able to communicate that plan clearly to all of the stakeholders, including the supervisor. If the voices of the LGBT campus community—students, faculty, staff, and alumni—are included in the planning process and in communications, the director should be able to articulate the plan with the supervisor and with the entire campus community.

NEW CENTER/NEW INSIDE DIRECTOR

Institutions hiring for the position of director of an LGBT campus resource center should certainly conduct a national search to recruit the best candidates. Internal candidates—those already at the institutions in other capacities—may be the best people for the job. While a successful internal candidate would have the same challenges as an external director of a new center, the internal director has added dimensions as there are great advantages to knowing the climate of the institution and the personalities of some of the key players.

Case Study 5.1
The University of Maryland College Park

The position of coordinator of LGBT equity was created at the University of Maryland (UMD) at College Park beginning on July 1, 1998. This assignment was a full-time job, reporting to the assistant vice president for academic affairs. I was appointed to the position on an acting basis at that time. Following a review of the usefulness of the position, a search was planned for later that academic year in compliance with University guidelines. Due to unforeseen circumstances, the search did not get under way until quite late, the acting appointment was extended, and a final permanent appointment was made on November 9, 1999, when I became the Director of the Office of Lesbian, Gay, Bisexual and Transgender Equity. The first proposal to create this Office came on November 6, 1996, in a report titled "Embracing Diversity: Lesbian, Gay, and Bisexual Students, Faculty, and Staff at the University of Maryland at College Park," submitted by the Lesbian, Gay, and Bisexual Staff and Faculty Association in conjunction with the Lesbian Gay Bisexual Alliance, a student organization. I was the lead author of this report. It grew out of efforts by the staff and faculty who had been active in advocating for domestic partner benefits and who then became interested in taking a more comprehensive view of the needs of the campus LGBT population. The proposal for an LGBT resource center was denied by the president, but he accepted the proposition to create a standing committee for LGBT concerns. This was named the President's Commission on Lesbian, Gay and Bisexual Issues, which conformed to the names and reporting structure of other university-wide standing committees dealing with well-defined segments of the campus population. The commission began its work in February 1997, and I was named the first chair. In the fall of 1997, the commission approached the president once again about an office dedicated to LGBT concerns, arguing that the language of the original denial betrayed a misunderstanding of the purpose of the proposed office. (The commission scaled back the notion of a center, replacing it with an office.) In December 1997, the president indicated that the next logical step would be to discuss it with the vice presidents of academic affairs and student affairs to determine their support and the most logical place for such an office. The commission determined that the scope and purpose of the new office were most similar to the Nyumburu Center, the Office of Multi-Ethnic Education, and the Office of International Educational Services, all of which are located within academic affairs. Locating this office within student affairs, as is common on other campuses, would have isolated the LGBT Office at UMD. With the first preference for academic affairs, we approached the provost who also serves as the senior vice president for academic affairs. Our provost had been recently appointed and had worked previously at the Pennsylvania State University, which has a coordinator of lesbian, gay, bisexual, and transgender equity. Shortly after arriving at UMD in the fall of 1997, he attended a speak-out sponsored by the commission in which many students gave compelling testimony regarding the difficulties that they faced on campus and the need for increased services. His attendance at this event exceeded the amount of time he had allocated. By February 1998, the commission had worked through its process of precisely what to request, and we had received guidance from the president on how to proceed. The provost indicated his support for such an office but cautioned that the decision would be made by the campus cabinet, which consists of the president, the four vice presidents, and other selected senior administrators. We followed his advice in submitting a short, one-page proposal to the cabinet. Although the deliberations of the cabinet are not public, it is believed that all supported the general concept from the beginning. Some think that the vice president for student affairs initially felt that the needs of the LGBT community would be met with a graduate assistant working 20 hours per week, which was about to be established within student affairs. The proposal to create this assistantship had not been communicated to the commission as a whole partially because all discussions initiated by the commission had been within academic affairs. Unfortunately, this information did not reach us before our proposal was submitted even though senior administrators from student affairs were members of the commission. Despite the initial competition of proposals, the cabinet ultimately decided by consensus to move forward with both. The name of the position in academic affairs had not been prompted by the commission and it matched exactly the position at Pennsylvania State University, coordinator of lesbian, gay, bisexual and transgender equity. Within student affairs, the LGBT assistantship was created along with two others, one for Asian American students and another for Latino/Native American students. (There was already a staff position dedicated to working with African American students.) This position is now known as the coordinator of lesbian, gay, bisexual and transgender student involvement and community advocacy. Although there is no formal link between the position in student affairs and the one in academic affairs, we have determined to consult regularly with one another and to work jointly on several projects. Key elements of our success include the following: tenacity in the face of initial denials and roadblocks; consistently pointing to similar institutions that already had dedicated resources for their LGBT populations; a comfortable working relationship with senior administrators and the person initially appointed; and the good fortune to have a senior administrator who knew first hand of such an office. I began working at the University of Maryland in July 1988 as the associate director of the Center for Studies in Nineteenth-Century Music. I later became active in our Lesbian and Gay Staff and Faculty Association, and in 1995, I became its co-chair. As a vocal and visible leader, I tried very hard to demonstrate my desire to do what was best for the institution without flinching in my advocacy for our LGBT population. As my academic training in musicology had not prepared me directly for some of the issues that I would face, such as incorporating LGBT studies into the curriculum, I often felt inadequate. Consequently, I relied on many colleagues and sought to educate myself in this area. I believe that my growth in knowledge and as a leader was visible to campus administrators, and that our ability to work together provided them with the comfort that they needed to move forward on these issues. (Submitted by Luke Jensen, director, Office of Lesbian, Gay, Bisexual, and Transgender Equity, University of Maryland, College Park)

EXISTING CENTER/NEW OUTSIDE DIRECTOR

The advantage of being an outside director, especially one who lived in another city, is that one is not yet entrenched in campus or community politics.

Case Study 5.2
University of Michigan 1994–1997

I began my career in higher education by being hired as the director of the Lesbian and Gay Male Programs Office at the University of Michigan, the oldest such office in the country. The office was in dire need of new ideas, skills, and energy. The situation was excellent because I knew that anything I did would almost automatically viewed as a success. I needed that thread of confidence since I was approaching 50 years of age, starting a new career, and moving 1000 miles from home to take that job. After three and a half successful and wonderful years at Michigan, I accepted a position at UCLA, whose center was fairly new and, like Michigan in 1994, was in need of a new vision and direction. My center at Michigan was now in great shape with programs built upon their own merit, and my relationships at the institution were solid. (submitted by Ronni Sanlo, LGBT Campus Resource Center, UCLA)

Case Study 5.3
University of Michigan 1998

My career as director of the Office of LGBT Affairs began at the University of Michigan in 1998 following a very powerful and successful director. While the LGBT community of students, faculty, staff, and Ann Arbor residents warmly welcomed me, it was challenging nonetheless. A year had passed since the former director had accepted a position at another institution. The university and the LGBT communities were very flexible with me. An added challenge, however, was that one of the founding directors, who is also well-respected and admired, happened to still work at the university. I knew that I was being compared to previous directors and there were people around who were still in grief over their departures. One of the first E-mails that I received at the university came from a disgruntled alum who was disappointed that the founding director was no longer in the directorship. He proceeded to lament the departure of that director and predicted my failure and downfall. This was, of course, very disheartening and disappointing, but this was by far the most blatant form of disrespect that I received from anyone missing a former director. Others did not complain in this fashion but were, instead, more subtle. For example, there were comments that the office did not run as smoothly, even though we had more staff. In small ways, I could see that while the staff liked and accepted me, they clearly missed my predecessor. I was able to have a very open, honest, and productive conversation about this with staff, and it seemed to help. I noticed several issues that needed to be addressed. One was an obvious underutilization of the office by women. This distressed me. I knew that we were at a disadvantage because men held the two most visible positions in the office, director and business manager, so I knew that we had to add women staff and create programs to address women's issues. Another challenging issue was race/ethnicity in the LGBT community. I found that a lot of the students of color felt frustrated about race issues within the LGBT community. As I am an African American gay man, students of color were communicating to me that they felt as if their particular issues don't always get the attention that they deserve and that LGBT Caucasian students often don't look at their own issues around race or privilege. As a result, students of color often felt as though they had not been as included in the community or that they had not been treated sensitively. Finally, one of the most challenging areas for me as a new director in an old center that had just recently added "transgender" to its name was how, exactly, to be fully inclusive of the transgender community. Despite, or perhaps as a result of, the challenges, it was a successful first year. I have an excellent working relationship with the former directors of the center and do not hesitate touching base with them for guidance and support. As I do this work, I know that I, too, will be available as a supportive director for new colleagues entering this exciting field. (Submitted by E. Frederic Dennis, director, LGBT Affairs, University of Michigan, Ann Arbor)

FULL-TIME VERSUS PART-TIME DIRECTORS

The decision to hire a director or coordinator of an LGBT center or office is often based on issues related both to funding and to commitment of the institution to provide professional services to the LGBT campus population. The one advantage to hiring a part-time person, whether one already on campus in another position or a graduate student, is money. The disadvantages are inconsistency of hours, programs, and services for existing staff and a reinvention of the wheel each time a new person assumes the position, which, in the case of students, may be annually. The institution needs to determine exactly what is expected of a person who is hired as a part-time director or coordinator.

The following is the national call in 1998 for a part-time intern/coordinator position for the LGBT Section of the Student Life Community at a Midwest university:

The Division of Student Life and Services seeks applications for the position of Community Coordinator– Gay/Lesbian/Bisexual/Transgender in the Multicultural Resource Center. This is a full-time, 11-month (July 15, 1998 through June 14, 1999), limited-term Intern appointment, reporting to the Assistant Dean of Student Life and Services. The appointment is made annually. In accordance with the mission of [unnamed] College as an educational institution, the position of Community Coordinator—Gay/Lesbian/ Bisexual/Transgender offers the unique opportunity to combine service to Gay/Lesbian/ Bisexual/Transgender and other students with personal and professional development in the arena of higher education. Generally, this internship is a one-year opportunity that provides hands-on experience in student development in higher education. The primary objective is two-fold: 1) to provide support for and develop Gay/Lesbian/Bisexual/ Transgender students, as well as other students, as they work toward completing an [unnamed] degree; and 2) to encourage the Coordinator's development as a professional in higher education. While supporting Gay/Lesbian/ Bisexual/Transgender and other students and advocating for their cultural, social and intellectual needs, the Coordinator will be exposed to the complex nature of an institution of higher education. He or she will be challenged to effectively balance student needs and concerns with administrative duties. The incumbent will have responsibility for assessing and addressing the specific cultural/ social/political needs and concerns of Gay/Lesbian/ Bisexual/Transgender students while also working with other students who belong to historically disenfranchised or marginalized communities. The other groups include but are not limited to the following: Asian American, Latino/a, African American, Native American, and multiracial communities as well as first-generation and low-income college students. Housed in the Multicultural Resource Center, this Coordinator acts as a link between the Assistant Dean and Gay/ Lesbian/Bisexual/Transgender students, as well as between the Multicultural Resource Center and the rest of the College communities.

Duties and Responsibilities:

Identify the social, cultural, educational, and political needs of Gay/Lesbian/ Bisexual/Transgender students, as well as those of other student communities;

Advocate to the Assistant Dean of Student Life and Services the concerns of Gay/Lesbian/Bisexual/Transgender students, as well as those of Asian American, Latino/a, African American, Native American, and multiracial communities as well as first-generation and low-income college students;

Serve as a liaison for the Multicultural Resource Center;

Maintain tangible links and public relations with students and other departments through the design and distribution of newsletters, brochures, and other publications;

Maintain records and provide narrative and/or written progress reports as directed, including program assessments/evaluations;

Under the direct supervision and guidance of the Assistant Dean, the incumbent will assist Gay/Lesbian/Bisexual/Transgender students and students of color in general to foster a strong sense of self, to strengthen individual communities, and to build alliances with other departments and communities;

Submit bi-weekly activity reports to the Assistant Dean of Student Life and Services;

Meet weekly with the other three Coordinators and the Assistant Deans;

Hold regular office hours.

This was an actual call for intern applicants at a Midwest university for an 11-month position. The position description is detailed and involved. The successful candidate for this position is expected to provide services that generally take full-time professional staff a year or more just to get started. Foundations need to be developed, action plans need to be defined, and familiarity with campus places, people, and, most importantly, students needs to be developed. It will likely take this intern the full 11 months of his or her tenure to have developed enough rapport with LGBT students that they feel safe enough to come to the office—and then the position is over, and a new intern will begin anew. The good news is that this is an incredible opportunity for a graduate-level student who wishes to learn about operating an LGBT center or office, but in all likelihood, she or he will have burned out by the time the 11 months is completed.

Following is another view of a part-time position.

Case Study 5.4
Iowa State University

Iowa State University (ISU) has had a part time director of LGBT Student Services (LGBTSS) since the program was established in 1992. Although there are disadvantages with this type of organizational structure, LGBTSS has utilized several strategies to overcome many of the problems associated with a part-time director. Due to budget and institutional priorities, LGBTSS is coordinated by a graduate student who holds a half-time assistantship. The coordinator is expected to work only 20 hours weekly fulfilling a vast array of tasks that are vital to the mission of the program. It is extremely unlikely that one person working only 20 hours weekly could fulfill these tasks. The shortage of time, therefore, is one of the most pressing challenges that LGBTSS has encountered in utilizing a part-time director. Another problem with using a part-time, graduate student director is the expected annual staff turnover. The resulting lack of continuity creates difficulty in establishing and fulfilling long-term goals. Also, LGBTSS is perhaps viewed as a "lesser" student affairs priority since it has no full-time or permanent staff appointment. Given these challenges, LGBTSS has utilized several key strategies. For example, having strong allies among administrators has helped to provide consistency, even through annual staff turnover. Nurturing a strong and active advisory committee has also assisted in providing consistency. In addition, the LGBTSS office has many programs that are designed to be self-service. Finally, LGBTSS counts on many volunteers, interns, and a work-study student in order to fulfill its mission. (Submitted by Sine Anahita, coordinator of Lesbian, Gay, Bisexual and Transgender Student Services, ISU)

FULL-TIME CENTER OR OFFICE DIRECTOR

The advantages of having a full-time director or coordinator of an LGBT Center or Office are many: one person responsible for directing, training, and supervising staff and volunteers; one voice with equal standing as the other directors in student or academic affairs; one person to assure the creation and implementation of all services, programs, advisory and other boards; and one person as a familiar focal point for the entire institution regarding resources, education, policies, and information. Appendix E is the actual position description of the full-time professional center director at UCLA.

It is the hope and the challenge of the National Consortium of Directors of LGBT Resources in Higher Education that every major institution will have an LGBT center or office with full-time professional staff. LGBT campus resource center directors understand the importance of college student development as well as the experience and knowledge of LGBT issues and people. They are resourceful and skillful programmers as well as creative and sensitive managers. They hold positive regard for all students and maintain a courageous commitment to leadership and advocacy. Regardless of how they came into the position, LGBT directors do this work out of love and respect for LGBT students, and they understand the importance—as Michigan vice president for student affairs Royster Harper emphasizes—of keeping students at the center of our focus.

Chapter 6

Developing a Strategic Plan

Strategic, long-range planning is necessary because we cannot predict the future. It is what we must do today to be prepared for the uncertainty of tomorrow. We make decisions for and in the present but not for the present alone. The decisions that we make today may commit us on a long-range basis. "It is the continuous process of making present decisions systematically and with the best possible knowledge of their futurity, organizing systematically the effort needed to carry out these decisions, and measuring the results of these decisions against the expectations through organized, systematic feedback." (Matteson & Ivancevich 1993, p. 103)

Planning is the conscious determination of courses of action to achieve preconceived objectives. It is deciding in advance what is to be done, when it is to be done, by whom it is to be done, and how it is to be done. It can range from the detailed, specific, rigid to the broad, general, and flexible design. It is a process of choosing from alternative courses of action and charting use of time, resources, and effort to achieve the objective sought. (Matteson & Ivancevich 1993, p. 115)

According to Smith (1994b), strategic planning should occur initially as an organization is created, then periodically to analyze whether the organizational mission is still relevant to the needs and expectations of the constituency. There should be a well-defined and understood strategic plan that the organization's staff as well as its board or other governing body uses to guide program activities, allocate resources, and assess the organization's achievements. It should be a proactive rather than reactive tool. "A good strategic plan will provide staff and leaders with the guidelines to establish the organization's program of activities; allocate human and financial resources to accomplish these activities; assess whether the objectives are being met; and evaluate programs, staff, and resources." (Smith 1994b, pp. 1-2).

A strong strategic plan is realistic. It takes into account changes that will take place both within and outside the organization in a specific time-frame. It requires that we "not only look inward at what we might desire for our organization, but also—and perhaps more importantly— that we look outward to the external environment to understand those forces and trends which will affect our organization's future and the accomplishment of its mission" (Smith 1994b, p. 2). It broadly maps the activities that the organization should pursue to maintain its desired character and identity and is a tool to guide decision making on which issues are fundamental to the organization. According to Smith (1994b, p. 2), "a well-developed strategic plan provides the framework for responding to a changing environment." Questions that should be asked during the planning process are: What is the essence of the organization? What are the core values and beliefs of the constituents? What is its mission? Who is served, and what do they get? Should the mission be amended? What does it do best, and how does it relate to what the world needs? What are it's strengths and weaknesses? What are the keys to the success of the organization? Of those factors making a difference, what is changing in the environment? How can the organization really make a difference in the lives of its constituents and in society? What activities are worth undertaking and committing to over the next three years? Five years? What must be done to implement the strategy?

When completed, a strategic plan should be short and focused, containing a vision, mission statement, principles, goals, and an action plan. It "says to the world: this is who we are and what we want to be, and here's how we plan to fulfill our mission" (Smith 1994b, p. 3).

Two maxims to remember: a strategic plan is a statement of important, but flexible, guidelines, not a rigid document, and the process of strategic planning—the development, implementation, and assessment of a plan—is not a single exercise but an ongoing continuous process that must adapt to internal and external environmental changes.

Strategic planning helps us develop our road map and keeps us on task. It's the opportunity to work with the stakeholders of our institutions who are lesbian, gay, bisexual, or transgender (LGBT) themselves or allies who care about the environment for LGBT students, faculty, and staff. Ronni Sanlo, director of the UCLA LGBT Center, prefers a three-year strategic plan, although some of our colleagues prefer a five-year plan. The strategic plan is that process that develops or reaffirms the vision statement, the mission, or purpose and revises the goals and action plan to be accommodate the needs of the students. The process presented in this chapter is one that Sanlo uses repeatedly and has continued to give her excellent results as well as provide for both continuity and change. To develop an excellent strategic plan, you must have the undivided attention of your advisory board or stakeholders for two full days.

Before you plan the strategic planning process, obtain the vision and mission of your student affairs division and the institution. Be sure that planning takes place within the expectations of the division or the entity responsible for the LGBT Center.

Six months in advance of your strategic planning retreat, select a date, location, and meals. If possible, hire a professional strategic planner. There are always folks on campus who do strategic planning work. Check with your business school, psychology school, or public policy school. If you do not have an advisory board, either create one or invite stakeholders to participate in a two-day retreat to either review or create your vision, mission, goals, and action plan.

One month in advance, send a thank-you and a reminder to the stakeholders for their willingness to participate on such-and-such a date. Make copies of your current vision, mission, goals, and action plan if you have them and send them to the stakeholders for their review prior to the retreat. If you do not have these items, compile vision statements, mission statements, and goals from other institutions to use as guides in your planning process. If possible, get the vision statement and mission of student affairs or wherever your center is housed and include those as well. Send these to the stakeholders.

One week in advance, contact your stakeholders by phone or Email to be sure that they will be attending and give that information to whoever is providing food. Get name tags (the pin-on kind work best for multiple-day events), four flip charts, 12 magic markers, folders with notebook paper and pens, and several boxes of the Avery multi-colored sticky dots.

On the first day, arrive early with the supplies and be sure the coffee, juice, and bagels are prepared. If the retreat is to begin at 9:00 AM, hopefully you told folks to be there by 8:30, knowing that we generally run on "gay-light standard" time, meaning that we're always late.

For an actual "how-to" read *Working Toward Strategic Change: A Step-by-Step Guide to the Planning Process* by Dolence, Rowley, and Lujan (1997). It is important that the following are accomplished at your retreat: a realistic list of center strengths, weaknesses, opportunities, and threats; a vision statement; a mission statement that reflects the mission of the division of student affairs or whatever area in which the Center is housed; goals to meet the mission; and actions to accomplish the goals. For example, if the mission includes "educate the campus community," a goal may be to create a speakers bureau. Action plans would then include the development of a training for speakers and the actual initiation of the speakers bureau.

According to Smith (1994b), the action plan should accompany a strategic, plan but it is unlikely that there will be time during the retreat to develop the action plan. However, the process for developing an action plan should be discussed at the retreat, and assignments should be made.

While your strategic plan focuses on the what, your action plan focuses on the how. It provides the real guidelines to activate the strategic plan. Details should include the outline of the specific tasks that need to be accomplished to achieve the strategic objective; exact dates (month and year) when each task should be completed; identity of who (staff, volunteers, advisory board, work-study) is responsible for completing the task; identification of all resources required to accomplish the task, including funding for supplies, equipment, staff time, travel, and so on;

specification of desired or anticipated results and what will be accomplished by the selected timeline; and how you will determine or evaluate that the task has been completed or that success has been achieved (Smith, 1994b).

Once the strategic plan is written, share it with constituents, stakeholders, and your supervisor. Use it as your road map. One of the most difficult things with which you will be faced is the temptation to move off the task. Certainly reserve the right to make changes if necessary, especially in emergency situations, but your students, your center, and your sanity will be best served by remaining with your plan.

Table 5
Five-Step Guide to Strategic Planning

Step One: What Is the Vision of Your Organization?

This question actually is asking, What is the philosophy of the organization? The vision of a group rarely changes, while its mission should be revisited every three to five years. The business (or mission) of a nonprofit organization is to make a difference in human lives. A well-drafted vision allows dissent or conflict to be constructive because you have unity on mission, purpose, and values. Question to pose to the planning group: What is your reason for being? Example from the Statewide Pennsylvania Rights Coalition (SPARC) vision (the philosophy of the coalition): The Statewide Pennsylvania Rights Coalition seeks to establish a unified statewide community by building the framework to create positive change for lesbian, gay, bisexual, and transgender citizens with the support of their allies in the Commonwealth of Pennsylvania.

Step 2: What Is the Mission of Your Organization?

This question actually is asking, How do you operationalize your philosophy? Pose the following questions to the group:

A. What are you trying to achieve?
    1. What is your direction?
    2. What results do we want to achieve?

B. What are the organization's major strengths?
    1. What have you done well?

C. What are the organization's major weaknesses?
    1. In what area does it lack the competence or the resources to be effective?

D. Whom are you serving, and what do they value? Need to consider the needs of the different types of people whom you are serving (e.g. an LGBT resource center may need to meet the needs of students, faculty, staff, and/or the local community)

E. If you already have a mission statement. does it need to be modified based on the responses to the previous questions?
    1. If not, why not, If yes, why is that?
    2. In what ways, if any would you rewrite or refocus the mission statement?

3. What would be the major benefits of the new mission?
4. What challenges would you be likely to encounter with the new mission?

Step 3: What Are the Goals of the Organization?

This question is asking, How does the organization achieve it's mission?
Pose the following questions to the group:

A. Where should we focus our efforts?
List the areas you believe the Alliance should focus on and how each one fits the mission.

B. Are there programs, activities, or constituency needs that the organization should add? If so, can the current structure handle them effectively and efficiently, or do you need to add committees, outsource, hire a staff person, and so on.

Step 4: What Are the Organization's Action Plans?

This question is asking the organization to identify specific actions that will allow it to meet it's goals.

A. Under each of the goals, identify a list of action items to fulfill the goal, the target date for completion, who has ultimate responsibility to see that it is achieved, and budget considerations. Use this worksheet example: Goal Actions Budget Target Date Support Implications Needed

Step Five: What Are the Organizational Responsibilities?

Review the organization's current structure. Is this the best structure to accomplish the mission of the organization? If the answer is no, create a new structure that will assist the organization in accomplishing its mission. If the answer is yes, identify specific responsibilities for each position and their responsibilities in assisting the organization in fulfilling the action plans

Source, Rankin and Associates, Consulting

Chapter 7

Developing Your Vision, Mission, Goals, and Evaluation: Building Your Action Plan

The vision, the mission or purpose, the goals to achieve that purpose, and the action plans to meet your goals are your road map for a successful operation. These four items are critical to keeping your center and your work focused and on task. A fifth item—a values statement—is also important to the focus of your work.

Developing your vision, mission, goals, and action plan are most productively accomplished when the task is shared. A shared vision and a shared mission or purpose mean that the road map belongs to all who have interest in seeing the center meet the current needs and plan for realistic future needs. Hopefully, you have an advisory board made up of stakeholders—people who have an interest or responsibility in the new or changing process (Komives, Lucas, & McMahon 1998), 25% of whom are undergraduates, 25% graduate students, 20% faculty, 20% staff, 5% alumni, and 5% allies—whom you invited to develop these items. If you have no advisory board, invite the same composite of people for a retreat to develop your center's road map to success.

Most institutions already have divisional vision and mission statements. For example, the UCLA Division of Student Affairs has its own vision statement, which fits snuggly with the vision statement of the institution. The vision ultimately developed for the UCLA Lesbian Gay Bisexual Transgender Campus Resource Center also fits snuggly into the vision of Student Affairs. The mission statement or purpose was developed in the same manner. The organizational goals of the Division of Student Affairs at UCLA (http://www2.saonet.ucla.edu/Strat_Plan/main.htm#misstate) has seven key points:

to be responsive, convenient, and cost-effective in supporting students in achieving academic success and personal development; to foster a campus community that is civil, respectful, and supportive of individual differences;

to forge meaningful, mutually-beneficial partnerships with other campus and community entities;

to be accountable for attaining high levels of achievement in advancing the Student Affairs mission, vision, values, and goals;

to have regular opportunities to assess their individual professional and work-related needs with their respective supervisor or delegate, and determine means to address identified developmental needs;

to acquire, judiciously utilize, and account for human, fiscal, technological, and facility resources essential to realizing its mission; and,

to provide the organizational infrastructure (policies, procedures, practices) to support its stated mission in an optimal manner.

The LGBT center's mission was developed to meet those seven key points while creating an action plan to do our work in the best possible way. The action plan allowed us the flexibility of meeting the goals of Student Affairs while also expanding and refining the center's goals to specifically meet the needs of the LGBT campus population and the entire campus community.

If you have been hired as director of an existing center or office, find the vision and mission statements. Are they clear? Are they visible for all to see? Do they describe the direction that you as director wish/need to pursue? Are the old action plans feasible? With new leadership come new ideas, new energy, new strength. Review the existing vision, mission, goals, and action plans with the center's advisory board or LGBT campus community stakeholders. With them as partners, review the plans to see if they work, or see if you need to develop a new road map that will guide you in the direction that you wish to see your center go.

VISION

The UCLA Lesbian Gay Bisexual Transgender Campus Resource Center envisions lesbian, gay, bisexual and transgender people as fully included and affirmed in every aspect of the UCLA community where justice, equality and respect for all people prevail (UCLA vision statement, January 2000).

A vision statement should be lofty. It should generate hope and inspiration (DePree 1997; Dreher 1997, Smith, Bucklin, & Associates 1994). It describes what a perfect world would look like for you in your position as director of an LGBT center or office. It's global, it's broad, and it's not impossible to attain. "The vision statement should motivate, inspire, be a stretch, be clear and concrete, be achievable, reflect high value, and be simple" (Komives, Lucas, & McMahon 1998, p. 207). DePree (1997) stated that "only with vision can we begin to see things the way they can be" (p. 117).

Smith (1994b) suggested these questions when developing a shared vision: What are the strengths and weaknesses of the organizations? What is the public perception? Is there a lack of awareness? To what extent are perceived weaknesses accurate? Are criticisms founded? How would you like constituents to feel about the center? How would the center operate in an ideal world? How would it be perceived?

Your vision statement should be available for all to see easily (Dreher 1997). It should be proudly displayed in your center and published in your brochure. It is an articulation of how the center—and you and your staff—perceives the world. Komives et al. (1998) said that unless the vision "is shared and owned by the members, nothing of significance will ever happen" (p. 208). The vision and the mission statement guide the organization. They "need to come alive and be kept alive through the actions of the leaders and the members of the organization" (p. 208).

MISSION

The UCLA Lesbian Gay Bisexual Transgender Campus Resource Center provides a comprehensive range of education, information and advocacy services. We work to create and maintain an open, safe and inclusive environment for lesbian, gay, bisexual and transgender students, faculty, and staff, their families and friends, and the campus community at large (UCLA mission statement, January 2000).

The mission is your statement of purpose. It "offers the compelling reason" (Komives et al. 1998, p. 207) for the center's existence. It broadly answers the question: Why does the center exist? It must reflect the personality of the organization. Komives et al. (1998) explained that an organization's mission—"the contribution the organization makes to the campus, community, or world—needs to be articulated in a way that is enticing to potential participants and motivational to those who have already joined the organization" (p. 207).

Smith (1994b) describes a mission statement as "a succinct statement which sets forth the organization's purpose and philosophy. Although brief, the mission statement will specify the fundamental reason(s) for the organization's existence; establish the scope of the organization; and identify the organization's unique characteristics" (p. 15).

Like the vision statement, the mission statement should be readily visible for all to see. It should be displayed in your center or office and be included in your brochure. There should be no guesswork as to what the purpose of the center is and who the center serves.

CORE VALUES OR VALUES STATEMENT

We recognize that sexual orientation and gender expression work through and are influenced by race/ethnicity, gender, culture, age, ability status, class, faith, and other social characteristics. In keeping with the ideals of UCLA to provide leadership and service, we commit to justice, equality, and respect for all persons in all of our endeavors. We acknowledge that:

All sexual and gender identities are valued equally and seen as a contributions to the diversity of the campus as a whole.

Every member of the student body, staff, and faculty must know about the center, understand our purpose and/or activities and use us as a resource.

The UCLA LGBT Resource Center must become a model for other universities in providing services to our LGBT population.

Students must be free to contribute to the UCLA community regardless and inclusive of sexual or gender identity.

Staff and faculty must experience no employment discrimination based on sexual orientation and must not fear coming out because of repercussion to employment status or to future opportunities.

The center will precipitate a better sense of community among LGBT students, staff, faculty, and alumni.

It is incredibly helpful to develop, display, and publicly articulate the core values of the center or office. "Without core values, any behavior would be justifiable as long as it moves the organization toward its mission or vision" (Komives et al. 1998, p. 208). Core values describe the way in which people are treated. According to Smith (1994b), the core values or principles are "statements which identify the philosophical guidelines for all of the organization's activities. Statements which identify the philosophical guidelines for all of the organization's activities Values and beliefs that recognize constituent needs and expectations can be captured as principles that define the philosophical guidelines for the organization's activities" (p. 18).

GOALS

Goals are the nitty-gritty to accomplishing excellent work. Smith (1994) described goals as "a limited number of statements which translate the association's mission into major policy direction. Goals are tools to assess the success of the organization in fulfilling its mission. Goals will necessarily be broad statements, limited in number, and focus on the unique characteristics of the organization" (p. 20).

Goals set out measurable tasks. Do your center's goals clarify your mission statement? Do they specify the overriding purposes of the organization? Do they provide the foundation for developing targeted programmatic activities and operational plans? Do they provide the basis for assessing the major priorities of the center? An example of one university's goals and action plan appear in Appendix F.

ACTION PLAN

The action plan is your day-to-day functioning system. It is a calendar of sorts that documents what you are going to do as a way to meet the goals that meet the purpose that strives to reach the vision of your center or office. Fayol (1993) said that an action plan "is, at one and the same time, the result envisaged, the line of action to be followed, the stages to go through, and methods to use. It is a kind of future picture. It entails running the business as foreseen and provides against over a definite period of time" (p. 93). Its broad features are unity, continuity, flexibility, and precision. "It utilizes a department's resources and the choice of best methods to use for attaining the objective. It suppresses or reduces hesitancy, false steps, unwarranted changes or course, and helps to improve personnel" (p. 99).

The compilation of a good plan demands that the director know how to ethically manage staff; have the energy necessary for constant vigilance; have the moral courage to make the required changes when even the best of plans do not work out; have the continuity of tenure; and have the experience and professional and ethical competencies to do the work. A good plan is compulsory, is made generally available, and is part of the unit's educational growth and process.

EVALUATION

It is imperative that you have methods by which to evaluate your work. The Council for the Advancement of Standards in Higher Education (CAS) has developed standards and guidelines specifically for LGBT programs and services. The CAS evaluation method is an excellent place from which to begin because it will help you assess where you are now, where you need to be, and what you need to do in order to achieve your goals.

According to Barr (1993), the CAS standards provide focus, direction, and perspective. These guidelines impact program development, staff development, comparison across institutions, development and enhancement of program credibility, definition of clear missions, improved political maneuverability, budgetary assistance, and program assessment. The CAS standards are "excellent tools to create, expand, and defend" (p. 513) imprint program and services. The CAS LGBT Standards and Guidelines may be ordered at www.cas.edu.

The CAS Standards were constructed to represent the minimum criteria that every institution and its programs should, with the application of adequate effort, be expected to meet over time. To clarify these standard statements, to assure they are being properly interpreted, and to enhance or strengthen programs, and because effective practice occurs and can be viewed as a continuum, there is need to provide users with additional criteria that *may* be used as circumstances warrant. Consequently, in addition to the standards, CAS has established guideline statements designed to clarify and amplify the standards and to guide enhanced practice beyond the essential levels of the various standards. That is, when a program has achieved effectiveness, according to the standards, opportunity to achieve enhanced effectiveness has been built into the statements and is referred to as *guidelines*. Guidelines use the auxiliary verbs *"should"* and *"may"* and are presented in small regular print to distinguish them from standards. (CAS Web site, www.cas.edu, July 2001)

Embrace the evaluation process as a celebratory event that assists with the benchmarking necessary to provide excellent services to students as you and your staff help them achieve their academic and personal goals.

Chapter 8

Advisory Boards

Campus centers and programs are most successful when they are consistent with their vision, their mission, and with the constituents whom they serve, whether solely students or also faculty, staff, alumni, and/or the surrounding community. The mission may be constant or in flux; constituents needs' may be continuous or changing. It is the responsibility of the organization's staff to stay in touch with the mission and the needs of the consumers. One highly effective way to achieve this end is to establish an advisory board.

PURPOSE OF THE ADVISORY BOARD

Advisory boards can serve three important functions: provide communication with center or office staff about the campus environment; offer advice based on their experiences at the institution; and act as advocates or lobbyists for the center or office.

Communications

Advisory board members communicate to program staff about the needs and concerns of those actually or potentially served. They not only speak from their own experiences but also report on the experiences of colleagues and friends. Board members may be belong to identity groups or organizations with which office or center staff members have no other direct connection. For example, an out varsity athlete may provide access to teammates who are deeply closeted but may share information about their experiences to that trusted athlete board member. The information that such board members may provide about the service and program needs of their friends is invaluable to staff in planning. Board members may also provide staff with data regarding the efficacy of previously offered programs and services.

This communication link works in both directions. Staff may solicit feedback from consumers, in general or about a specific service or program, via board members. They can also convey information through board members that they feel is vital for constituents whom they may not be able to reach by any other means, such as the availability of new programs or warnings regarding potential risks or threats to the community. Information such as the operation of on-campus HIV test sites or recent increases in harassment of LGBT students in certain neighborhoods could be communicated this way.

Advice

Whether in a one-time strategic planning process, in regular annual reviews, or in periodic informal discussion, advisory board members help the staff and university administration set and abide by the organization's mission and, especially given limited staff and funding, identify priorities for services and programs. Based on board advice, activities that are generating limited interest and drawing small audiences may be eliminated with focus placed on more vital and popular programs.

Advocacy

Finally, advisory board members make powerful lobbyists and advocates for the center or office. They may communicate either regularly or as needed with the central administrators responsible for making decisions about the organization's funding and staffing. Certainly, if there is a threat to funding or other vital area (such as changing the program's reporting line), board members can mobilize their respective support systems and lobby, individually or collectively, to counteract potentially harmful decisions. Of course, such actions must be undertaken selectively. If board members went into combat mode each time that an obstacle was thrown in the program's path, they would soon be disregarded and their lobbying rendered futile. It may be unwise to include the lobbying function in the advisory board's formal statement of purpose. It is probably better for this role to be understood rather than explicitly stated.

While providing a link between consumers and program staff (and vice versa) and contributing to the organization's mission and priorities are the foremost purposes of an advisory board, there are other potential functions for such an entity. Advisory boards to centers or programs can serve as campus-wide sounding boards regarding LGBT issues. For example, even though the LGBT center or program may have nothing to do with housing, residence personnel may seek in-put from the center or program advisory board in making decisions affecting their area of responsibility, such as whether or not to provide cluster housing options for LGBT residents. In addition, advisory boards may, from time to time, decide to take a stand on a significant campus issue not directly related to the program or center, such as domestic partner benefits or the presence of military recruiters or Reserve Officers' Training Corp (ROTC) on campus. As with lobbying, such actions are most likely to be compelling and meaningful only when they are taken very selectively.

Central administrators within whose portfolios LGBT centers or programs fall may want to consult with advisory board members, or at least advisory board leadership, when personnel decisions are being made. Some people who serve on the advisory board are logical participants in the search for a new director or when administrators are considering promoting the present director, reclassifying the position, or increasing salary.

It is important that all involved—board members, staff, and central administration—be clear that this board is consultative, not directive. This body does not have fiduciary responsibilities, as boards of directors of non-profit organizations (such the institution's trustees) do. Formal and financial decisions must remain the province of the programs' director and those above them in the reporting line within the institution. This does not mean that the director or central administrators should minimize or ignore the perspective of advisory board members. In fact, savvy directors and administrators will listen carefully to, and, whenever possible, heed, the advice of board members, but, should a conflict arise between the program's advisory board and the institution's administration, the final word will rest with the latter.

MEMBERSHIP

The composition of the organization's advisory board may have been specified in the deliberations and reports leading to the establishment of the center or program. What is more, some members of the task force or committee that advocated for the founding of the center or program may wish to serve on its advisory board—or may even be mandated to do so. In such instances, the degree of freedom regarding board composition is limited.

Many considerations need to be taken into account in composing an advisory board, where leeway does exist. First, to as great an extent as possible, all segments within the campus LGBT community, actually or potentially served, should be represented on the board. This includes women; men, and transgender people; lesbians, gay men, and bisexual men and women; Caucasian people and people of color; students, both undergraduate and graduate/professional; faculty; and administrators/staff from a variety of schools and departments within the institution; alumni; and campus activists and others who may be less out and less vocal. Since the number of members may be limited (though not necessarily—see later), it is difficult, if not impossible, to "have it all." This is a familiar dilemma on college campuses and indeed elsewhere in life, as are the compromises or trade-offs necessitated by such circumstances.

The matter of including heterosexual men and women on LGBT program advisory boards can be seen as akin to the inclusion of white people on African American resource center boards or men on women's center boards. Virtually all LGBT centers and programs include education in their missions. The emphasis may be on events aimed at LGBT community members, but it almost always includes some efforts to reach out to the entire campus and to reduce bias and increase inclusion through education. Further, on many campuses, heterosexual students and employees, often self-labeled or referred to as "allies," seek to educate themselves and work to counter heterosexism and homophobia. These activities may occur through these allies' participating in the work of the LGBT center or LGBT student groups or through a separate organization founded by the allies. In light of these factors, representation on center or program advisory boards of the campus heterosexual population can be seen as both logical and desirable.

It is true on virtually all college campuses that power is not distributed evenly and that certain constituencies or individuals have greater clout in important institutional decisions. This very real phenomenon needs to be taken into consideration in determining advisory board membership. Clearly, senior faculty members, those with endowed chairs or other forms of high visibility, make very attractive board members, ones whose opinions will be listened to by the central administration. Student leaders, those who hold elected office, especially in large and vital organizations, are similarly heeded by the institution's administration. Moreover, these individuals are likely to have the ears of many community members and can thus provide staff a lot of useful feedback and distribute information as well. As previously mentioned, individuals who have access to less visible and less vocal communities are also important participants.

Though at first it may seem illogical, it may also be sensible to include on the board individuals who have previously been vocal critics of the center or preceding similar efforts on campus. Membership on the board provides these people a place for their concerns and criticism to be voiced, a venue where some of their suggestions may be taken and their contributions valued. Further, they may be less likely to express their negative comments outside advisory board meetings, since their board colleagues could rightly regard that as unproductive or even disloyal.

Program or center directors need to bear in mind that all board members are undertaking this activity over and above their other responsibilities, whether studies or full-time jobs. They are volunteers, with all the valuable contributions, as well as the occasional disappointments, that go along with that status. It is challenging to find ways to guarantee that members will follow through on assigned tasks and be held accountable if they do not. Both the staff and the board leadership need to be aware of these factors in determining which assignments members take on.

Some take the position that boards can be effective only when their numbers are kept low, that large meetings can be unwieldy, that too many opinions are impossible to manage. This view may not apply to advisory boards. The question of the number of members is related to the nature and volume of the work that the particular advisory board takes on. Those responsible for forming advisory boards need to assume that only a certain percentage of members will attend meetings and otherwise be active. There seems to be no harm in having individuals listed as advisory board members who may turn out to have fairly little time to participate in a substantial way. Powerful individuals willing to lend their names—if only for the letterhead or the roster or the occasional meeting with high-level administrators—can still make a valuable contribution. Most of the work of the advisory board will need to be carried by those individuals who can make a larger contribution of time and energy.

After the advisory board has been formed initially, decisions will need to be made as to how new participants are selected when original members leave for any reason (such as graduation). If a formula has been provided in conjunction with the founding of the board, this procedure can be followed. Otherwise, as needs demands, some process has to be developed.

One question that needs to be addressed at the start or as it arises is whether all or some of the seats on the board are "dedicated," that is, are designated for, or "belong to," certain groups or constituencies. Does the undergraduate student organization always get to designate a representative to serve on the center's advisory board—and when that person resigns or graduates, is the student group entitled to select a replacement? Or does the body have certain members managing nominations who are paying attention to representation of undergraduate students on the board in a less formulaic way? Such considerations could arise regarding any group or constituency. Especially if serving on the advisory board has evolved to the point of carrying with it some prestige, care will need to be taken (hopefully without burying the board in red tape) as to how new members are selected.

LEADERSHIP

Advisory boards need some, if only limited, leadership that is selected, by some agreed-upon process, from among its membership. Having a form of shared leadership, such as co-chairs, means that responsibilities are distributed so that one individual is not unduly burdened. Shared leadership can also make a statement about parity when, for example, the co-chairs are a student and an employee or a man and a woman or a person of color and a Caucasian person. Also, since the board leaders are likely to have some contact with the chief student affairs officer or other highly placed administrator who oversees the LGBT center or program, there is some advantage to having a senior faculty person or a student leader as a chair or co-chair. Since such individuals are likely to have a substantial number of other responsibilities, boards may not always be able to realize this advantage.

The director works most closely with the board leadership. The leaders are the individuals with whom the director needs to have most frequent contact between board meetings—for consultation about day-to-day matters when necessary and to plan the activities of the advisory board. Together, leaders and director set agendas for board meetings and review progress on projects taken on by board members. Certain activities can be undertaken by board leaders without the involvement of the director. These might include notifying members about meetings, following up with absent members, taking and distributing meeting minutes.

The director needs to strongly resist the temptation to manage the advisory board and relate to members as if they were staff. She or he should direct inquiries about the board, such as how one becomes a member, to board leaders. While board leaders may need reminders or encouragement from the director, these reminders are important, practically and philosophically, for only they fulfill responsibilities such as encouraging members to complete assigned tasks, increasing attendance at meetings, and asking an inactive or problematic board member to consider resigning. If directors were to take such actions, the results could be harmful to the organization and possibly to themselves.

Directors need to deliberate and decide, according to their particular circumstances, to what extent they wish to involve board leaders in the day-to-day management of the center or program. As already established, it is useful for directors to consult with leaders, and, frankly, for them to do so from time to time, even regarding matters that may not truly require another perspective, may gratify leaders and bolster their investment. Micromanaging by board leaders is to be avoided, just as directors may aim to give staff members autonomy in program development and service provision. Most importantly, board leaders need to recognize—and perhaps, occasionally and diplomatically, be reminded—that the director does not report to them in the same way that an executive is beholden to a board of trustees.

It is possible that advisory board leaders may have differences of opinion with center directors. Optimally, these differences can be resolved behind closed doors, not expressed in front of the board or acted out in some other destructive way. Regular meetings even once a semester, between board leaders and the administrator(s) to whom the director reports, contribute to keeping all involved on the same page regarding program management and priorities.

STRUCTURE

In light of their purposes and composition, center or program advisory boards can function, and may function best, with less rather than more structure. In almost all cases, the nature of the board's charges does not demand that there be many formal or codified regulations and procedures. As with any such entity, as the advisory board evolves, its structure may be developed and refined. This evolution is common to most non-profit organizations, including their boards of directors or advisory boards. The aspects of structure discussed here are meetings, communication, board activities, and associated costs.

Advisory boards do need to meet regularly. In most instances, twice or perhaps once each semester will suffice. Meetings are necessary, even if there is not urgent business to conduct, so that board members can see each other and the staff face-to-face with some predictability. The agenda should be established and sent out to members, in advance of the meeting. At minimum, it should contain a report from the director that up-dates members on development in the center or program since the last meeting. It may include more or less detail, such as utilization statistics, as suits the director and the board. Some directors provide written reports to reduce the amount of meeting time spent talking about past activities. Some review, if only of highlights, is necessary even when written reports have been provided, because, as would be expected, not everyone will have read or will read written reports provided. The director should suggest at least one item at each meeting that requires discussion by, and a recommendation from, the board. Discussion of, and subsequent support from, the board regarding such matters increase the likelihood of favorable decisions from the institution's administration. Shifts in emphases, a change in the name of the organization, and major personnel or budgetary deliberations are examples of matters that could benefit from board discussion and recommendation. It is not suggested that such items be fabricated if none exist. In such a situation, there is probably little need for a meeting.

It is useful if a representative of the central administration, perhaps the chief student affairs officer or other individual to whom the director reports, can attend at least one advisory board meeting each academic year. Other guests can be invited as discussion topics merit. While the organization's director is the liaison between staff and the advisory board, it is often helpful for staff members to be present for part or all of each board meeting. They should be given the opportunity to share directly with the board particular services or programs on which they have been working. Since the board gets to meet the staff and is informed by their sharing, and the staff gets to interact with board members and have their diligent work acknowledged, this kind of arrangement seems to benefit everyone.

The designated board leader(s) should chair meetings. In addition to presenting a report, the director should be ready to give in-put where needed in board deliberations but should avoid any appearance of running the meeting or calling on people who wish to speak. Though participants may be likely to regard the paid director as the actual leader of all endeavors related to the program or center, the director should studiously avoid that perception during board meetings and in the conducting of board business. Any such regard from members should be gently re-directed to the board leadership.

Frequent and accurate communication with and among advisory board members is crucial to the success of the operation. Electronic communication is a boon in this regard. The creation of a listserv for the advisory board is a simple step that returns manifold the investment of time and technology resources. Announcements of meetings, minutes, and notification about, and discussion of, important matters between meetings can easily take place via the listserv. Periodic telephone calls or personalized electronic messages from the director help to keep board members involved. As noted earlier, advisory board members are volunteers—and all volunteers need to be recognized and thanked by paid employees from time to time.

Much of the work of the board can be done between meetings. Many advisory boards have evolved to include committees or working groups for specific projects. This is an efficient use of such volunteers. It provides a way for members who have more time to give (in contrast to those who can only lend their names to the roster) to be more involved. These members are expressing willingness to "do," not only to "advise." Care must be taken, however, in identifying which projects will be undertaken by advisory board committees or work groups. If the planning of a center program or event were undertaken, lines of responsibility may become blurred. Advisory board members would be serving in the same way as volunteer event planners. Activities that seem more within the province of a board and less likely to get conflated with the day-to-day operation of most centers or programs include development or fund-raising, alumni relations, volunteer recognition events, strategic planning, and any projects that help maintain or strengthen the advisory board itself.

Organizational costs associated with advisory boards are minimal. There are certain expenditures, but they are generally low and provide good value. That part of the director's salary that goes to communicating with the board and its leadership and attending board and committee meetings is the most significant item. Other costs include maintaining the board listserv, some photocopying, and light refreshments at meetings.

Case Study 8.1
LGBT Center Advisory Board, University of Pennsylvania

Every individual given the opportunity to serve in a leadership role of an advisory board for an LGBT center experiences personal satisfaction and oversees a group of volunteers who are working toward institutional goals and objectives. This has been our experience serving as the co-chairs of the LGBT Center Advisory Board at the University of Pennsylvania. You will have the good fortune to work with colleagues from campus and the community. At Penn, our ability to successfully establish and maintain an effective working group who represent a broad range of ideologies is crucial to supporting the center staff and advocating when necessary with the central administration. The initial trepidation to assume the role of a "recognized leader" quickly dissipates as you understand that the advisory board members typically have no hidden agendas. Most, if not all, of the board members are truly serving as volunteers, committed to sharing thoughtful and creative insights. Each board undergoes evolution and changes within its membership. This evolution also impacts the role and selection of the board leaders. As with any dynamic organization, different sets of issues and challenges may arise. The appointment of new members may require an adopted procedure; likewise, the selection and approval of board leaders should also follow an agreed upon structure. When considering board leaders, one or more of the following may need to be addressed—the number of leaders, their actual role and responsibilities, and the length of their appointment. We believe that the two most useful skills for the board leader(s) are communication and the ability to follow through. As chief facilitators for the board, you will be responsible for establishing meeting agendas, recording and distributing minutes, managing the discussion, cajoling members, and listening and sharing with the center director, staff, and central university administration. Since the role is more consultative than directive, your relationship with the center director and staff is not about micro-managing but rather to provide a platform for the staff to articulate and implement strategies, policies, and program possibilities. In spite of any frustrations (and they will inevitably show up), our experience has been very enlightening and enjoyable. As co-chairs, we have been able to play a direct role in assisting the center in identifying its mission, shaping its goals, and creating a vision for its future. We have been able to witness the bridging of personalities and ideas from students, faculty, staff, and alumni to foster the vibrant intellectual environment that academic institutions strive to maintain. We have grown to respect the commitment of our board members and value the influence that we all bring to this campus. (Submitted by Janice Austin and Christopher Nguyen, co-chairs, LGBT Center Advisory Board, University of Pennsylvania)

This case study describes the experiences and accomplishments of two long-term LGBT center advisory board member-leaders. Their testimony, coupled with the information provided throughout this chapter, makes clear that center or program advisory boards are relatively easy to establish and maintain and serve a variety of valuable purposes, benefiting the institution, the center or program operations and staff, and advisory board members themselves. Following are the advisory board guidelines of the University of Pennsylvania:

Purposes:
To provide advice and input to the director and staff on planning, implementation, and operational aspects of the center; to assure that the overall planning and implementation are consistent with the expectations of the Division of Student Affairs; to advise on the coordination of the activities of the center within the context of the university and the greater community; to serve as ambassadors for the Center's goals and objectives.
Procedures:
1. The Advisory Board will meet at least once a term, with meetings scheduled six months in advance. Special meetings may be called as necessary by the chair of the board or by the director of the center.
2. An agenda will be established prior to each meeting, and minutes will be taken and circulated to all advisory board members. Minutes will be available to the public in the center.
3. All written materials regarding or representing the center or any of its programs must be reviewed by the director of the center before duplication and distribution occurs.
4. Membership of the advisory board will be determined by the director of the center with 50% of the membership comprising of students.

Expectations:
To meet periodically to provide direction and input into the center; to assist in planning activities; to act as public relations agents for the center; to assist in developing the center as a program model; to conceive and create ways for the center to interact with the university and the greater community for the enhancement of lesbian, gay, bisexual, and transgender students, faculty, staff, and community; to advise on program evaluation; to formulate and participate on committees when needed; and, to participate in activities and events.

Part III

Identifying and Providing Programs and Services

Chapter 9

Selecting and Implementing Services:
The Basics of an Active Center or Office

Whether a higher education institution is in the process of planning an LGBT office or center, has just initiated one, or has had one for some time, careful deliberation needs to take place about how to deploy the resources—funding, staffing (both paid and voluntary), and space. This chapter presents a variety of services offered at most centers or offices that are thought to be the most basic and the most needed. However, the combination of services offered will depends on variables such as the organization's mission, its consumers, its locus and reporting line with the institution, the unique profile of the particular institution, its lesbian, gay, bisexual, and transgender (LGBT) community, and the key players making the determination. No attempt is made to suggest which services described are best suited for specific missions, staffing patterns, or institutions. Each center needs to make that determination based on the campus climate and the campus LGBT communities.

Throughout Part III the term "center" is used to inclusively refer to a center, office, or other program unit that provides LGBT services on campus. While the term "center" has a specific meaning, any other related term may be substituted without changing the meaning of the discussion. Consumers of the services described may be students (undergraduate, graduate, or professional), employees (faculty, staff, administration), alumni, or people from the surrounding community. Only when a service is unique to one of these is the constituency specifically mentioned. Specific services that are available at nearly every LGBT campus resource center— information and referral, crisis intervention, discussion groups, student organization advising, community service, mentoring, and communications—are presented in this chapter, while others are presented as individual chapters.

INFORMATION AND REFERRAL

Regardless of how many services and programs a center offers, nearly every center provides a wide range of information and referral to many other units on campus and to organizations in the surrounding community. Requests for information and referrals come from various sources, including visitors, telephone callers, and E-mail. (E-mail is particularly useful to those who wish or need to make anonymous requests). The importance of an information and referral service cannot be overstated. Luckily, its value comes at a relatively low operating cost to a center.

The most common requests are for information regarding events of interest to LGBT people that occur on campus and in the community—meetings, socials, educational programs—and services such as counseling and health care that target the LGBT community. Such requests are fairly easy to provide, especially if someone within the center is responsible for maintaining up-to-date calendars and services that are then available for center staff members as they respond to such requests. Some centers provide such information via their Web site, listserv, voice mail bulletins, newsletters, and/or resource guides. Others have telephone hot lines that are staffed by informed volunteers in the LGBT community. Such hot lines are usually available during evening and weekend hours.

Providing the service is relatively cost-free. However, making sure that providers are LGBT-supportive is more time-consuming. Be aware of how LGBT-supportive your institution's counseling and health services may be. Create an inventory of questions for those and other services on campus. An example of such an inventory is found in Appendix G.

Offer to provide training if providers are not completely aware of LGBT issues or if you receive complaints from students about the ways in which they've been received in those units. Once there is an understanding of the awareness of on-campus services for LGBT students, referrals may be made without hesitation. If necessary, until all practitioners in the on-campus units are prepared to work with LGBT students, make referrals only to specific practitioners who have demonstrated bias-free practices.

Referrals may need to be made to off-campus facilities either because appropriate on-campus practitioners are not available, the requestor is ineligible for on-campus services, or the campus simply does not provide the service, such as a domestic violence abuse shelter. If a caller asks for a referral to a local mental health therapist, provide a list of at least three and encourage the caller to make her or his own decision based on a personal interview with the providers. However, before such referrals can be made, the center must query local practitioners regarding their inclusiveness and welcome of LGBT people. A center may create a survey to be sent to local practitioners in health, law, or other services (see Appendix H). These surveys, or some variation of them, must be accompanied by a cover letter explaining who you are and why you are making this query.

Personal preferences and individual experiences vary widely. A counselor or health care practitioner's style may suit one student perfectly but may be seen as troublesome by another. A practitioner or service should be eliminated from the referral list when complaints have been received and explored with the practitioner or service in question. At some institutions, there is close proximity to, or no real difference between, the campus and the community in which it is located. In such instances, referral options are more limited, boundaries are more fluid, and the need for confidentiality, while always important, is particularly crucial.

On campuses and in communities with very limited resources or a high degree of anti-LGBT sentiment, regional and national resources become especially important. There are hot lines for a number of regional and national organizations such as Parents and Friends of Lesbians and Gays (PFLAG), which can be very helpful in these circumstances (see Appendix I).

CRISIS INTERVENTION

A variety of crises—or potential crises—may arise that require some involvement on the part of LGBT center staff. The more prepared staff members are about the potential for such eventualities, what their respective roles are, and what procedures are to be followed, the less likely it is that any long-term damage will be sustained.

Most institutions of higher education have procedures outlining various crises that may befall students. These procedures usually specify point people within student affairs and provide action steps and 24-hour contact information. The LGBT center director should be an integral part of such a system, given the variety of scenarios that could involve LGBT students in crises—such as a gay student disappearing from campus or being a victim of a hate crime or other emergency situations.

Case Study 9.1
University Crisis

A fire bomb was thrown into the residence hall window of a second-year student who was a lesbian. Luckily, neither she nor her roommates were in the room, but excessive damage was done to the building. The student affairs core crisis committee—the dean of students, the director of counseling services, the director of housing, the judicial officer, and the campus police chief—gathered immediately. Realizing, at the very least, that the targeted student was a lesbian, I was also called into the initial meeting. Since the perpetrator—a former girlfriend of the victim—was still at large, we immediately found secure housing for the student until the perpetrator was found. The perpetrator, who was heavily armed and suspected of at least one murder, had an extensive arrest record. She was located and jailed two days later. She committed suicide while in custody. In the meantime, the student had been placed in a safe housing location. The crisis team met with her and her parents to provide every effort not only to keep the student safe but to ensure that her academic success was compromised as little as possible given the horrifying situation. (Submitted by Ronni Sanlo, LGBT Campus Resource Center, UCLA)

Individual crises occur without the need for intervention from a campus crisis team. It is not unusual for a student to verbalize suicidal ideation because of the loss of a partner, harassment from peers, and/or the anticipation of coming out to parents and family. It is imperative that center staff be trained to deal with these situations, whether a student calls on the telephone or appears in person. Obtain crisis intervention training for your staff from your campus' student psychological services.

Crises may also be defined as relating to the entire community rather than just to individuals. Sometimes these situations arise precipitously and unexpectedly or with particular furor.

Case Study 9.2
Managing Campus Public Sex Complaints from a Sex-Positive Perspective

Aggressive cruising and public sex activity were obvious and disruptive in the locker, shower, and sauna rooms of a recreation facility used by general university community members and student athletes, generating numerous complaints. Other staff complained when student athletes were groped and propositioned. Facility staff complained about destruction of property and their deteriorated work environment. A coach complained of finding men engaged in sex in stairwells and bathrooms. Athletes complained of sexual harassment, including public masturbation. A sense of crisis ensued among high-level administrators; they demanded action before a public relations nightmare erupted. I convened a team to address the problem, defining our goal as reducing and/or eliminating complaints, *not* stopping public sex activities. Other team members included two Student Affairs assistant vice presidents (one of whom is the athletic director), the university police chief, the coach of an affected team, and the manager of the facility in crisis. I was designated to serve as the spokesperson on campus regarding public sex. I prepared talking points on the subject and worked to assure provision of a consistent message to all concerned parties, particularly the media. An initial task was educating the team to recognize the history and cultural significance of public sex in the queer community. I debunked myths (e.g., that the main practitioners of public sex on campus are visitors to our university), and I reminded team members that university community members at all levels might be involved in public sex. This tactical move was to dissuade team members who thought arrests and public shaming would be effective, efficient methods of deterring the behaviors that were drawing notice. I stressed the need for a non-judgmental, sex-positive approach. The primary strategy for reducing complaints was communicating to men who have sex with men that the recreation facility had become a potentially dangerous place to cruise. I passed the word that police (in uniform and under cover) and facility staff would patrol on a random basis and that ID checks would be made of anyone deemed to be "hanging out" too long. Unauthorized facility users would be ejected and threatened with a trespassing charge if found on the premises again. I also reminded the team and other university administrators that we would merely be shifting traffic to other campus venues. I communicated the information in various culturally-appropriate forums, to local gay media outlets, Internet sites, several university news groups, the queer student listserv, gay campus opinion leaders, and gay travel guides. In addition, I posted "public service announcements" to gay AOL chat rooms. As maintenance, I routinely survey team members to learn if they have received new complaints. I monitor other campus sex venues for potential explosiveness, conducting periodic tours of those venues with queer student leaders and building administrators, tracking property destruction and situations that might elicit complaints. In order to forestall a "sex panic" situation, I remind public sex participants to follow common sense etiquette to avoid creating complaints, encouraging arrest, and endangering their own activities through unwanted notice. (Submitted by Willa Young, Director, Student Gender and Sexuality Services, Ohio State University)

The Chinese symbol for crisis means both danger and opportunity. While individual or institution-wide crises may be frightening, even perilous, they may also encourage growth. Individuals and institutions have the opportunity to learn from these occurrences and be better prepared to deal with similar situations should they arise in the future.

DISCUSSION GROUPS

Discussion groups are easy and inexpensive to organize and are popular among students. These groups are different from therapy or support groups that are usually offered by the campus counseling service. Discussion groups focus on informal chat about particular topics of interest to those involved. While participants may find these groups supportive or even therapeutic in the broadest sense of the term, such is not the intent of the activity.

Groups may be scheduled for men, for women, or for both men and women together, although some topics found compelling by men and women may be quite different. Decisions as to which to offer are dependent not only on the nature and needs of the LGBT community on a particular campus but also on staff or volunteers available to facilitate the discussions. Some campuses may not have a sufficiently large number of students to merit two groups nor staff available to assist with them. Variant interests, combined with the fact that most LGBT student organizations are co-educational, suggest that, where possible, students may value the time in the single-sex environment that discussion groups may provide. Some campuses may be large enough to have multiple discussion groups. For example, UCLA has a men's group, a women's group, a bi group with both men and women attending, a transgender and questioning group, a coming-out group, a residence hall group, a group for non-traditional-age undergraduates, and an Alcoholics Anonymous (AA) group for LGBT students, faculty, and staff.

If the group offers nothing else, it should be consistent. Its time and location should not change from term to term, year to year. Therefore, in planning your groups, decisions need to be made about which kind to offer. How long will each session last? (Generally, less than 90 minutes does not provide sufficient time to address a topic [especially given late arrivals], but more than two hours leads to loss of attention and diminishing participation.) Will the discussion groups be offered for a single semester or throughout the academic year? Will they occur weekly, biweekly, once a month?

Unlike therapy or formal support groups, discussion groups usually do not require participants to commit to regular attendance. Students may attend whenever they are free or if a given topic motivates them.

If possible, the weekly topic should be advertised in advance, and facilitators should offer some information about the topic at the beginning of the session. This provides a "trigger" for the discussion that follows. Student participants may be assigned in advance to offer information. Students could also take turns facilitating discussion, but they must have some awareness of group dynamics and potential problems or pitfalls. Though clarity must be provided from the beginning—and affirmation received from participants—that this is not a therapy group, discussions may become contentious or emotional, so it is recommended that trained facilitators—either staff or volunteers—be present or at least available to assist student facilitators.

While topics may be decided from session to session, it is probably more useful to poll participants early in the semester or the year to construct a list of potential topics. Then, at the end of each meeting, the topic for the following meeting may be chosen from the list. Knowing the topic in advance also provides staff the opportunity to prepare for the discussion. On occasion, guest facilitators from the university or neighboring community who are expert in specific topic areas may be invited.

Topics frequently chosen are coming out; developing and maintaining relationships; drug and alcohol use in the community; meeting people via the Internet; gay men/lesbian women having children; ages and stages in the lives of LGBT people; lesbian women and gay men relating to each other; bisexuality; body image, dieting, and eating disorders; interracial relationships; and stereotypes about LGBT people. In reality, the list is endless.

Case Study 9.3
Michigan State

First, we developed collaborative working relationships between the LGBT student organization, the LGBT Concerns assistant/counseling center liaisons (staff consultants), and the discussion groups. This mutually collaborative training model includes philosophy, training components, and format, as well as discussion group leader selection criteria: self-awareness, interpersonal communication, group facilitation, co-facilitation, and multicultural competence. The specifics of the training model are operationalizing the components of the model, initial fall training and selection sessions, skill development areas, weekly in-service meetings for discussion group leaders, and advanced training sessions. Student response is important. We include in our training how to elicit feedback from participants via formal assessment tools and from discussion group leaders via discussion and process. We look for successful outcomes, including high participant satisfaction with discussion groups. The benefits of the collaborative model include enhanced services for LGBT students, skill building for student leaders, opportunities for training and mentoring relationships, preprofessional experience for discussion group leaders, maximal use of existing university resources with low cost, consistent with the move toward more pro-active, cross-campus partnerships to meet student needs, and the opportunity to build "allies" with other units on campus. (Submitted by Brent Bilodeau, assistant for LGBT Concerns, Multicultural Development Office, Michigan State University)

STUDENT ORGANIZATION ADVISING

Requirements and procedures regarding staff or faculty advising of student organizations vary widely from institution to institution. Advising LGBT student organizations should naturally follow each institution's model. Even where student organizations are not mandated to have advisers, LGBT organizations, particularly those comprised primarily of undergraduates, are likely to reach out to a friendly and knowledgeable faculty or staff member to serve in that capacity. Directors or staff members of LGBT centers are logical, but not inevitable, choices to fill these positions.

The role of adviser may be both rewarding and frustrating. As is true in working with any student organization, there are opportunities for sharing suggestions based on experience that will be heeded and produce success, and at the same time there are ample opportunities to incur students' projections and sometimes wrath. These are, in a nutshell, the two sides of serving in loco parentis.

The primary value of extracurricular activities, apart from the aspired organizational goals, is preparation for students' future lives—both in their professional work and in their volunteer service. Students are in the process of establishing themselves as independent and self-reliant adults. As a result, while advice from advisers may be helpful in a present situation as well as a useful strategy for later in life, it can sometimes also feel contrary to their sense of personal development. Advisers may prefer to allow students to learn from their mistakes rather than to incur their displaced parental scorn, but only if the mistakes are not likely to be very costly, either financially or in other consequential ways.

Potential advisers must also be aware that student organizations change their styles of operating from year to year, depending on the leadership and other factors. As a result, in some years, the advisers' in-put will be actively sought. In other years, students may not want or feel that they need advisers.

There are some particular considerations regarding the LGBT staff serving as advisers of record for a student organization. First, with limited, if any, staff and many LGBT organizations on campus, it would be nearly impossible to provide advisers from the center. Second, student organizations are not likely to hold their general meetings or board discussions during conventional professional work hours. Most center personnel are used to working some evenings or weekends, but student organization boards often opt for meetings at what might be considered extreme hours for working adults—11:00 PM. on Thursday nights, for example, or 7:30 PM. on Sunday evenings. Attending meetings at such times is not realistic for most professional staff.

Third, it is vital for campus LGBT centers to maintain solid working relationships with student organizations. If the center's director serves as adviser to one organizations, relationships with other LGBT student organizations may be jeopardized. Additionally, tensions may arise between an organization's leaders and the center director pertaining to the work of the organization and the suggestions or intervention of the adviser in that work that may easily carry over into the relationship between the organization and the center. It is not always easy for students to divide the two roles of the director as organization adviser and LGBT center director.

Finally, at some institutions, people sense a conflict of interest when the director is also the adviser for the LGBT student organizations. At one Midwest institution, for example, the campus commission on LGBT equity felt that the LGBT director was alienating the students away from the work and people of the commission and towards the center. When an institution is involved with turf issues, as occasionally happens, the director as the visible campus LGBT leader is sometimes placed in an awkward position regardless of the accuracy of the information. Many faculty and staff would love to take on the adviser role of an organization—if they were only asked.

Case Study 9.4
Brown University

As assistant dean/liaison for LGBT concerns at Brown University from 1991 to 1997, I developed the role of liaison, which included both advising a burgeoning group of LGBT student organizations and providing leadership training to both volunteer and paid student leaders/staff. Prior to becoming a dean, I worked in student activities for two years, during which I advised a number of student organizations and created a leadership development program for all student groups. A center director may be called upon to formally or informally advise student organizations and use various models for promoting leadership development among LGBT students. Depending on the location of the office within the institution and institutional requirements for faculty advisers to student organizations, the director may be asked either to take on formal advisory responsibilities for LGBT student organizations or to assume an informal advising relationship with student leaders. Each of these standpoints has advantages and challenges. For example, in the case of a formal adviser, the roles are clearly defined, but there may be less flexibility and more accountability for the professional. In the case of an informal advising relationship, students generally have more autonomy and can take more risks, but the informality does not provide structure for resolving some of the difficult situations that can come up when students take activist stances or come in conflict with other campus administrators. (Submitted by Kristen Renn, Michigan State University)

COMMUNITY SERVICE

Many colleges and universities are encouraging students to become involved in volunteering in the communities surrounding their campuses. Apart from the assistance that such efforts provide to community initiatives and organizations, students benefit from what is being called "service learning." Students may then document what their volunteer endeavors taught them in preparation for their professional and even personal lives. Sometimes this learning is formal, connected to courses offered for credit in various academic departments, and sometimes it is a gift of time that one may include on a resume.

LGBT students should be encouraged to participate in service learning and to provide assistance to the LGBT community through its many agencies and organizations. Centers may assist students with this objective in two ways: collaboration with offices on campus whose primary responsibility is matching student volunteers with worthy community organizations or, where no such office exists or may not be called upon, assigning center staff members to make such arrangements.

In working with campus volunteer placement offices, centers may provide the names and contact data for key LGBT community organizations. This information is likely to be known by center staff already as a result of previous outreach and referral efforts. Volunteer placement offices are less likely to have this information and may be less able to assess which among the many community organizations are most likely to provide students with meaningful and instructive experiences. Conversely, those same community organizations may not know how to contact appropriate officials at the college or university to request LGBT student volunteers.

This kind of collaboration strengthens the relationships between campus centers and LGBT community organizations. Positive outcomes regarding volunteers will increase the likelihood that cooperation will occur regarding other projects. The flow of traffic—and resources—may be two-way. Collaboration between campus centers and community organizations may encourage community people to attend center-sponsored programs and events, may convince some community members to apply to college or university programs, and/or may introduce local LGBT funders to this important center on campus.

Case Study 9.5
Alternative Spring Break

University of Michigan (UM) Student Affairs encourages students to participate in Alternative Spring Break—a community service learning program that engages students during a week-long period between semesters in early March. In 1996, the LGBT Center sponsored an Alternative Alternative Spring Break especially for LGBT students and their allies. Ten students and a center staff person obtained a UM van and drove to Washington, D.C. There the students spent a full day at each of the offices of the two largest LGBT national organizations—the Human Rights Campaign and the National Gay and Lesbian Task Force—to learn first-hand how these organizations operate. The students spent their third day with Ann Arbor U. S. Representative Lynn Rivers, who showed them the legislative process in action and let them see how bills become laws. On the fourth day, the students spent nearly six hours at the U.S. Holocaust Museum to understand in visceral terms how unchecked hatred and bigotry can swiftly lead to murder. The students were generously hosted by the Washington, D.C., Metropolitan Community Church. The week was an intense learning opportunity for these students, a number of whom graduated and have returned to Washington, D.C., to live and work. (Submitted by Ronni Sanlo, LGBT Center director, UCLA)

COMMUNICATIONS

Communication with consumers is an essential function of every LGBT center or program. The specific forms of this communication depend on the institution. While electronic communication has become predominant at most colleges and universities in recent years, there is still a need for print communication as well. Assuming the presence of basic technology, electronic communication is easy to establish, highly effective, and, apart from costs associated with set-up, relatively inexpensive.

Many LGBT campus centers have some sort of electronic bulletin that is disseminated via a distribution list. These publications are able to reach hundreds of readers in a matter of seconds. They may be sent to students, faculty and staff, alumni (anywhere in the world), and to people from the community surrounding the campus.

Bulletins can be issued monthly, weekly, or more frequently if there are demand and staff to manage this activity. They may contain campus, local, or national news of interest to the LGBT community. The center passes on to readers stories received, at no cost, from news services offered by national organizations such as the National Gay and Lesbian Task Force (NGLTF), the Human Rights Campaign (HRC), Lambda Legal Defense and Education Fund, the Gay Lesbian Straight Education Network (GLSEN), and others. An astute and efficient editor can regularly and quickly sift through the significant amount of information received and decide what will be of particular interest to recipients. Electronic bulletins may also include announcements of campus and community events, calls for papers and for participation in local, regional, or national conferences, and classified ads, such as for roommates or about apartment sublets available.

Another way to quickly provide information about events is a voice mailbox with only outgoing messages. This is a service available through the sophisticated telephone systems used on most college campuses. Consumers call the designated number—most desirably one that is easy to remember and dial—anytime, day or night, and instantly receive information about upcoming events. Messages are easily deleted once the events are over. A staff member such as a work-study student may easily learn the voice mail technology and up-date the events line regularly, optimally no less often than once a week.

There is still a need for printed newsletters to be distributed on a regular basis. Such publications provide space for stories—news, opinions, fiction—that are not suitable for electronic bulletins. They may also contain longer-range calendars of events, such as one for a full semester. Of course, newsletters will take more staff time than electronic bulletins. Staff members need to recruit people to submit articles, and they need to edit, copy, and distribute the newsletters. The advent of sophisticated desktop publishing software makes the layout and editing of newsletters in-house fairly simple. Most campuses have some form of intramural mail. The utilization of this system as much as possible cuts back on postal expenses. Invariably, however, some newsletters need to be sent through the U.S. mail, and some expenditure of funds is thus entailed. Buying paper is an expense, but purchasing in bulk—say, for an entire year of publications at one time—lowers the cost to the center.

Case Study 9.6
Queer-E & Outlines *at the University of Pennsylvania*

Communication between PENN's LGBT Center and its constituents is vital to inform people about events, provide a forum for student ideas and opinions, and enable dialogue to emerge between segments of both the LGBT and non-LGBT communities. Queer-E is a periodic E-mail-based bulletin maintained by PENN's LGBT Center that includes LGBT events on the campus of the University of Pennsylvania and in the Philadelphia area. It serves as a vehicle for most of the announcements for the PENN LGBT community and is seen by hundreds of people, and it is therefore one of our most reliable and immediate methods to disseminate information. Each edition of queer-E is divided into organized sections, such as "PENN events," "mark your calendars," "announcements," "on-going events," "can you help?" "conferences," and "internship opportunities." Such a classification system as well as chronological listings allow users to find events quickly and to plan ahead. Events are submitted by campus organizations and queer/queer-friendly people or businesses in the Delaware Valley either via a form on the center's Web site or directly to the queer-E editor. Other events are gleaned from local queer newspapers and listservs. When possible, contacts are listed with an event so that subscribers can find out further information. Each entry reads something like this: "January 24, 1999, at 7 P.M. —LGBT Center Film Series: *Watermelon Woman*. The story of a young African American lesbian's search for an old-time Philly film star nicknamed 'the watermelon woman' whom she discovers was queer. The movie will be shown at the LGBT Center (3537 Locust Walk, 3rd floor) with snacks and beverages provided. For more info, please call (215) 898-5044."

To receive queer-E, persons contact the editor and have their E-mail address added to a nickname list in the center's E-mail account. Confidentiality is ensured by placing the nickname in the "blind carbon copy" (BCC) line, meaning that the only name that people see when reading queer-E is that of the center's director, which is listed in the "To" line. Moreover, the subject line states only "Electronic Newsletter #__." Consequently, many students feel safe reading queer-E regardless of their level of "outness" because of the precautions taken. Due to the anonymity of E-mail and specifically of queer-E itself, the center reaches students who may otherwise not be directly involved in the queer community or are just beginning to question their sexual orientation. The center's newsletter, *Outlines*, on the other hand, does not always reach questioning individuals but works well for individuals who are on our postal mailing lists. *Outlines* is published at least four times during an academic year and is a forum for reporting the news and expressing thoughts of interest to both the LGBT and general community at PENN. A general call for submissions of essays, poetry, articles, art, and stories is made approximately one month before an issue of *Outlines* is published. Additionally, work-study students at the center submit something to each issue, and the editor approaches students who she feels will have an interesting perspective on a story. Using more than one method to attract writers allows for diversity in contributors. For instance, a member of our ALLIES group wrote about his impressions of B-GLAD (Bisexual Gay Lesbian Transgender Awareness Days) from a heterosexual standpoint; an undergraduate chronicled his first year in college in several installments; alumni are featured in a profile in each issue; and creative poetry and reaction to current events (e.g. Matthew Shepard's death or Jesus Week on campus) are often found in the pages of *Outlines* in addition to the "usual" reporting in a newsletter. Once stories have been submitted, *Outlines* is edited, graphics and photographs are added, and the final multi-page product is printed. We then send copies to everyone on our mailing list, including current students, faculty and staff, alumni, and allies. For students, it is fun to receive something in the mail, and *Outlines* also keeps them and other constituents abreast of what is happening at the center without subscribing to a listserv or queer-E. It is created in PageMaker and is usually 8 to 12 pages long. Overall, both queer-E and *Outlines* have proven to be effective ways to communicate with students and other constituents about news, ideas, and general happenings at PENN's LGBT Center. (Submitted by Erin Cross, University of Pennsylvania)

Resource Guides

Providing lists of campus and community resources is a very valuable service. Especially for institutions located in urban or other densely populated areas, the assembling and distributing of resource guides can be very time-consuming and expensive. This is a project that could be undertaken in conjunction with a local community center or other organization in an effort to share costs and enhance accuracy. Resource guides are useful to almost everyone in the community but are of particular value to those new to campus or to the LGBT community.

Among the resources worth including in the guide are campus LGBT organizations (student groups and campus programs); campus offices with services tailored to meet the needs of LGBT students and employees; other student and youth groups and agencies in the community; hot lines and information lines; organizations in the community concerned with politics and civil rights, health, religion, hobbies, recreation, or sports; groups providing personal support; bookstores and libraries; organizations for professionals (e.g., gay lawyers or social workers); media (magazines and television and radio programs); and restaurants, bars, and nightclubs.

Because campus and community organizations wax and wane and change their locations and contact information frequently, the publication of printed resource guides may be undertaken only periodically, say every other academic year. However, a version of the resource guide may be located on the center's Web site. That version should be easily up-dated on a regular basis.

Web sites

Web sites are another facet of electronic communication that are vital for campus LGBT centers. The initial design and establishment of a Web site can be complicated and costly, but the benefits are substantial. Contemporary college students are frequently familiar with the technology necessary to set up a Web site and can be of considerable assistance in the process. Moreover, many campuses have technology offices or student organizations that can provide consultation regarding Web site construction at no or low cost.

Center Web sites may contain, among other components, basic information about the organization, its programs and services; profiles of center staff, both professional and student; lists of campus and community resources; a calendar of upcoming events; and links to other campus and community programs likely to be of value to consumers viewing the Web site. Such Web sites also almost always provide readers the option of sending E-mail messages to staff members directly from the Web site.

Some center Web sites receive thousands of "hits" annually. The mechanisms that monitor these Web sites indicate that the visitors are not only from campus but also from all over the world. The costs associated with establishing and maintaining Web sites seem well worth the useful information and services that they offer.

LIBRARY SERVICES AND READING ROOMS

LGBT campus centers are usually intended, at least in part, to support the academic mission of the institutions in which they are located. This goal may be achieved through the provision of reading rooms or lending libraries and consultation to students and others doing research regarding LGBT people and the LGBT community.

Most institutional libraries, especially on larger and more progressive campuses, have some books and periodicals about and of interest to LGBT people. How extensive this collection is depends on who is determining acquisition policies and making decisions about specific materials. It is useful for LGBT center staff and LGBT community members to encourage library officials to be as broad and inclusive as possible in their deliberations.

However, regardless of the size of the collection, library officials report that materials related to LGBT people and concerns are among the most frequent to disappear. Though the behavior may seem paranoid to some, it is possible that some of those seeking to use such materials may be afraid to take them to the circulation desk to sign out.

A reading room or lending library within the LGBT center may provide materials not available within the institution's main library system and, possibly, a safer place in which to utilize them. This may include publications provided in substantial quantities to the center at no cost, such as community newspapers, which are then distributed to consumers. Many centers also receive national magazines, which, though not free, may be subscribed to for fairly reasonable rates. Because they contain news and many stories of interest to LGBT consumers, they are often seen as a worthwhile investment. Further, back issues may provide useful archival information. Books are sometimes quite expensive but often provide vital resources.

Reading rooms offer books and periodicals that can be used only in the center. Lending libraries make some of these materials available for circulation. In most instances, consumers are not allowed to borrow newspapers and magazines of which only one copy is received. This is because they are more easily lost or forgotten and never returned. This is less likely with books. Nevertheless, some books are never returned, either because consumers were as afraid to sign them out as they would have been in the main library, or simply because they are misplaced or taken intentionally.

Greater staff time and costs are associated with lending libraries than with reading rooms. In either case, some kind of database needs to be used to list the center's book collection. Though sophisticated library software is available, more general database applications may provide the options required by most centers—to list books by author, title, subject matter, and category. These systems may be up-dated and maintained fairly easily. A version of this database may be uploaded to the center's Web site, thus making it possible for potential consumers to view the center's collection and perhaps even the availability of a specific volume from some distance.

Since virtually all centers have finite funds with which to purchase books, some policy regarding acquisition needs to be established. Scholarly volumes and collections of articles in fields such as history, psychology, and science, which are generally very expensive, are most likely to be used for course-related research and less likely to be seen as justifiable purchases on limited student budgets. Fiction and biography are most often be signed out for personal reading. Though some literature sought by students may be for course work or papers, centers are likely to purchase them, especially if they are relatively less expensive. Self-help books are useful for a short time in consumers' lives and, hence, are also less likely to be seen as wise personal purchases. Using the logic provided, centers with limited purchasing power may wish to concentrate on scholarly volumes and self-help books rather than fiction or biography. They would also be wise to buy books once or twice a year, rather than piecemeal, thus making a bulk discount more possible from a friendly local bookstore or national mail order business.

There are ways for LGBT centers to acquire books other than buying them. Directors may write to publishers, especially those known for offering books of interest to LGBT readers, and request copies of books at no cost. These may be either samples or review copies or remaindered books. It is important in such requests to comment on the center's limited budget and to establish its nonprofit, tax-exempt status. Donations of books, either new or used, may also be sought from alumni or community members. Giving books is an excellent way for people to provide an important resource while also receiving a legitimate, in-kind income tax deduction.

Most centers with lending libraries allow consumers to borrow books for a specified period of time. Unless the software used by the center provides reminders, responsible staff will need to review the list of signed-out books regularly and call the borrowers to ask that they be returned. Staff members may need to call before a book is due if another consumer needs to use the book sooner.

Someone should be available in the reading room as many hours as feasible, given staff size. Those staffing the reading room can help consumers find what they are seeking, via the database or their own familiarity with the collection, and then assure that books are properly signed out, with current and accurate telephone and E-mail information provided, to decrease the occurrence of loss or theft.

An inventory of the collection should be undertaken at least once a year, most usefully near the end of the year. Unreturned books may be pursued and a list of books permanently missing constructed. Decisions will then need to be made as to replacing the missing volumes or eliminating them from the database.

Center staff may provide consultation to students and faculty conducting research on LGBT people and concerns. Staff may first need to help students— both LGBT and non-LGBT students—understand or narrow their topics. They often arrive with ideas or aspirations that are off-base or unrealistic to achieve, especially in the time frame available to them. Then, those doing research need to be directed to relevant resources in the library or reading room. They may also need to be familiarized with archives of magazines or periodicals or to less widely available resources, such as clippings files.

Often, researchers contact the center seeking respondents or participants for surveys or interviews. This may range from a sophomore's seeking one gay person to interview for a sociology paper to a doctoral student or faculty member's doing a large-scale study that requires dozens of participants. Following a set of carefully considered guidelines about cooperating with such research, center staff may be willing to contact potential volunteers through its listserv or other outreach mechanisms.

Case Study 9.7
Requesting to "Do" Research through the UCLA LGBT Center

I get very concerned and somewhat protective when people contact me about "doing" research with our LGBT students. Sometimes non-LGBT students want to interview "a homosexual" and want me to produce a "homosexual" student for them. At other times faculty (or non-faculty professional) researchers want me to distribute a "bazillion" surveys. Upon occasion, researchers have asked for entrée into the LGBT students support/discussion groups. The bottom line is that rarely a week goes by when someone hasn't asked for access to our LGBT students, as if the students lived in a fishbowl simply waiting for someone—anyone—to ask them about their lives. I finally developed two policies for allowing accessing to students through our Center. First, regardless of one's standing, whether a UCLA undergraduate or a researcher with the Ford Foundation, the researcher must have UCLA institutional review board approval—and be able to prove it. Second, if researchers are undergrads at UCLA, they are invited to subscribe to our gay-bruins listserv and solicit participants themselves without the center's being the middle person. Finally, if the researchers are students who want to know more about LGBT people and culture, I assist them with fine-tuning their topic area then provide them access to the center's library and Web system. (Submitted by Ronni Sanlo, LGBT Center, UCLA)

It is vital that the availability of the library be widely advertised throughout campus. Libraries and reading rooms support the institution's academic mission and offer valuable resources to consumers. Though some staff time and expenditures are required for effective operation, they pay off in the long run. For a comprehensive listing of information resources, see Appendix J.

CONSULTATION SERVICES

LGBT centers can provide valuable consultation to other departments on campus. This consultation usually relates to how those offices can provide services to LGBT consumers sensitively and effectively. In some instances, the departments reach out to the center, either because they have experienced problems with, or complaints from, LGBT consumers or because they anticipate concerns and want to avoid them. In other cases, the LGBT center or a campus administrator may recommend or require such consultation. Naturally, consultation sought willingly is more likely to be received graciously and appreciated than advice that is mandated.

Campus departments often seeking or needing consultation include residence life; counseling and psychological services; fraternity and sorority affairs; career services; admissions; campus police; athletics and recreation. Some general principles apply to all organizations seeking consultation, but there are also considerations that are specific to individual offices. The considerations of an organization providing mental health services to LGBT consumers will clearly be different from those of the campus police. Those providing consultation need not be only center employees. A campus psychology professor might be involved in consultation to the counseling service, while a gay or gay-sensitive community cop might be included in consultation provided to the campus police.

In general, consultants need to regard this as a somewhat delicate operation. Sexual orientation and gender identity are subjects that are challenging for some to discuss openly, perhaps because they are uninformed but seek to be politically correct, because they are ambivalent or even hostile because of religious upbringing or other homophobic socialization, because they are themselves gay or lesbian and closeted, or because of a variety of other factors. Consultants may encounter ignorance or antagonism. They need to remain as calm and rational as possible, referring frequently to institutional policies that ban discrimination or mistreatment on the basis of sexual orientation. Generally, consultants should not be trying to change people's personal beliefs or attitudes. Rather, they need to stress that institutional practices should be sensitive and inclusive and that the institution has the expectation that student and employee consumers be treated equitably. This is accomplished not as a result of changes in beliefs or attitudes but rather through enlightened behavior. Consultants who can provide service using this approach are more likely to be effective and, as a result of word of mouth, to be invited to consult with other college or university offices.

Case Study 9.8
Consulting with Other University Departments and Units

At Washington State University, the GLBA Program is available as a resource for all university departments. Units contact our office as they identify needs, and occasionally we'll offer our services to departments that we know could use our assistance. Our ongoing relationship with the campus Police Department is an example of this kind of consultation. When I began as director of the program, I scheduled a meeting with the police chief right away, so that we could talk over safety issues and share concerns, goals, and plans. A few months later, he called my office to discuss strategies for dealing with the public health and safety issues raised by public sex in a well-known campus cruising area. He was reluctant to increase patrols and was adamantly opposed to arrests but needed to respond to complaints by custodial staff and others. We were able to create positive alternatives, including some education of patrol officers, the alerting of an informal communication network of gay men that the location in question was receiving police surveillance, and the distribution of safer sex information around the cruising location. These strategies produced results that satisfied both the LGBT community and the police department. Since then, we have continued to work together. For example, I take part each year in the department's cultural awareness training. The Police Department often sends a representative to participate in educational programs at the GLBA Center, such as brown-bag discussions or panels on criminal justice-related issues. The department's senior officers came to the center's vigil for Matthew Shepard. During the high-profile (and still unsolved) disappearance of an area gay student, the Police Department shared up-to-date information with our office in order to reduce rumors and misinformation. In turn, we have been able to reassure students that the Police Department will respond appropriately if they file complaints or report malicious harassment. Individual officers have made referrals to the center for follow-up when students reported incidents of homophobia. Our most important joint venture is communication: keeping our respective offices in the loop about ongoing issues. Our working relationship is not without its stresses, of course, but continued communication and mutual education keeps us working together, even in challenging situations. Though some barriers remain, the police administration's commitment to a safe campus and to community policing, as well as their willingness to be publicly identified as allies have helped resolve some familiar, lingering concerns in the LGBT community. (Submitted by Melyndah Huskey, GLBA Program, Washington State University)

SPEAKING OUT: LGBT SPEAKERS AND TRAINERS ON CAMPUS

According to Kerry Poynter at Duke University, speakers panels are educational interventions in which volunteer gay, lesbian, bisexual, transgender, and supportive heterosexual allied people share their personal stories and respond to questions and comments from an audience. These panels are frequently used on a college/university campus to reduce homophobic/heterosexist attitudes. Often these panels are used in a classroom setting to provide personal experience in addition to course material.

Panels usually consist of two to four people who identify as gay, lesbian, bisexual, or transgender, or as heterosexual allies. Panelists may be students, faculty, staff, or people in the local community. Coordination of a panel program can come from a student organization or university office. Coordination usually consists of recruiting new panelists, training, advertising, signing up panelists for panel dates, and evaluation. Some universities such as the University of Michigan offer academic credit for panelists.

Advertising of the program should go to residence halls or student organizations as well as academic departments that include LGBT issues in course material. Many professors/instructors are happy to utilize a panel as part of their course as long as they are aware of the program. As your panel program gains a reputation as a worthwhile educational intervention, many professors will plan a panel into their course syllabi every semester. Some departments to consider contacting for your panel program include counseling psychology, social work, education/professional development, psychology, women's studies, philosophy, and sociology. Be creative and seek out specific courses that cover LGBT issues.

Case Study 9.9
University of Maryland

Our Speakers Bureau is mostly student panels (i.e., occasionally faculty/staff volunteer), but for the past two years they've been coordinated through my office, and I have provided two days of training at the beginning of the fall semester. Next year we hope to implement a for-credit system using our sexual health peer education program as a model. They train for a full week before the fall semester (I'm thinking that might be a bit much) and meet one hour a week during the fall and spring semesters. Each class member must do a certain percentage of the total number of presentations; then they get three semester credits at the end of the spring semester, so it's a commitment for the entire academic year with credit coming only at the end. The faculty for the proposed undergraduate certificate in LGBT studies want (1) those who take it for credit to have had at least one LGBT course as a prerequisite or the permission of the instructor to make sure that they have at least some foundation before doing panels and (2) a volunteer component so that newly out individuals who do not have much of a knowledge base can participate (but they would not get credit). The idea is that each panel will have at least one person who is taking the course. That person will be responsible for putting a panel together from the pool of volunteers or other members of the class. The volunteers will receive the same training being offered now. The problem, of course, is that you have panels with some people getting credit and others not. The justification is that the for-credit panelists have more responsibility in putting panels together, have greater knowledge, therefore ensuring the content of the presentations, and are receiving instruction on what may be primarily a course on queer pedagogy. It's a bit complicated, but we're going to try to make it work. I imagine that through experience we'll refine it considerably. (Submitted by Luke Jensen, director, Office of Lesbian, Gay, Bisexual and Transgender Equity, University of Maryland, College Park)

There are many excellent resources available to assist with the development of speakers panels and peer educators on campus. Three exemplary resources are The National Gay and Lesbian Task Force's *Campus Organizing Manual*; *Toward Acceptance: Sexual Orientation Issues on Campus* by Wall and Evans; and *Homophobia: How We all Pay the Price* by Blumenfeld. Other recommended sources are found in the annotated resource list that follows.

RESOURCE LIST

Croteau, J. M., & Kusek, M. T. (1992). Gay and Lesbian Speaker Panels: Implementation and Research. *Journal of Counseling & Development*, 70, 396–400.
    This article covers two basic and important areas, implementation and research, concerning LGBT panel presentations. Student affairs professionals will find this helpful if they are assisting LGBT students in organizing and training. The article covers previous research on attitude change after attending LGBT panel presentations while making suggestions on how to implement panels. Although it does touch on how panelists should answer audience questions, it does not offer a typical listing of questions that may be asked.

Geasler, M. J., Croteau, J. M., Heineman, C. J., & Edlund, C. J. (1995). A Qualitative Study of Students' Expression of Change After Attending Panel Presentations By Lesbian, Gay, and Bisexual Speakers. *Journal of College Student Development*, 36(5), 483–492.

Two-hundred sixty students who attended presentations by lesbian, gay, and bisexual individuals were asked to write about their experiences. In this article, writings from these students were analyzed to determine how they perceived and explained their own changes as a result of attending the panel. Since this article provides examples of student responses to positive change after attending a panel it could be a good resource to help solicit panel presentations in a classroom setting.

Gray, J., & Poynter, K. (1996, October). Developing a Speakers Panel Program to Provide Curriculum Content on Gay, Lesbian and Bisexual People in Baccalaureate Social Work Education. Paper presented at the 14th Annual Baccalaureate Program Directors Conference, Portland, OR.

This paper is a basic overview of how a panel program was used in social work courses. It also includes information on how the panel program was implemented and how the social work department allied itself with the campus LGBT student organization. Contact Judith I. Gray, Associate Professor, Dept of Social Work, (765) 285-1012 or E-mail at 00jigray@bsu.edu.

Lucksted, A. (1998). Sexual Orientation Speakers Bureaus. In R. Sanlo (Ed.). *Working With Lesbian, Gay, Bisexual, and Transgender College Students: A Handbook for Faculty and Administrators*. Westport, CT: Greenwood Press, 352–362.

A good starting place for those interested in developing their own panel program. This chapter covers different structural models, speakers, a basic panel, common questions, suggestions, and effects on the speakers. There is no specific mention of how to train or use heterosexual ally or transgender panelists.

McCord, D. M., & Herzog, H. A. (1991). What Undergraduates Want to Know about Homosexuality. *Teaching of Psychology*, 16, 243–244.

The best part of this article is that it is short, concise, and to the point. The authors collected about 300 questions prior to inviting a LGBT panel into their psychology courses. The questions were placed into 13 separate categories and numerous examples are given. While LGBT panelists will find the example questions helpful, professionals will find the article useful in preparation for LGBT classroom presentations.

Poynter, K., Gray, J., & Zimmerman, J. (1996). *Challenge Bigotry: A Training Video and Booklet for Lesbian, Bisexual, and Gay Speaker Panels*. Muncie, IN: Ball State University.

This is the only known resource available, a video and booklet, that documents how to implement, train panelists for, and coordinate a panel program. A very good resource for common questions for LGBT and ally panelists, example scripts to use, designing an evaluation component, major ideas to get across, and points to remember. Although this video/booklet includes information for supportive heterosexual ally panelists, it does not include any information about transgender panelists. This is available from the office of Academic Research and Sponsored Programs at Ball State University (www.bsu.edu/provost/oarsp/info) or by calling (765) 285-1600. Profits from the sale of this video/booklet go to the campus LGBT student organization Spectrum. Cost for this video/booklet is a modest at $50 for colleges/universities and $30 for student organizations.

Source: Poynter, Kerry. Frequently Asked Question (FAQ). National Consortium of Directors of LGBT Resources in Higher education. www.lgbtcampus.org.faq

Chapter 10

Safe Zones and Allies Programs

Lesbian, gay, bisexual, and transgender (LGBT) students, faculty, and staff often feel invisible and isolated on their college campuses. There are few indications that they are welcome and little recognition that their lives and achievements as contributing members of campus communities matter. Although some institutions are now developing LGBT campus resource centers, most colleges and universities in this country offer no official recognition to, or provide services for LGBT students. To address the issues of support and visibility, some institutions developed safe zone programs. (See Appendix K for an example of a letter introducing the program.)

THE PROGRAM

Safe zone programs appeared on several campuses almost simultaneously in the early 1990s. Since the death of Matthew Shepard in October 1998, a growing number of institutions have initiated safe zone programs. The safe zone program concept is simple. "The college community identifies, educates, and supports campus members who are concerned about the well-being of LGBT students" (Hothem & Keane 1998, p. 364). The goals of safe zone programs are to increase visibility, support, and awareness of LGBT people and issues on campus (Iowa State, 1999).

Typically, a safe zone marker, such as a sticker, magnet, or mug, identifies people who are knowledgeable about LGBT issues. On some campuses safe zone participants must attend one or more group or individual training sessions before receiving a safe zone marker. On other campuses, people receive a marker simply by requesting one. The markers usually have a common, identifiable symbol. When LGBT students need to talk or require assistance, they find someone with the identifying marker and know that they are in the company of a welcoming person. Markers are not necessarily invitations to discuss one's sexual orientation with every person who displays one; rather, LGBT students simply feel more comfortable if they knew they could speak freely about issues affecting their academic success (Gaumnitz 1996).

Symbols on safe zone markers are almost universally some version of a pink triangle or rainbow flag, both with historical significance. Gay men were forced to wear the pink triangle in Nazis concentration camps (Marcus 1993). The LGBT community has reclaimed the pink triangle as a symbol of power and pride. The six-stripe rainbow flag, also a symbol of pride, was designed in 1978 and designated as the official LGBT Freedom Flag by the International Flag-makers Association (Marcus 1993).

Safe zone programs are typically funded by student government, student affairs offices, equal employment or affirmative action offices, LGBT campus resource centers, or by internal or external grants. Some safe zone programs receive no money at all. One chose to have no official recognition (and therefore receive no funding) so that the program was free from campus constraints.

THE PRACTICE

Safe zone programs theoretically are important statements of welcome and inclusion for LGBT students on college campuses. Do they work? Some issues may prevent them from being as effective in practice as they appear in theory.

First, safe zone programs tend to be labor-intensive. They require knowl-edgeable people—nearly always volunteers—to facilitate on-going training ses-sions. "Nobody has stepped forward to relieve the initial group of trainers. The original team of six has dwindled to four, and despite our constant advertising we remain a small band trying to do this in addition to our 'regular' jobs on campus."

Second, upon occasion, anti-LGBT people have become safe zone partici-pants to continue the victimization that LGBT students already experience. One quickly removed, but honest, participant said that "he would need to share his belief that homosexuality is a sin to anyone who brought up the issue."

Third, in multiple staff settings like reception areas, there is sometimes confusion over whether the entire area was considered safe or just the individual who displayed the marker.

Fourth, some LGBT supporters verbalized discomfort with an identity group marker on their doors. Gaumnitz (1996) noted that some people worried that the markers might inadvertently mean that they were trained counselors about sexual orientation issues. Additionally, there was concern that while offer-ing visible support for one group of students, another group may feel discour-aged and not ask for needed services, especially in helping areas like the campus counseling or a health center or a dean's office. One senior student affairs offi-cer lamented that although he was a strong supporter of LGBT students, faculty, staff, and programs (that he generously funded regularly), he was called homo-phobic because he would not affix a safe zone sticker to his door.

Fifth, in least one institution, some faculty and staff feared—and actually experienced—harassment and marker defacement when they posted safe zone stickers on their doors. Likewise, some residence hall students were similarly harassed when their stickers were displayed.

Finally, some people viewed the program as "evidence of 'special privilege' for LGBT people" (Iowa State, 1999). Others questioned whether some heterosexual participants were simply being "politically correct" by participating.

THE GIFT OF SAFE ZONE PROGRAMS: VISIBILITY

While these and other issues may plague many safe zone programs, some are quite successful. At Iowa State (1999), LGBT students "felt that the project had validated their efforts to improve the environment." The Princeton program brought people together who had connected previously only via E-mail. "We heard stories of colleagues coming out to each other when they see an ALLY sign on each other's doors. Most importantly, the program has given straight supporters 'in-roads' to the community which hadn't previously existed." At some institutions, students asked LGBT faculty who had posted safe zone stickers about LGBT issues related to their fields of study. Additionally, service utilization increased on one campus' LGBT resource center following the initiation of the safe zone program.

The Iowa State program is considered very successful. However, there is an unspoken feeling that administrators may point to the safe zone program to show that LGBT issues are being addressed while "more significant underlying issues facing this community continue to be ignored."

Safe zone markers provide important cues that LGBT people are welcome on campus. University of Michigan's John Mounsey shared that the resident adviser in his residence hall had a safe zone sign on her door. "For me it helped a lot. I knew there was someone I could talk to, and she was right upstairs, and she was supportive." Bev Tuel at Colorado said, "I think that the visibility issue and the safe space issue are related. It's done a lot to influence the campus climate. We just need to keep up with the other visual messages that come up in terms of graffiti, particularly in rest rooms. I think the concept of its not being cool to be homophobic is slowly becoming part of the culture here."

Margie Cook at Northern Illinois University (UNI) spoke of the impact that the safe zone program has had on allies of LGBT people:

What allies learn in the process of identifying themselves as safe zones is a positive outcome just as important as having welcoming signs posted around campus for LGBT students to see. Safe zone allies are writing me not so much about what has happened in terms of students' feeling able to come talk to them (which does happen, but not in great numbers), but more so about their own internal process. For many, it is a profound experience of identifying themselves with a marginalized community and beginning to understand the experience of being targeted for abuse and intolerance. At NIU, we are trying to build an identifiable network of educated allies. It is a labor-intensive project, and it has developed slowly. But I think we are reaching our goal. (E-mail Communication, June 2000)

Many centers have sponsored or at least assisted ally and safe zone services. They are distinct endeavors but related in some respects, and they have pros and cons, depending on the particular campus and other factors. In this context, allies are usually, but not invariably, heterosexual students, faculty, or staff members invested in supporting individual LGBT people and the LGBT community. Safe zones services identify places and people on campus where LGBT or questioning students can go for information and support that they can be assured will be accurate and provided without judgment. On some campuses—and this is where the overlap occurs both in concept and in terminology—allies are the individuals whom LGBT and questioning people find in the safe zones.

Safe zone programs vary in their structures and operations. What they have in common is a sticker or poster that indicates that LGBT and questioning people may feel safe in locations bearing the safe zone symbol. In some instances, individuals need only request a sticker or poster. In other cases, there are rigorous training programs that one must attend, and, only upon successful completion of such a program, plus occasional in-service training sessions, will one receive the desired designation. We believe that there is a serious flaw in programs which do not require training and certification. Anyone who wishes to be designated as "safe" may be so. Some people may seek to participate because they think it is "cool." Other more disturbing motivations can be imagined. Though a training may not guarantee that an individual has the skills and knowledge necessary to assist troubled LGBT people or those in the process of coming out or questioning their sexual orientation, it is more likely that some training will be better than none and that attendance at training does indicate at least some untainted motivation.

An allies program may exist on some campuses where there is no safe zone service. Allies— who are usually heterosexual—want to support the LGBT community and contribute to the eradication of homophobia and heterosexism. This is done in one or both of two ways: working within a campus LGBT student organization or through a separate campus allies organization. In the first instance, allies are members of an LGBT student organization and join in the planning and implementation of that organization's programs, including some that may focus on allies. One significant way for them to contribute is participation in the organization's speakers program. At speaking engagements, they may act as heterosexual educators of other heterosexual students through sharing their personal experience in recognizing and countering their own homophobia. Or they may not initially disclose their heterosexuality, thus helping to make the point that it is easy to make incorrect assumptions about people and not so easy to identify who among a group of students is lesbian or gay.

It is useful for allies to form their own organization and to undertake projects that are not merely supplementary to those of the LGBT student organization but rather aimed at the achievement of their own, unique objectives. The case study from the University of Pennsylvania demonstrates how this can be accomplished and to what effect.

Case Study 10.1
ALLIES at Penn

It is difficult to summarize our experience during the creation of the ALLIES group because it has been filled with so many different feelings: from triumph and joy, to confusion and anger. Our freshman year, we were both new to the University of Pennsylvania atmosphere and the dynamics of students and politics on the campus. Although we were faced with these issues in high school, it was not until college that we realized the necessity for dialogue and student action. After attending Penn's Matthew Shepard vigil in October 1998, we were quite unimpressed by the number of students there. Although this was one of the best turnouts the Penn LGBT community had seen (about 300 people), we felt that many more individuals should have joined to show their support. The next day, in an animated conversation with another friend, we expressed our desire to do something, even if our contribution was as minor as licking envelopes. Filled with innocent passion and healthy anger, we stomped up the stairs to the LGBT Center. We found that, among the numerous groups and resources, none specifically addressed the questions and responsibilities of straight people. Even more shocking, there had not even been much interest expressed in such a group. We were appalled. However, for us, our shock on that day was also the birth of a new idea and a new organization. With infinite support and help from the LGBT Center family, we were able to start a group geared toward the mission and goals that we hoped to achieve. We named it ALLIES.

The process was encouraging from the beginning. Our first meeting consisted of eight of our closest friends, but we gradually grew, and more people became involved. ALLIES now has amazing and dedicated members, and the group continues to develop and succeed.

ALLIES' goals are to raise awareness, to provide education about and discuss LGBT issues, to make it known that it is Ok to be straight and care about LGBT issues, and to inform the community at large that queer issues affect straight people. Our mission statement is ambitious, to say the least, but with continued effort and patience we hope one day to witness the equality for which we strive. We have sponsored educational programs during B-GLAD (Bisexual Gay Lesbian Awareness Days) and at other times. We have been part of the LGBT Center's Speakers Bureau, sometimes identifying ourselves as heterosexual during speaking engagements and directing our remarks to other straight people in the audience, sometimes remaining ambiguous to reinforce the fact that sexual orientation is invisible.

The process of starting this organization has been a learning experience for us, not only as leaders but also as individuals. We have been able to recognize the magnitude of LGBT issues and that there is much to learn. Through listening to people speak about queer issues and struggles, we have realized the gravity of the situation. We now share our own feelings more openly and have more confidence dealing with people whose ideas differ from our own. Most of all, we have discovered that, as individuals, it is our responsibility to be aware of, and try to counteract, all injustices because they affect our lives no matter how distant they may seem. (Submitted by Heather Lochridge and Leily Saadat-Lajevardi, University of Pennsylvania)

CONCLUSION

We agree that our campuses must be safe environments for all students to learn and all faculty and staff to teach and to work. We understand that this is the vision, not the reality. Safe zone programs may or may not work as they were originally intended: to educate many people about LGBT issues so that they will post safe zone markers on their doors and to be available for LGBT students. However, as a visibility program, safe zone programs appear to be extremely successful. Through signs, posters, magazines, and other visible means, LGBT students learn that, at least in some areas, they are welcome. Admissions, counseling, and residence hall forms with inclusive language are not difficult to create. Peer education programs in classrooms and professional development sessions on LGBT issues must occur in every area of campus from dining services to facilities and clerical staff to campus police. Documentation of campus hate crimes and the creation of an anonymous reporting system should be developed and well-advertised. Finally, administrators, faculty, and invited campus speakers must use inclusive language in their speeches, in their policies, and in their practices.

Take an inventory of your campus climate. Ask your LGBT students what the campus is like for them. Ask yourself if you believe that your campus is safe enough for your own child if she or he were lesbian or gay. These suggestions are not the end; they are just the beginning for a campus that invites, welcomes, and values *all* students, inclusive of their sexual orientations.

Chapter 11

Mentoring Programs

Patricia Alford-Keating

Mentoring services have been effective in several communities on college campuses. Their success among students of color has been particularly noteworthy. Within the last few years, mentoring services for LGBT students and those questioning their sexual orientations and/or gender identities have been initiated at several institutions, some under the auspices of campus LGBT centers and others based elsewhere. The case study from the University of California, Los Angeles describes a very successful mentoring program, sponsored by Student Psychological Services, which has served as a model for mentoring activities at several other colleges and universities.

Case Study 11.1
The UCLA Mentoring Program

Gay, lesbian, bisexual, and transgender (GLBT) people encounter many challenges as they attempt to master the intrapsychic and social processes of coming out. Many have felt alone and different as they struggled through one of the most difficult periods of their lives. This "oppressed in isolation" phenomenon stands in contrast with the experience of other minority groups not compelled to suffer intense, cultural oppression alone. Ethnic and religious minorities can usually count on family support. After all, the whole family may be stigmatized and know the pain of it. Further, they usually have built-in communities of others in the same circumstance. GLBT people, on the other hand, do not enjoy the inclusion born of immediately accessing a community of like others. Instead, at least initially, they must contend with an unwelcoming world solo. Coming out in a hostile cultural milieu alone works against the development of a positive GLBT identity.

Moreover, since families are often hostile or uninformed, GLBT youth do not typically receive positive parental guidance related to sexual orientation issues. Even well-meaning heterosexual parents are usually ill-equipped to guide the youth regarding how to develop into productive, happy GLBT adults. Without guidance and support, self-esteem may be damaged. Consequently, some GLBT people succumb to serious health risks, including substance abuse, unsafe sex, clinical depression, or even suicide.

In light of these risks and in an effort to partially make up for the missing guides needed during the developmental years, the University of California, Los Angeles provides GLBT mentors who serve as supportive guides and resource persons for students in the coming-out process. Volunteer mentors are students and staff members who have successfully worked through their own coming out and are in a position to serve as positive role models for others. Mentees are UCLA students dealing with coming out to self and/or others. Both mentors and mentees are diverse in age, gender, ethnicity, sexual/affectional orientation, and gender identity.

Potential mentors are carefully screened for maturity, responsibility, commitment, appropriate boundaries, and interpersonal skills. Once selected, mentors go through 30 hours of training covering a variety of topics, including coming out, internalized homophobia, relationship issues, sexuality, safer-sex practices, bisexuality, transgender issues, active listening skills, religion, racial and ethnic diversity, gender issues, subcultures within the LGBT community, and managing difficult situations. After successfully completing the training, mentors attend bi-weekly team supervision meetings, facilitated by a psychologist. Mentors sign a contract agreeing that they will *not* use alcohol or drugs while mentoring; will *not* become sexually involved with a mentee; will attend biweekly team supervision meetings; and will maintain the confidentiality of their mentees.

During meetings with mentees, mentors function as confidants, tour guides, or supportive companions. Casual discussions take place about once a week, usually occurring over lunch or coffee. During these conversations, mentors answer questions, provide information, or simply listen with an insider's understanding. Mentors help mentees sort out issues such as coming out to parents. Also, they recommend helpful reading materials or videos. During field trips, mentors unveil positive community resources. Mentors and mentees visit GLBT community centers, bookstores, coffeehouses, movies, plays, restaurants, pride events, and so on. Afterward, they discuss the mentee's questions and reactions. Mentors also function as advocates by accompanying mentees to group meetings, until mentees feel comfortable attending alone.

The primary objective of this program is to help GLBT students feel comfortable in their own skin by developing a positive GLBT identity. Then, they are free to lead healthy, productive lives, unencumbered by the weight of internalized oppression. (Submitted by Pat Alford-Keating, director, UCLA LGBT Mentoring Program)

In general, mentoring services are intended to provide assistance in a variety of ways to students who are new to the campus or new to the LGBT community as a result of either recently coming out to themselves or questioning their sexual orientation. Students are matched when an individual seeking service, the mentee, is connected with an individual possessing greater familiarity with, and experience in, the LGBT community, the mentor.

In most services, mentees are students only. Mentors may be only students or employees as well. There is no doubt that faculty and staff members may offer student mentees useful advice. But the concerns of mentees are not usually academic, nor do they pertain to the many areas of expertise of staff from a variety of disciplines and special skills. Their concerns tend to be personal and social, so it is logical that mentees would prefer to be matched with individuals whose life experience is close to their own in some way, whether in gender, age, stage in development, or major. For this reason, most programs have opted for student-to-student matches. This may not be feasible at small institutions, as the number of individuals available to serve as mentors is limited. Even at large universities, it may not always be possible to provide an exact match, for example, a Latina undergraduate who identifies as bisexual.

Mentors need to be carefully selected from among those who apply. They should be provided with some training and must be familiar with the rules and procedures of the mentoring service's operation.

Applicants should complete an application, either hard copy or via the Internet, that provides a basic self-description and some indication of their reasons for wishing to serve as mentors. Applicants should then be interviewed by the center director or other person managing the service and one or two current mentors. Interviewers need to find a way, in a relatively standardized interview format, to assess the appropriateness of the applicants' motivation, their knowledge about, and understanding of, the multifaceted LGBT community, and their maturity, empathy, and communication skills.

The opportunity to serve as mentors should be publicized near the end of each academic year. If interviews and training sessions can take place before the end of the year, mentors can be ready to serve at the beginning of the following year—when the availability of the service will be publicized among the cohort of students new to campus. At that time and throughout the academic year, those interested in having a mentor will also be asked to fill out a brief questionnaire, either hard copy or via the Internet, providing basic autobiographical information and a statement regarding their reasons for requesting a mentor at this time.

Training may be as extensive and inclusive as time and resources allow. At a minimum, it must address listening skills and needs assessment, an overview of campus and community resources, and a review of the program's rules and procedures. Including seasoned mentors who share their practiced wisdom with mentees is very helpful to new volunteers. In-service training sessions may be scheduled from time to time to enhance competence and provide the opportunity for those currently serving as mentors to exchange ideas and experiences. Trainees should be provided relevant materials, such as information about campus and community resources and a manual of some sort containing policies and procedures of the mentoring service.

Trained mentors should sign an agreement of service prior to being matched with mentees. This fairly formal document should embody the rules of the service, including that sexual activity between mentors and mentees is strictly forbidden. Though the presence and discussion of this requirement risk reinforcing the stereotype of gay men as sexually indiscriminate, there have been situations in which such inadvisable interaction has taken place. Those new to being gay or questioning may be craving sexual experience as a way of resolving their uncertainty or moving ahead with their newly acknowledged self-identities. They may honestly believe that a sexual experience with their mentor is what they need. But sexual activity will jeopardize or even destroy a relationship that may bring them many long-lasting benefits. Mentors may think that they are supplying useful experience if they offer or acquiesce to a mentee's request for sexual activity. Nevertheless, it is their responsibility—and their obligation according to their signed agreement of service—not to engage in any form of sexual activity with their mentees. Mentors should avoid any behavior that may be construed as seductive or sexually playful. Staff should help them understand that, in response to a mentee's request for sex, they can let the mentee know that the proposal is understandable, even flattering at some level, but one that must be declined in the best interest of all involved. To complicate this matter further, it is not forbidden or even inappropriate for mentor and mentee to talk about sex. In fact, mentees may have several questions relating to sexual activities. Assuming that the mentors are comfortable and prepared to address these inquiries, there is no reason, in the context of a developed and comfortable relationship, that they should not do so.

Case Study 11.2
Interviews with a Mentor and His Mentee

Mentor: Steven Leider

So far, I've worked with five mentees, helping them to negotiate the sometimes turbulent waters of the coming-out process. As a mentor I introduce young lesbian, gay, bisexual, and transgender (LGBT) people to their culture. Society does little to help people discover their lives and their culture as LGBT people. That's why I participate in the Mentoring Program. When people come out as gay, lesbian, or bi, they may want only to be "social," limiting their participation to the club or rave scene, trying to make up for lost time. Many also complain about not finding what they want in these scenes in terms of friendship, romance, or intimacy. The club scene is only a narrow slice of the pie that comprises LGBT culture. Many people, especially those just coming out, tend not to explore other areas of LGBT culture because they don't know about them. That's where I come in. I help them learn that there is more to queer culture than clubs, bars, and raves. As a result they begin to enjoy and appreciate the breadth of LGBT culture, usually understanding it better and thereby achieving better integration into those parts of our culture that most interest them. Some, perhaps most who are just coming out don't want to be "political." But coming out is in itself a political act, not because we perceive or desire it to be so but because others, especially conservative politicians and religious groups, have *made* it so. The struggle for gay civil rights begins twice for each of us, the first time when we come out to ourselves and again when we step out of the closet door and try to make contact with others like ourselves and with our culture. Letting others know that we are a part of this culture is the "political" part that I try to work through with my mentees. Sometimes, because they are either unable or unwilling to deal with the intense emotions and feelings that everyone who goes through the coming-out process experiences, the young men I work with bolt from the Mentoring Program. So far two of my mentees left. Luckily, however, both eventually had successful coming-out experiences and are now doing well, adjusting to their new lives. The other three mentees, although they have "graduated" from the Mentoring Program, continue to learn about LGBT culture and what it is to be gay. My first mentee, Charles, continues to work with me and has even become a mentor himself in the program. For me, the toughest part of being a mentor is dealing with religion. Two of my mentees were raised in very religious families. Trying to undo years of hateful indoctrination without invalidating the mentee's religious beliefs is delicate and frustrating work, especially since it's usually impossible to know how successful I am in this area. The best part of being a mentor, though, is the joy in seeing a mentee such as Charles grow as a person and a gay man, one with self-worth, self-respect, with compassion and appreciation for the many facets of his community and who has successfully integrated himself into LGBT society.

Mentee: Charles Harless

Being a mentee was an opportunity to see into a whole new world, a culture that I didn't know existed and of which I'm a part—a fabulous culture that I otherwise might not have had access to. Steven was a guide—a shining light in the darkness. I knew I was gay, but I didn't know what that meant. Could I have become a happy gay man who's fully integrated into his culture? Well, yes, but coming from a small town in Alabama where LGBT people were viewed as "outsiders" and "other," I never dreamed that the world was so different and vast beyond my narrow view. Eventually, I would have had my field of vision expanded, but working with a mentor helped to accelerate that process. Because I am comfortable with myself as a gay man, I think that my work and academic relationships are much better than they would have otherwise been. A year ago, when I became a mentor myself, I confided to the other mentors with whom I was being trained that my mentor was my hero. I think every LGBT should have an LGBT hero, especially on campus. (Submitted by Steven Leider and Charles Harless, UCLA Mentoring Program)

The frequency of contact between mentors and mentees—and what they do together when they meet—is left up to the pairs. Some communicate almost entirely via E-mail, though at least one face-to-face meeting is always arranged at the start of the relationship. Others meet regularly and become, in effect, friends, without the facts of how their relationship began being disclosed to others. There are almost invariably question-and-answer discussions over coffee or on-line. Mentors may accompany mentees on their first visit to an LGBT meeting, party, or club. Such events often lead to mentees' meeting others with whom they can socialize. Though not without exception, the mentee's need for a mentor usually diminishes, and, unless they have become true friends, the relationship drops off and eventually ends.

Those charged with managing the mentoring service check in periodically with mentors and mentees as a way of keeping track with how the relationships are going. Some services include requirements that the mentor make periodic reports without being asked for them. Procedures are in place through which changes may be made in matches that are not working, from the perspective of either the mentor or the mentee. These are usually handled without judgment or consequences, unless the problems experienced were substantial or against the program's regulations.

Someone, most logically the service's manager, needs to be available for consultation or back-up should a mentor report a particularly challenging situation arising from the circumstances in the life of the mentee. These occurrences are rare, but a plan needs to be in place in the event that a matter of this nature should be presented.

In summary, the service manager recruits, oversees the selection of, and trains mentors; arranges periodic in-service training sessions for mentors; finds mentees; arranges mentor–mentee matches; and monitors the progress of the matches; re-assigns mentors and mentees when necessary, and provides support and back-up to mentors dealing with particularly challenging situations.

Mentoring services require little by way of financial resources. The one significant cost is the salary for the manager of the program. The number of hours required for this position is greater at certain times of the year, but unless the number of actual and potential mentors and mentees is vast, a full-time person may not be necessary. Other expenses include printing and copying of materials, refreshments for periodic training sessions or social gatherings, advertising, and, if resources are available, a get-away retreat for training.

For further information about the UCLA LGBT Mentoring Program, access the Web site at http://www.bol.ucla.edu/~mentors/

Chapter 12

Advocacy and Judicial Response

Advocacy is an important, if sometimes complicated, service for LGBT center staff. It is essential that the term "advocacy" is clearly defined and that center staff understand precisely the requirements of their role in this area. Advocacy, both formal and informal, on behalf of the campus LGBT community is almost always considered an appropriate and important role for center personnel. This function involves lobbying for institutional policies and practices that are inclusive of, and sensitive to, LGBT students, employees, and alumni and entails offering education about the needs and concerns of the campus LGBT community. This is a complex endeavor with multiple benefits and pitfalls.

Advocacy roles require thorough familiarity with institutional policies, procedures, and resources; good listening skills; sensitivity to varying personal values; and the ability, under sometimes challenging circumstances, to preserve confidentiality and remain focused on those bringing the grievance. This powerful set of skills requires considerable preparation and practice.

Sometimes advocacy involves grievances. Usually, the investigative, mediative, and adjudicative aspects of grievances are assigned to other institutional personnel such as a judicial inquiry board or affirmative action officials or the ombuds office. However, helping aggrieved individuals to understand and access institutional procedures and offering personal support during the process are seen in many colleges and universities as appropriate functions for LGBT center staff to serve. Effective performance of these roles not only serves the involved individuals but also, through word of mouth, promotes trust in the center and center staff in both community members and colleagues within the institution.

Some of the issues that have provided the impetus for advocacy efforts in higher education in recent years are safe spaces for LGBT students and prevention of discrimination and harassment; funding and other forms of support for LGBT student organizations; equitable domestic partner benefits; the continued presence on campus of military recruiters and/or ROTC units, which, by virtue of their sponsorship by the U.S. Department of Defense, engage in discrimination on the basis of sexual orientation, which, in many colleges and universities, is prohibited by institutional policy; and the availability of a range of campus housing options for LGBT students and their partners and families.

With the pun fully intended, campus LGBT centers are in a queer situation. This may be true in several senses, but none more compelling than their unique position regarding advocacy. The mission statements of many such centers include engaging in at least one form of advocacy, either on behalf of LGBT individuals and/or on behalf of the LGBT community within the college or university.

The first type of advocacy involves situations in which LGBT students, employees, or alumni feel that they have been aggrieved in some way. This usually relates to institutions' policies of non-discrimination on the basis of sexual orientation or perceived sexual orientation (and in a more limited number of instances, gender identity or perceived gender identity). Staff of a few centers may be empowered to investigate such claims and intervene with the alleged offenders. Most centers' staff can provide advice regarding procedures or personal support to the complainants but must refer the aggrieved individuals to other offices if they seek investigation, mediation, or adjudication of such complaints.

The second type of advocacy entails lobbying within the institution for, among other things, policies and practices that are equitable and sensitive in terms of sexual orientation and gender identity. This activity includes education regarding the needs and concerns of sexual and gender minorities and consultation regarding ways to develop greater comfort in working with these populations to achieve the equity sought. A wide range of causes has, of necessity, been taken up by LGBT advocates within colleges and universities in the United States in the last 20 years. These include the presence of military recruiters and ROTC units on campuses with anti-discrimination policies; provision of full benefits to the same-gender life partners of lesbian and gay employees; attempts to curtail the funding or the mere presence of gay student organizations; housing options for sexual and gender minority students; guaranteeing protection for sexual and gender minority students and employees against assault and various forms of harassment; academic freedom for students and faculty doing research pertaining to sexual orientation or gender identity; and a myriad of others. Some of these matters have ended up in courts, and several of the battles are still being fought.

Many in the LGBT community have advocated for worthy causes. What is unique, or at least certainly challenging, for directors and staff of campus LGBT centers—the "queer" situation alluded to earlier—is that they are often battling the very institutions that have hired them and that will, hopefully, continue to pay their salaries and support their professional development. They are, in effect, in-house watchdogs and advocates.

THE IN-HOUSE ADVOCATE

Being the in-house advocate involves a tricky balancing act. LGBT center staff must be attuned to, and sympathetic with, the concerns of their student, staff, faculty, and employee constituents, while, simultaneously, remaining aware of the complex realities faced by those up their reporting lines, all the way to the president and trustees of their institution.

It is easy to say that, under such circumstances, these individuals must learn to "choose their battles" carefully. It is a cinch that they will not win all that come to their attention, even all that truly move them. But what, then, do they say to those students or colleagues whose concerns are not chosen for battle, either because they are losing prospects or because they do not merit staff's taking the chance that capital spent on this particular concern will diminish resources for the next, more worthy fight? In such a situation, the staff's honest rationale will provide little consolation to the aggrieved or discontented. Harsh criticism may be leveled against the staff members. Charges that they are out of touch with their constituents, or that they are too conservative, or that they have "sold out" to the administration are common in such situations. In an ultimate irony, these complaints about center staff may end up on the desks of the very administrators with whom the discontented individuals were originally annoyed.

At the same time, LGBT center directors must be prepared to incur some irritation from their superiors each time they do wage battle. This is, of course, despite the fact that the directors are doing exactly what they are being paid to do. Directors could take the cowardly course and try to shield senior student affairs officers, deans, and presidents against all complaints from LGBT students and employees. This strategy may win praise from central administrators for a short period of time, during which they are fighting fires within other campus populations. But soon the LGBT community will be up in arms, justifiably, and establish direct contact with the central administration to complain. The briefly praised director will no longer be in favor with either the community served or his or her supervisor.

SO WHAT'S A DIRECTOR TO DO?

The answer is largely providing education through well-maintained lines of communication and an ear held solidly to the ground. Directors must anticipate times of crisis, whether they are the result of issues or of personalities becoming inflamed. Maintaining regular communication with various members of the constituencies served often provides warnings. The organization's advisory board, if effectively constituted and structured, may be an excellent source of data. Regular, at least monthly meetings between the directors and their supervisors, even when there is not much formal business to conduct, are very important—both to keep the supervisor apprised of any possible problems and to gain information from the administration's perspective.

Individuals who hold key leadership positions, whether in the communities served or in the general student body and even the central administration, may be key informants. Such relationships must be carefully cultivated during periods of relative tranquility. Center directors need to spend a certain amount of time outside their own community, asking questions and showing interest in the endeavors of others. Collaboration with other organizations reduces costs and leads to more effective programs and services, particularly when aimed at those who belong to multiple communities. But this work also produces information about issues and, perhaps most importantly, about "how things work" within the institution, which can be extremely useful in tense situations later on. Furthermore, it is well documented that familiarity with informal structure is as important as knowing official procedures and reporting lines.

Casual conversations and collaborative efforts provide excellent opportunities for education, which is, after all, a director's constant goal. Directors must continuously instruct consumers, colleagues, and supervisors about the lives and concerns of LGBT people generally and within the communities that hey serve specifically. If they are thus informed, they are most likely to recognize and pass on information that is useful to directors in challenging situations. If a particular conflict seems a strong possibility, directors' giving consumers, colleagues, and supervisors a "head's-up" is appreciated and may ultimately reduce the severity of the conflict.

A second key component of directors' ongoing education of consumers, colleagues, and supervisors is sharing, in a general way, something about the challenging nature of being an in-house watchdog and advocate. This should not be done in a grumbling or apologetic manner. Nevertheless, in times of lower stress, it is useful for directors to explain that fighting for every cause would lead to a poor track record, very few satisfied consumers, and a reputation within the administration as someone who "cries wolf" or who "sheds more heat than light." Their understanding this position may help soften the blow if, at some later date, their concern is not one that the center or program considers a high priority.

Not elevating a concern to the level of a campus-wide battle does not mean that LGBT centers or programs cannot provide assistance. There are many, less provocative, less public, and less costly ways to help individuals and communities deal with their concerns. The informal networks mentioned earlier may offer ways to accomplish this. Personal connections and collecting repayment of personal "favors" from colleagues may also provide possible assistance. Coalitions can be formed or connections between individuals with similar concerns established; such alliances can also produce effective solutions. This opportunity makes clear the need for centers to keep detailed (but, of course, highly confidential) records regarding issues and complaints brought to their attention.

It is vital that directors not minimize, in their minds or in their responses, the importance to complainants of the concerns that they bring. Providing a sympathetic ear is always possible and usually appreciated, even if a full-fledged battle is not likely to come about. This human connection costs little in energy and time but can yield substantial returns.

The role of in-house watchdog and advocate may be slippery and complex, but careful strategizing and generous use of diplomacy and personal skills can lead to the detriments being far outweighed by the gains.

STUDENT PERPETRATORS OF ANTI-GAY BEHAVIORS

When a student at UCLA is found responsible for anti-gay behavior, he or she is adjudicated to the LGBT Center director for 40 hours of service. The center staff people are unaware of the adjudication; they think the person is just another volunteer. The director, who, of course, is aware, does several things immediately: first, she spends at least two hours with the student to learn where she or he may be in terms of her or his own thoughts, feelings, reasoning, and reasons behind the anti-gay behavior. Then the student writes an apology—to the victim if there is an identified one or to the LGBT community in general if there is no identified victim—but the apology goes to the director, who reviews it with the student.

Case Study 12.1
UCLA
I remember one student who said that he wasn't homophobic, just drunk, and since he is 21, the drinking was okay except that it caused his bad behavior. We decided to work on his drinking issues first, then his attitude.

Perpetrators are assigned one of several standard projects. One may be to review every video at the center and write a synopsis about it. Another may be to go through all of the center's information files and explain how they could be better organized based on subject matter. The director tries to keep the student busy and disengaged from other students initially. The student—the perpetrator—is already on the defensive and usually feels both angry and embarrassed. Later, though, in the course of the work, the student may be required to do something more visible like staff an information table with other students from the center. Students' final project is tough and often heart-wrenching. They must write a paper on what their life would be like—given everything that they know about themselves and in their current social, educational, and family situations—if they discovered that they were gay or lesbian.

The program seems to be successful. There have been no repeat anti-gay acts from the students who were adjudicated to the center. One—an elite, well-known athlete—became a volunteer when the AIDS Quilt was displayed on campus. When he saw me, he hugged me hard. I saw the tears in his eyes as he went back about his assigned duties. No words were spoken and none were needed. (Submitted by Ronni Sanlo, UCLA)

Some perpetrators who spent time at the center ultimately acknowledged their struggles with their own sexual identities. Others may do so later, but the that time they spent at the center was time during which they learned about difference, about being invisible, and about being respectful of other human beings.

Early in 1999, Angela Nichols, the LGBT community coordinator at Oberlin College, queried the National Consortium of Directors of LGBT Resources in Higher Education for a list of suggested activities for anti-gay perpetrators on campus. The list follows:

Development exercises from the Gay Lesbian Straight Educators Network (GLSEN) book entitled *Tackling Gay Issues.*

Have the student spend time with LGBT students and vice versa.

Have the student attend LGBT campus meetings and/or support groups for LGBT students.

Have the student make bulletin boards on harassment and violence.

Have the student read *OUT* magazine, the *Advocate*, *Curve* magazine, *Girlfriends* magazine, and others and compile articles on violence against LGBT people.

Have the student do an environmental "walk-through" assessment of campus to document examples of homophobia and heterosexist assumptions.

Have the student review every video in the resource center and write a blurb about them.

Have the student read Warren Blumenfeld's *Homophobia: How it Hurts Us All.*

Have the student provide general help with support of LGBT programming on campus.

Have the student write a reflective paper or keep a journal about the experience and what has been learned.

Have the student write an apology letter to the victim.

Chapter 13

LGBT Faculty, Staff, and Alumni Organizations

Many campuses have LGBT faculty and staff organizations as well as LGBT alumni associations. In some instances, these kinds of groups can lead, or have led, to the founding of an LGBT center. The presence of an LGBT center can encourage the continued existence of such organizations or lead, indirectly, to their dissolution. The latter has occurred on a few campuses where the faculty-staff organization had lobbied the administration for the creation of an LGBT center or the hiring of professional staff to serve as a point person for LGBT concerns. Once the center was established, or the professional staff person hired, faculty and staff members seemed to believe that their goal had been achieved and, hence, that the need for their organization to exist had dissipated.

Though there are many purposes that such organizations may serve, it seems that they remain most vital when they are working toward the accomplishment of a specific, terminal goal. These groups could—and some do—function over lunch or coffee on a monthly basis as a forum for the informal sharing of concerns, frustrations, or even successes related to their status as LGBT faculty or staff. This purpose is more likely to be viable on campuses, such as in rural areas, where few other such opportunities are available to participants. In urban environments, faculty and staff are more likely to be members or volunteers in organizations in their communities that fulfill similar purposes.

Several such organizations have been successful in lobbying regarding matters of importance to faculty and staff. The provision of domestic partner benefits in a number of colleges and universities was the direct result of the influence exerted by faculty-staff groups. Other similar causes include supporting colleagues in tenure, promotion, or research struggles; involvement in discrimination cases; and advocating for changes to institutional practices that assure equity for LGBT people, such as policies that ban discrimination on the basis of sexual orientation and gender identity.

FACULTY AND STAFF GROUPS

The Faculty-Staff organization at Michigan State has become successful in soliciting funds to assist LGBT students.

Case Study 13.1
Pride Scholarship Benefits LGBT Students at MSU

A new scholarship fund has been created to assist LGBT students at Michigan State University (MSU). The Pride Scholarship was established by Bill Beachler, an MSU alumnus, working with GLFSA and the university's fund raising office. "I see a day when one or more lesbian, gay, bisexual, or transgender high school students will be honored, by receiving a full-ride scholarship to MSU," Beachler said. "I wanted to create a program that will reward LGBT students for who they are, rather than shame them." Beachler has inaugurated the Pride Scholarship with both a cash gift and a pledged bequest.

Scholarship recipients will be selected by members of GLFSA, an organization of LGBT faculty, staff, and graduate students at MSU. "I am very excited about this program," said Val Meyers, president of GLFSA and assistant director of financial aid. "Bill's generosity and vision will benefit many students in the coming years, and we are grateful to him for initiating the Pride Scholarship." The Pride Scholarship will initially award $500 annually. A companion endowment fund will enable contributions to accumulate interest under the financial management of the university, which will eventually make larger awards possible. The endowment fund has already received $1,500 in cash and several bequests of various sizes.

Beachler and Meyers both indicated that the Pride Scholarship will make a significant difference for college-bound LGBT youth. "I attended MSU as an out-of-state student on a scholarship," Beachler said. "It was as affordable to come to MSU as it would have been to stay in my home state, so I am aware of the important role that scholarships can play in recruiting students." "We know that LGBT students sometimes have particular difficulties attending or staying in college," Meyers said. "Often, these students are estranged from their family and peers, and their academic progress can be hampered because they are struggling with their sexual orientation or their gender identity."

Beachler anticipates that other alumni and employees of MSU will contribute to the scholarship. Donations of cash, securities, and bequests may be directed to the University Development office at MSU, or to GLFSA. For additional information about the Pride Scholarship, applications, and instructions for making a donation, contact: GLFSA, P.O. Box 6951, East Lansing, MI 48826, GLFSA@msu.edu or on the Web at www.msu.edu/~GLFSA (E-mail announcement, February 2000)

Faculty-staff groups may also sponsor educational programs. On some campuses, they offer seminars of interest to LGBT employees, co-sponsored by the institution's human resources operation. Topics have included explanation of particular benefits for same-gender domestic partners; advice about investing tailored specifically to LGBT employees; and retirement planning discussions of same-sex couples. Educational programs sponsored by the faculty-staff organization that have a less practical focus are not as likely to be compelling to potential consumers. The bottom line, especially in times of restructuring and down sizing, is that faculty and staff have multiple and complex commitments on campus and, generally, as a result, very limited time to give to their own edification or pleasure.

Some LGBT centers sponsor faculty-staff organizations or provide some staffing for their planning and programmatic needs. This may be a good investment in terms of the potential return of support of the center and affiliated students and student organizations by faculty and staff constituents. However, if meetings and programs are unlikely to be well attended for any of the reasons suggested, the time and effort expended by staff may have little or no pay-off. Therefore, it is probably best for center staff to take their cues from actual or potential faculty and staff leaders. If the leaders are motivated to keep a faculty-staff organization vibrant, some investment on the part of the center is more likely to be worthwhile.

ALUMNI ORGANIZATIONS

The prevalence and success of LGBT alumni organizations have waxed and waned. In the mid- to late 1980s, there were not only several colleges and universities that had such organizations, but also an active national umbrella organization—NetGALA—comprising LGBT alumni groups. That network fell into inactivity in the mid-1990s, though many individual alumni organizations continue to thrive. Their foci have changed to some extent—and relationships between them and campus LGBT centers have developed as the latter have come into being.

Alumni organizations (LGBT and in general) are most vital and successful when they are operated by alumni. Alumni, generally, have many commitments, both personal and professional. It is challenging to find individuals who are willing to make service to their alma maters a high priority among the demands for their time. This may be particularly true among LGBT alumni, many of whom may have had somewhat unpleasant or even oppressive experiences during their student years related to the development or management of their sexual identity. Some LGBT alumni may wish to reward schools for the ways in which they were supported (regarding sexual orientation or other aspects of their experience; after all, coming out or being LGBT was most likely only one, if a major, aspect of their college lives). Others may get involved with alumni organizations in an attempt to prevent current students from facing some of the challenges that they once encountered.

It is therefore easy to see how alumni may wish to see LGBT center staff manage alumni organizations and how center directors and staff may be tempted to do so. At first glance, this may seem like a logical and practical plan. However, many LGBT centers are not specifically mandated to work with alumni organizations, and the alumni relations operations on campus—some quite elaborate and perhaps territorial—or the administrators to whom center directors report may not support this endeavor. Further, this work may take considerable time, often more than can be afforded given other obligations. Finally, unless alumni are directly involved in setting priorities and planning programs, the efforts of center staff may be misdirected and ineffective.

None of this is meant to imply that it is not appropriate for LGBT center staff to be involved with alumni work. On the contrary, it may be richly rewarding for current students and for the center itself. However, certain conditions are essential for the work to be effective. The center's alumni work needs to be undertaken in cooperation with, and to a certain extent, driven by alumni and carefully coordinated with the institution's alumni relations operations.

Contacting Alumni

Since many LGBT alumni organizations pre-date campus centers, and, in some instances, alumni may have been involved in the efforts to create them, a cadre of LGBT alumni volunteers already exists at some institutions. If that is not the case, center staff will need to reach out and find such volunteers. Some may work on campus or live in the immediate vicinity. They will be relatively easy to find through advertisements or calls for volunteers through campus newspapers or magazines, local queer publications, and so on. Reaching and involving alumni at a greater distance may be more challenging. One useful method is to place notices in the alumni magazine or newsletter provided editorial cooperation can be secured. Some organizations have reached alumni at a distance through placing classified ads (often free to non-profit organizations) in local LGBT newspapers around the country, focusing on metropolitan areas where there tend to be larger LGBT communities. Many institutions do periodic surveys of their alumni. It is reasonable to ask those managing these surveys to include questions that will produce useful information. Questions about alumni involvement in particular undergraduate organizations or about current community volunteer service are good sources for the names of potential volunteers. Encouraging the survey authors to use orientation-neutral language, such as "name of spouse/significant other" or "partner" may also yield potentially useful data. Assuming release of this information to the center has been arranged (this is standard practice with regard to, e.g., academic departments, athletic teams, and performing arts organizations), center staff can make discrete follow-up calls or send letters to respondents assessing their interest in becoming involved in an LGBT alumni organization.

There are both pros and cons to alumni organizations being formally recognized by general alumni societies and connected to alumni relations personnel. Confidentiality is always a concern. It is usually preferable, when possible, for alumni volunteers or center staff to control the organization's mailing list. Some alumni who would not be willing to give provide their names and mailing addresses if they thought that the organization's database were in the hands of college or university officials. This does add work for center staff, something, as previously noted, generally to be avoided.

The process of achieving recognition for the LGBT organization by the general alumni structure may be bureaucratic and time-consuming. Again, however, the benefits seem to justify the investment. Official recognition may result in the organization's being given some time by alumni relations staff members, and funding may also be available.

There is another possible outcome, though only in the longer term. The perspectives of alumni are valued by the institution's leadership (partly because of the financial support, often in significant amounts, provided by alumni), and alumni organizations usually have a voice in the selection of college or university trustees. In fact, many institutions have a designated number of seats on their boards for alumni representatives. There is probably no more significant way in which alumni can influence the lives of current and future students, especially in terms of policies and practices, than through service at the institution's highest levels of management.

How Do Alumni Help the LGBT Campus Community?

Apart from those already mentioned, many purposes may be served by alumni organizations. The first is bringing alumni together to renew acquaintances, socialize, reminisce. In addition, alumni may be an important source of support to current students by helping them financially through scholarships, book or travel reserves, or emergency funds. This support may be provided through capital campaigns, annual giving, or direct contributions.

Second, alumni may influence administrative decisions, not only through the service on boards already mentioned but through telephone calls or messages about specific issues or concerns. Finally, alumni may be helpful to students seeking counsel regarding career development or opportunities or geographic relocation. Some centers publish lists or directories of LGBT alumni willing to talk with current students about particular careers, specific employers, or the part of the world in which they live where students may be considering taking a job, attending graduate school, or merely visiting. Some centers sponsor career-planning seminars and invite alumni back to campus to talk about their professional lives.

Alumni organizations are an important component of LGBT centers' overall operations. While considerable center effort may need to be expended upfront to launch—or rebuild— these groups and help them function effectively and with appropriate recognition status, the longer-term investment of center time and resources will be minimal and the potential benefits substantial.

Case Study 13.2
YALE GALA, the Integration of a GLBT Alumni Organization into the University Structure

Yale GALA was established in 1983 by a group consisting principally of recent graduates who had been active in the then-still-new gay and lesbian organizations on campus. Yale GALA in the early days focused on campus reunion events and on mustering a crowd to march in the New York City Pride Day parade. The founders of Yale GALA likewise had ambitious plans for multiple regional chapters as well as a national umbrella group. This model succeeded for a while, but by the late 1980s Yale GALA had been reduced to a very active New York City chapter with only occasional events staged by alums in other cities like Boston or Washington, D.C. The New York chapter of Yale GALA— advantaged by the greatest concentration of alums and by proximity to New Haven—had become the defacto national chapter of GALA.

In the year that I joined the Steering Committee, Yale GALA was in a process of regrouping and refashioning the New York Chapter of GALA into something larger. In

1989 we started sending the New York Yale GALA newsletter, hitherto produced for the benefit of the New York chapter, to the full national mailing list. This newsletter, published quarterly, quickly became the glue that held the organization together. With the restructuring of Yale GALA as a single national organization came the recognition that GALA had to shift from social activities centered in New York to activities that would engage the interest and support of all gay, lesbian, and bisexual alumni. This suggested a more visible and active presence for GALA on campus.

Alumni relations at Yale have, since 1972, been organized through the Association of Yale Alumni (AYA). The AYA is built upon three categories of component alumni organizations: geographic Yale Clubs, Classes of Yale College, and Graduate and Professional (G&P) School Alumni. Each of these alumni organizations is entitled to designate a delegate for a three-year term to the AYA, and from the general AYA delegacy a 21-person Board of Governors is elected. In addition to the delegates from the clubs, class, and G&P Schools, the Board of Governors names 33 (11 each year, for three-year terms) "at-large" delegates, selected from under-represented constituencies (traditionally, meant women and racial minorities) and recent graduates. Twice a year all AYA delegates—a group, these days, of about 300 alumni—convene in New Haven for three-day assemblies. It is at these AYA Assemblies that alumni are briefed on current university affairs, meet with university administrators, and have the opportunity to express opinions on matters of importance to their alumni constituencies.

When I assumed the presidency of Yale GALA, one of my first objectives was to obtain for GALA recognition by the university and a defined relationship to the AYA. Petition to the AYA and conversations with its executive director led, with very little fuss, to the creation of a category that the AYA chose to call "Special Interest Alumni Groups." In 1996 a number of such groups were for the first time listed in Yale's Leadership Directory and subsequently in the Yale Alumni Magazine. By this initiative, Yale GALA gained official recognition within the Yale Alumni establishment not only for itself but also for (by latest count) 42 organizations of singing group alumni, religious-affiliation alumni, sports team alumni, ethnic alumni, and the like. It was also quickly recognized that, with about 700 members, GALA was (aside from some of the sports team alumni groups, which are assiduously nurtured by the Athletic Department) the largest and most active of these "special interest" groups—indeed, larger than most geographic Yale Clubs.

Listing in university publications immediately increased GALA membership. Also, once the university bureaucracy recognized Yale GALA, it became much easier and more natural for us to avail ourselves of Yale's professional alumni relations staff. We started holding more frequent events on campus and hosting, for example, GALA's receptions for graduating seniors in Rose Alumni House. It is now routine for the AYA staff to include GALA events on reunion calendars and GALA literature in registration packages for reunion classes.

The professional staff of AYA has always been more than friendly toward GALA. One lesson learned is that professional alumni relations people love alumni groups that help themselves. Many times I have been told that, in contrast to the life-support measures that they administer to moribund Yale Clubs in the hinterlands, the AYA staff love helping Yale GALA plan our always-successful parties. Also, Yale GALA has never asked AYA for financial support. On the contrary, GALA has been busy raising money for the new Lesbian and Gay Studies Program. At the end of the day, the best way for an alumni group to endear itself to a university is to raise money.

Currently, GALA is negotiating with the AYA and Yale Information Services for maintenance of GALA's mailing list. Keeping the mailing list up-to-date and printing labels for the quarterly newsletter and other mailings are GALA's most time-consuming, on-going chore. For an organization that depends on a small core of volunteer workers, it would be a colossal boon to have this task shifted to university computers. List keeping, however, for reasons of cost, staff time, and privacy, is a sensitive issue for the university, and, while they have helped GALA with specific fund-raising appeals, AYA is still reluctant to assume continuing responsibility for the mailing list.

As for my personal journey as a gay Yale alumnus, after I completed my terms as president of Yale GALA, I was invited by the board of the AYA to become an at-large AYA delegate. My nomination was clearly recognition of my work with Yale GALA, and during my three years as a delegate I freely identified myself as the GALA representative to the AYA. At the end of my term as an at-large AYA delegate, I was pleased to be nominated and elected to the Board of Governors. Naturally, as a governor of the alumni association my concerns extend beyond those of the gay and lesbian constituency from which I rose, but as the highest ranking "out" gay person in the alumni hierarchy, I know that I am perceived by people within the administration as a resource of specific value. I was, for example, placed on a special task force to examine ways in which the AYA can better serve and develop the "special interest" alumni groups. I have also been consulted many times by the provost, the dean, and others on matters concerning the GLBT community at Yale. I find it very amusing that I should be recognized today as an important alumnus because I am gay. The irony is particularly rich because, 30 years ago when I was an undergraduate, I was so intimidated by the culture of Yale and by my own conflicted feelings that I remained deeply hidden in the closet until after I left. To be back at Yale now as a proud gay alumnus gives me tremendous satisfaction. (Submitted by Belmont Freeman, an architect in New York City.)

Case Study 13.3
Rebuilding an Alumni Group

It was wonderful to see that there is some interest in continuing Lambda Alumni for UCLA's lesbian, gay, bisexual, transgender, queer (LGBTQ) population. I have hope that others will come out of the woodwork to help us continue to be a supportive organization to past grads and future grads. At the meeting I spoke of Lambda Alumni being a string within a web of support. As LGBTQ people we often lose many connections within our web of support when we come out and start to be real with the world. We have many difficulties because of these strings that break or unravel, usually at the times when we could use them the most. This organization can be one of the first and most enduring strings that graduating students can join upon entering the real world. In a world that is full of homophobia and bigotry Lambda Alumni could be a great supportive organization that allows them to thrive and prosper for years to come. We all must rebuild our webs of support, and this is one perfect opportunity to do just that. With connections as people, free thinkers, friends, our career paths or aspirations, us as students, teachers, parents, kids, and so on, we have the potential to make this world a greater place. If you want to rebuild some of the connections that you have been ignoring or were missing or broken, I implore you to use this vehicle, Lambda Alumni. That's what it is here for and why we continue to hand out scholarships and whatever else we can. Start that process of rebuilding, healing and network building. I am always hopeful and do what I can do to help others, my community, and myself. The one thing that I have come to realize is that by doing one of these things I am actually doing all three. By helping others I end up helping myself and my community. Any way you put it, it means that something healthy, love-filled, and productive is taking place. Please help us rebuild Lambda Alumni and help yourself and your community in the process! It really works, and it feels awesome.

(E-mail message from Ritch Johnson, president of UCLA's Lambda Alumni organization following a re-building meeting, February 2000)

Chapter 14

The Power of a System-Wide Organization: The University of California LGBTI Association

Jonathan Winters

The 11-year history of the University of California Lesbian Gay Bisexual Transgender Intersex Association (UCLGBTIA) cannot be thoroughly conveyed nor detailed nor nuances of its history analyzed in one short chapter. What can be gleaned, however, is that through sheer determination and persistence of an organized force, progress on lesbian, gay, bisexual and transgender (LGBT) issues is possible in large university systems. The even distribution of resources among campuses and the power dynamics between campuses and constituencies (students, staff, faculty, alumni) continue to be daunting tasks at any large, multi-campus system. The experiment of an "umbrella" LGBT organization throughout the University of California (UC) and its nine campuses is strong and continues to develop in new directions, and it is subject to the politics of the time. Just as the student political movement raises new demands on a campus, so too the agenda of UCLGBTIA continues to develop throughout the University of California system.

Founded in 1990 at UC Santa Barbara as the University of California Lesbian Gay Bisexual Association, what is now known as the UCLGBTIA began as a student initiative to organize on LGBT issues among all the campuses in the University of California and among students across the state. Two important influences from that time are important to consider when assessing UCLGBTIA's early history.

First, the University of California campuses were major centers of the anti-apartheid and anti-racist movement. From 1984 through 1989 college campuses across the country erupted in solidarity with the anti-apartheid up-surge in South Africa. A common call of the American solidarity movement was for divestment of large holdings so as to cripple the apartheid economy. The demand was strongly felt at the University of California where the system-wide retirement fund alone was one of the largest customers invested in companies doing business in and with the government of South Africa. Due to political pressure from students, staff, faculty, and alumni, this demand was won when the regents of the university made the historic vote to divest in 1986. Of note were the lessons learned from this united political action, and networks of activists were built among the campuses.

Second, a new political trend was emerging, borne out of the struggle against AIDS, that changed the nature of gay and lesbian organizing. AIDS Coalition to Unleash Power (ACT UP) was founded in New York in 1987. By 1991 chapters had sprung up across the country. After a bold action by a group called Stop AIDS Now or Else (SANoE) that blocked traffic on the Golden Gate Bridge, the West Coast version of ACT UP San Francisco was founded in 1989 by some of SANoE's members.

ACT UP also gave rise to a group called Queer Nation which aimed to redefine LGBT people and reclaim the word queer itself. Anything remotely shocking such as public kiss-ins, girl-cotts or zap demonstrations of unfriendly businesses, was the order of the day for the life of their flash-in-the-pan existence. These groups and actions appealed to students and youth just coming of age and coming out in the age of AIDS. Though Queer Nation is now gone, the vernacular they provided remains: in youth and campus populations, queer is used as a positive term to include anyone who identified as other than heterosexual.

FROM IDEAS TO ACTION

Among LGBTI students at the University of California campuses was a desire for greater communication and coordination of their work to achieve progress on common issues. The coordinated anti-apartheid actions at each campus had drawn on support from students, staff and faculty. There was a feeling that despite the disparity among and within campuses regarding services and support for LGBTI students, staff, faculty and alumni, there was a common basis for working together.

The early days of the UCLGBA were very busy. From May 1990 to April 1991 there were 6 meetings held at 6 different campuses at which members drafted a constitution and ratified its first five paragraphs. While the constitution of the time demanded much from its members, it attempted to be as democratic and egalitarian as possible. While people shared common ideals, early leaders had to balance several factors: the differences between campuses in the northern part of the state and the southern part; representation from students, staff, faculty, and alumni; consideration of different sexual orientations, gender identities, races, ethnicities, and socioeconomic backgrounds; religious views; and physical abilities. The group consciously turned the institution's non-discrimination statement into a pro-active agenda rather than a stale promise.

The group often locked itself some difficult processes that didn't always bear fruit. Originally the group operated on complete consensus, both among the full membership (general assembly) and the leading members (steering committee). When the constitution was ratified, the general assembly had rules for decision-making: simple majority and special decisions by three-quarters vote. The original constitution also placed a high demand on steering committee members by requiring the body to meet at least three times a year in addition to the general assembly which was meeting twice in a year. Just as the group formulated its central demands, it was having difficulty maintaining the level of work it placed on itself to achieve them.

"PROMOTING AND PROVOKING," GROWING AND EXPANDING

In the Fall of 1991 the steering committee approved documents that addressed their views of why and how the organization should operate as well as its first central demands. These documents guided the work of the group through the end of the 1990s. One document referred to UCLGBA as the tool to promote and provoke communication among gay, lesbian, and bisexual people in the UC System. Its purpose was to get the attention of all strata UC-affiliates and build a united organization that was truly representative of all sectors of university life: undergraduate and graduate students, staff, faculty, and alumni.

The first central demands put in writing and made available for distribution were to: establish a chancellor's committee on LGB issues on every campus; establish LGB resource centers on every campus; discredit ROTC within the UC system; and establish domestic partnership rights in married/family student housing and with employee spouse benefits. Thus the work began to achieve these demands and organize all these people at all campuses.

The movement for these demands did not proceed in a straight line nor did it follow the same timeline at each campus or take the same direction. Much depended on the enthusiasm of members to organize on their home campuses which led to much unevenness among campuses. For example, by 1992, five campuses (Davis, Irvine, Los Angeles, Riverside, and Santa Cruz) had chancellor's advisory committees; four campuses (Berkeley, Davis, Los Angeles, and Irvine) had staff organizations; Berkeley and Los Angeles had alumni associations; three campuses (Berkeley, Riverside, and Santa Cruz) had LGB radio programs on their campus stations; and all had a variety of LGB student organizations. This incredible progress was made during those three years due to local efforts coordinated with the system-wide demands of UCLGBA.

Change and expansion were constant challenges. In 1994 the inclusion of the National Laboratories as member campuses was formalized. In 1996 the inclusion of transgender concerns yielded massive education and adoption of a name change for the group. In 2001 intersex issues were included after a somewhat divided debate at the 12th Annual General Assembly following two years of education by the Intersex Society of North America (ISNA). These milestones also precipitated name changes.

Since 1997 an internal comparison of each campus' LGBT resources was compiled by UCLGBTIA and used to establish benchmark standards. It also allowed the UCLGBTIA to organize to level the severely disparate and unequal resources among campuses. By 2000 every campus had a chancellor's/campus advisory committee (CAC) for LGBT issues as well as a professional director managing an LGBT resource center. The last campuses to implement centers (San Diego and Santa Barbara) were moved to do so in the wake of sentiment and outcry after the 1998 killing of University of Wyoming student Matthew Shepard.

Until 1993 much of what had been demanded within the UC was addressed primarily at the local level. While each demand was a burning issue at each campus, other campuses benefited when a demand was heard and implemented. But there was still not a defining project that drew all campuses together in concert that would require addressing the system-wide UC Office of the President and senior administration.

NEGOTIATING WITH THE CENTRAL UNIVERSITY ADMINISTRATION

Between 1993 and 1997 the demand for implementing domestic partner benefits (DPBs) occupied center stage. It would test UCLGBTA in dealing with the system-wide administration as well s with the university regents, the highest officials of the university. It was timely that UCLGBA involved itself in that particular fight because in 1992 the system-wide academic council had undertaken a study of DPBs and was poised to recommend the implementation of "symmetry" in benefits between married spouses and domestic partners and for full health and pension benefits for same-sex and opposite-sex domestic partners. This recommendation was based on conclusions from a report of a subcommittee of the University Committee on Faculty Welfare (UCFW).

There was doubt about how such a demand could possibly be won at that time, and the issue would vex the UCLGBA leadership for the entire period. At precarious moments, the steering committee was criticized both for holding out too much hope that the administration would move on DPBs and for not doing enough to fight for campus resource centers. This criticism was particularly sharp at the February 1997 General Assembly. There was no way of knowing that 9 months hence, after three regents' meetings and heavy media attention on the subject, that health benefits for domestic partners would be a reality at the university in what was a huge political watershed moment in the state.

The restive mood then was understandable. Under the Peltason administration (1992 to 1995), there was no commitment to implement DPBs. Two decisions were taken to lobby the president through a letter writing campaign. The first, in 1993, was to give visibility to the issue and give support to the UCFW report which was still under review by campus' academic senates. The second, in 1995, was to support the UCFW recommendations after they were approved by the system-wide academic council and to seek a meeting of the UCLGBA steering committee with the president. Based on the UCFW report, a sample letter was circulated to campus groups. As a result dozens of letters were generated to the president.

The requested meeting between UCLGBA and the president took place but yielded only a few positive results. As a pre-requisite to meeting with the president, the UCLGBA was requested to designate an officer representative through whom to communicate. This was confusing to the UCLGBA as it had no officers, just a board of equal representatives from each campus. The selection of a chair for the steering committee to organize these meetings—and to take on a new internal leadership role—became the method of addressing the issue. Of course, the decision to do this would affect the composition of the UCLGBA steering committee because it led to the adoption of a constitutional revision for elected officers who directed the work of the group. This change served the organization by providing for a rotation of leadership in the steering committee. The model of a chairperson was modified to allow two co-chairs to be a check on the power of just one person. The co-chairs had staggered terms to maintain continuity between a seasoned and incoming chair. Slowly, a strong leadership core with elected officers replaced the loose, ultra-democratic model of initiation.

When the first meeting with the University of California Office of the President (UCOP) occurred, Peltason agreed to recognize the organization as a system-wide group. He also agreed to circulate a statement on the university's commitment to non-discrimination based on sexual orientation. However, it was clear that the president had no intention of taking the matter of DPBs forward. He did not want to carry a "political" issue to the board of regents, and he was not personally in favor of the idea of implementing such benefits. This was evident in a report from UCOP on the DPB proposal of June 1995 that made no recommendation to implement, and worse, it raised the specter of huge costs to the university and rampant fraud by subscribers.

UCLGBA criticized this report mightily. While the criticisms were respectful and objective, the bald-faced nature of the report was personally insulting to steering committee members. A second meeting with Peltason in May 1996 did not change the report dramatically but only refined the details slightly. It became obvious that no progress would be made on this issue until after Peltason retired which occurred in October 1996.

When President Richard Atkinson came into office changes occurred. In December 1996, during a meeting with UCLGBTA, he said that he thought approval of DPBs was both possible and necessary to remain competitive, and to recruit and retain the best staff and faculty. While there were still delays and setbacks, the issues made it to the regents' agenda.

WORK ON DOMESTIC PARTNERSHIP BENEFITS

The first regents' meeting to have the matter of domestic partnership benefits on their agenda was in July 1997 at the UC San Francisco-Presidio Heights campus. Passionate testimonies, including a moving statement by Dr. Rose Maly, a faculty physician at UCLA, caught the regents' attention. (See Appendix L)

In November 1997, years of work on domestic partnership benefits at the UC came to fruition in the historic vote by the board of regents when they approved DP health benefits by one vote. It was one of the greatest victories for the UCLGBTA because it was the first time a demand was won that affected all campuses simultaneously and that had state and national significance for the discussion on DP benefits. The next legislative sessions would harken back to the public testimony at those UC regents' meetings to make their cases for several DP measures that have since been enacted, including the California Domestic Partner Registry. The two years following the regents' vote saw hundreds of public and private employers adding DP Benefits for their employees.

UCLGBTA's diplomacy and skillful lobbying of the regents was praised from a number of sectors. The UCLGBTA strategy relied heavily on personal appeals to the regents in letters, postcard campaigns and public testimony at regents' meetings. People's stories ranged from sharing outrage over potential unequal treatment to those whose partners had died without secured healthcare.

UCLGBTA press strategy involved contacting some 45 mainstream, college, and LGBT print, radio and television media across the state to get the UCLGBTA position out, and collected some 61 statements and letters to publicize the issue to the world and enter into the meeting record. The co-chairs and other campus representatives contacted regents thought to be supportive on the issue and got important information and insight from them. UCLGBTA representatives' gained stature and were highly regarded by a number of supportive regents.

The effect of UCLGBTA's organization and persistence led to a close vote against Governor Pete Wilson who had vowed to pull every dirty trick he could muster against approval. He lost. It was a huge defeat for Wilson and for his stand against DP benefits. Pundits at the time confessed their surprise at Wilson's tactics and rhetoric in opposing the measure. Some speculated that this defeat—or at least its methodology—doomed his presidential ambitions. Many analysts added this to the list of reasons why the Democrats swept the 1998 state elections.

In May 2001 UCLGBTIA was recognized as an official "advisory group" to the UC Office of the President on a wide variety of LGBTI issues. UCLGBTIA continues to work with the UCOP on the enhancements to DP benefits, especially pension equity, housing policy, and availability to opposite-sex domestic partners. At the end of 2001 there is still a plan that UC benefits will equalize pension benefits.

TECHNOLOGICAL CHANGE

When most of the UC campuses implemented email account access for students, staff, and faculty in 1995, new opportunities for communication between steering committee representatives on different campuses were opened. The role of computer networking and email access had a tremendous effect on the grassroots organizing effort for DP benefits and other UCLGBTA initiatives. Much of the strategies and tactics for the regents' meetings and lobbying campaigns were formulated by the DP team at UC Berkeley and communicated via email to the other campuses and laboratories. Through email members at all campuses could share ideas and information, documents and flyers, and make plans and coordinate decisions among themselves or to a list of people at once, instantly, without leaving their workstations. It was a quantum leap in the speed of communication for the group. Without this tool, the monumental work on the DP benefit issue would not have been so well organized.

The group utilized email listservs that disseminated tactics to an even wider audience. News of the latest wrinkle or an appeal for more letters and phone calls could generate a response at all campuses immediately. Respondents could also use email as their tool to deliver their letters to the administration. By late 1996, UCLGBTA had established a presence on the Web. With the subsequent explosion of this medium, UCLGBTIA has been highly regarded for the useful historical record presented on the website.

DEMOGRAPHIC CHANGE

Typical of groups on campuses in higher education, there is constant turnover of students. For UCLGBTIA an important demographic change occurred early on and continues to change. By 1993 the students who had founded the organization in 1990 were graduating. And no new students were volunteering to take their places because the movement was beginning to ebb. This phenomenon made staff members more visible and allowed for more staff members to join the steering committee. Partly due to staff members' self-interest and also to events taking place outside the organization, the challenge for DPBs began to occupy center stage.

Coincidentally, it appeared the group was feeling the effects of having run a long time on enthusiasm alone. After the first two years of a full calendar of meetings, it became difficult to sustain such a high number of meetings and expect people to attend. One particularly bad moment was a 1993 steering committee meeting which was to have occurred at UC Riverside. It did not take place due to confusion and burnout of the local group charged with convening the meeting. Former steering committee staff representatives promoted the view that students were "unreliable" and shouldn't be allowed to hold responsible positions within the group. This became a low point in the cooperative relations that were sought among UC affiliates.

Although a united front among students, staff, and faculty was among the original demands—and the loftiest goal of early student organizer—this working relationship unlocked previously unspoken prejudices and divisions between staff and students. At worst was the view that staff were "taking over" and that soon UCLGBA would be "irrelevant" because it "only represented" staff. And some staff members felt that students were "undisciplined" and "irresponsible". While such views were the minority, they affected the cordial, positive working relations between these constituent groups. The dynamics of the relationship between students and staff would dominate the group's politics and continue to be one that required careful management during the original DPB campaign and through to today.

COMBATING MEMBER BURNOUT

Another dynamic—burnout—among steering committee members and officers has also been an issue and continues to preoccupy the steering committee in its deliberations about how to organize effectively. The group excelled at deciding on tasks and piling assignments on its members but not at delegating work evenly or rotating and developing new leadership in its ranks.

The nature of activism among university students lends itself to periods of infectious hyper-activity on an issue which cannot be sustained over a long period. Over-commitment to a level of activity (number of meetings, reports, tasks, and so on), poor planning (advance notices for meetings/events, proper coordination among campuses) and inflated expectations of what can be realistically accomplished by individuals who have lives in the "outside world," are all elements of burnout syndrome. Members who burn out become alienated from the group that makes the demands of them and then turn pessimistic about achieving genuine results. Often, rather than facing their own shortcomings and limitations in an unreasonable situation, members abandon responsibilities they had assumed.

The job of tackling LGBTI political work in a multi-campus university is daunting and occasionally intimidating. Members of UCLGBTIA are often challenging their administration to adopt new policies, to consider innovative solutions and think outside the box, all of which are anathema to bureaucracy. UCLGBTIA members make political demands to support and protect a minority within a minority on all campuses. It is difficult political terrain with much of it is uncharted.

Officers and steering committee members make great personal sacrifices to forward the work of UCLGBTIA. Officers and steering committee members are often asked to make public presentations to campus and outside organizations, produce documents on organizational work, and make phone calls, send letters or emails to move the work forward, nearly all of which occur on members' own time and expense.

The amount of sacrifice has increased as the group's visibility and success has increased, yet the financial and infrastructure support has kept up. The annual conference and general assembly has grown in attendance each year, and costs more to produce, but has not gained steady financial support to assure its proper production. Six years after formal recognition of the UCLGBTIA by the UC office of the president, there is not the same material support given to it as to comparable system-wide advisory groups. This places an extraordinary burden on the members of the organization. It is not difficult to comprehend why burnout is a factor, and why it is difficult to retain officers and leading members.

BUILDING FOR THE FUTURE

The University is now a very different place for LGBTI students, staff, faculty and alumni than when UCLGBA was founded. UCLGBTIA has had great successes and is at a new era of its history. It has accomplished most of its original demands and made a positive impact at the local campus and system-wide levels. The achievement of these hard-won victories only raises new demands on the organization.

Just as questions that the organization faces today could not have been foreseen in 1990, so it is impossible to forecast where it will be ten years hence. As UCLGBTIA enters into its second decade of existence, it carries an air of authority as an institution with great experience. As an organization, it has a sound structure in place and many tools with which to operate. At the same time it is still a delicate experiment that struggles to navigate the way, and is nourished with the energy of new members only when it can fully nourish those members in return. There is still a long road ahead.

Chapter 15

Selecting and Implementing Programs and Services

Last night, Ruth Ellis was the guest of honor at a campus showing of the film about her life, *Living with Pride: Ruth Ellis at 100*. Ruth is living history, a 100-year-old Black lesbian who spent the first 37 years of her life in Springfield, Illinois, before moving to Detroit and becoming the first woman to own a printing business in Michigan in the 1940s. She is tiny and beautiful and fragile, yet tough as they come, a feisty Leo femme who loves to dance and loves to flirt. After the film, Ruth took questions from the audience, so I asked her about something that she had said the first time that I met her four and a half years ago as part of the LGBT Office's intergenerational research project. She'd told me then that she wanted a younger girlfriend, to which I'd replied that pretty much *any* girlfriend she had would be younger, and she laughed. Anyway, last night she said that she was just enjoying the flirting. Afterward I got to talk to her alone, and she told me that she's not had the chance to do much flirting lately because she hasn't been able to get out dancing much, so—I still do not know why I did it—I stood up and offered her my hand and asked, "May I have this dance?" She took my hand and stood up and stepped into my embrace, and I just kinda tucked her into my arms with one arm around her waist, holding her tiny hand in mine, curled against my chest. As she placed her head against my chest, I started singing "Let Me Call You Sweetheart," and we danced slow and gentle to the music that we were making. At first I thought that she was chuckling a little, but then she looked up at me, and there were tears in her eyes, and she said, "That's one of my favorite songs. What made you sing it?" I didn't know, but she was humming with me, and we finished that dance. It was *magic*...pure magic. After we finished our private little dance, she looked up at me again and kissed my cheek and said, "I sure do love gay people and lesbians." I raised her hand to my lips, kissed it, and bade her farewell for the evening. A little later it hit me—I had held a woman who has seen an entire century pass by, and I had hummed a song to her that I don't even know all the words to, and she had looked at me with diamond tears in her eyes, and for those few moments there was *no* one else in the world—no one. It still amazes me now, the privilege that Miss Ruth Ellis gave me of that brief magical moment when she took my hand and danced with me. Without the opportunity that I had with the LGBT Office's research program, I never would have met this powerful, beautiful woman. (Submitted by Beth Harrison, doctoral student, University of Michigan. Ruth Ellis died on October 5, 2000, at the age of 101.)

INTRODUCTION

Chickering and Reisser (1993) wrote that services and programs "assist students to move successfully through the college or university" (444). The services proposed in the previous chapters are essential for developing a sense of identity: interactions with others, commitment to personal goals, a positive self-concept, and availability of information and support. Programs, however, are broader. They provide student interaction on both a campus and community level, encourage leadership, improve interaction skills with students, faculty, and staff, and facilitate involvement in college activities. The goals of successful programs "should be to support learning in out-of-class settings" (Andreas 1993, p. 10) and should be "framed in terms of a particular theoretical or conceptual framework."

Andreas (1993) listed what administrators might do to create successful programs. The list is appropriate for LGBT center directors as well:

Understand the mission of the institution and of student affairs if that is where your center is located.

Learn about the students and other constituents to be served.

Conduct research to help the campus understand a problem or need.

Involve students as completely as possible.

Attend to politics. Know the political influence structure and key players. Anticipate opposition and plan how to deal with it. Involved affected persons.

Use the media—tell them what the program is trying to accomplish.

Seek help. Use campus consultants to provide specialized skills.

Some LGBT centers are funded to provide programming along with their services. Others are not. For example, while UCLA has a generous operating budget, it is not funded to "do" programming. Although the LGBT Center and other administrative units may assist students with their programs and events, programming must remain a student-initiated function.

Case Study 15.1
University of Southern California (USC)

Student programming at USC is offered primarily through student-run assemblies, and the Center for Women and Men works in close partnership with the Gay, Lesbian, Bi Assembly and with the Women's Student Assembly to provide speakers, educational events, National Coming Out Week programming, and so forth. A Student Affairs Advisory Group on Gay, Lesbian, and Bi Issues monitors the campus climate and advises both the center and the student assemblies. Recognizing that one center cannot provide the programming to end all programming, faculty, and staff, and students, and alumni alike share the load, offering mentoring programs, support groups, rap groups, festival programming, and speakers bureaus. The center, nonetheless, is the place to which all the spokes of the wheel are connected. Though we could always do with more staff and more money, we do a lot with the staffing and budget provided. We like being able to explore queer identity in ways that parallel the academy's focus and to address issues of ambiguity around gender in ways that say, "This center is for you whether you're gay, straight, bi, trans, male, female, or any combination of the above." It's great value for money: two for the price of one. (Submitted by Elizabeth Davenport, assistant dean for student affairs, director, Gay, Lesbian, Bi Student Support, University of Southern California.)

INCLUDING PEOPLE OF COLOR IN YOUR PROGRAMMING

Dr. Saralyn Chesnut, director of Emory University's Office of Lesbian/Gay/Bisexual/Trans-gender Life, wrote that the best way to be inclusive and to involve LGBT people of color in your programs is to have LGBT people of color in your center or office as employees or volunteers (National Consortium, www.lgbtcampus.org). She offered three basic strategies:

1. Offer programs that focus on LGBT people of color. There are many good films and videos, speakers, and other programming options that focus on LGBT people of color. The film distribution companies Third World Newsreel (www.twn.org), Women Make Movies (www.wmm.com), Frameline Distribution (www.frameline.org), First Run/Icarus Films (www.echonyc.com/~frif/), and others are good sources for films and videos. Make sure that a substantial number of your programs each year focus on LGBT people of color and their issues.

2. Do good outreach to LGBT people of color, including both campus and community-based people of color organizations. Someone from your center should build a relationship with both on- and off-campus LGBT people of color organizations, so that you can be sure that their members know about programs that they may find of interest. At the least, find out what types and avenues of publicity are most likely to reach the LGBT people of color community. You may want to ask groups to co-sponsor events with you; this is a good way to build a relationship and get members of the groups to come to the programs.

3. Build strong relationships between your office or center and any offices or centers on your campus that work primarily with racial/ethnic minority students. You should also build strong relationships with your colleagues in campus-based offices or centers that serve racial/ethnic minority students and employees. Establish personal relationships if possible; invite your colleagues to lunch or other social occasions. Offer to co-sponsor or help with their programs. Support and attend their programs. Once you have established a relationship, you can ask these colleagues to help you with outreach to the people of color communities on campus.

BRINGING MAJOR SPEAKERS TO YOUR CAMPUS

David Barnett and Shane Windmeyer wrote about obtaining speakers for your campus (National Consortium FAQ Web site). Money is scarce on many college campuses, and entertainment may be costly. As with most things, the best deals are obtained by shopping around and doing your research. If you have certain budget limits, remember that your money goes further by planning ahead, thinking creatively, and calling different agencies/speakers. Do not hesitate to negotiate a price for the speaker you want. Many are willing to lower their fees when they know that your center is not able to obtain further funding from your institution. Following are a few suggestions and a listing of entertainment resources to get you started.

1. Check out local resources. You may be able to find local speakers or entertainers who will come to your campus for free or for a very reasonable fee. Sometimes the best programs are lower-cost, "homemade" programs that build community or bring diverse groups together.

2. Know the basics about agencies. Realize that some LGBT speakers are represented exclusively by an agency while others may be represented by more than one agency. Some lower-cost speakers may not even be represented by an agency and prefer to work directly with schools to keep costs down. As an industry standard, agencies get a commission of the artist's booking at your school. By shopping around, you may save a few dollars. Remember, this is a money-making business.

3. Ask for referrals from other campuses. We know it's not an "original" idea, but call other college and university GLBT groups/centers and ask what speakers/entertainers they have brought to campus in the recent past. This way you can hear what worked on other college campuses and maybe learn about a few speakers who you did not know were on the circuit. You can also get good ideas by asking questions at your Regional LGBT College Conference.

4. Share the cost with other campuses. Another way to get good deals on entertainment is to work with other college/university GLBT groups in your area. Find out what they are bringing to campus. If you are interested in the same entertainment, you can usually get a better honorarium price for both of you by block booking with the speaker/agency. Block-booking means that he or she goes to one school on one night and the other school maybe within the next two nights. You can also save money on travel this way.

5. Be careful. Don't work with "fly-by-night" agents or promoters. Ask questions! How long has the agency been around? What colleges/universities have they worked with before? If they utilize the National Association of Campus Activities (NACA) Entertainment directory (See Appendix E), these agencies have proven track records and are evaluated by NACA schools on a yearly basis.

6. Know the procedures for contracts on your campus. Don't ask for a contract unless you are ready to make the deal. Before you ask for your contract, go over the terms of the deal specifically over the phone and take notes. Read your contract to make sure that everything is listed or negotiated from honorarium, to travel, to lodging, and so on. Some schools require a paid university official to ask for a contract, others do not. Many schools also require a designated university official to sign the contract (e.g. director of student activities). The person who signs the contract is legally bound to the terms of the contract, so ask questions before signing.

Keeping those suggestions in mind, review the list of resources in Appendix E. These resources represent links to other associations and agents that provide speakers/entertainers on LGBT issues.

OUT IN THE WORKPLACE

A usual program on campuses provides information on workplace issues. This programming generally takes three approaches: one focuses on faculty and staff by addressing their workplace needs; one focuses on the intergenerational opportunities of bringing faculty, staff, and students together to dialogue about what may be the experiences of "out" LGBT professionals on campus; and the third offers information to students about what they may expect as they prepare to graduate and enter the work world.

Case Study 15.2
"Out in the Workplace" at the University of Pennsylvania

"Out in the Workplace" at the University of Pennsylvania is a discussion series designed to expose undergraduate and graduate/professional students to the various ways in which people have managed their sexual identities in the workplace. The series has been co-sponsored by the Lesbian Gay Bisexual Transgender Center and Career Services in alternating years since 1983. Each series consists of three to four panel discussions, featuring topics ranging from those of current importance (e.g., AIDS in the workplace), to specific occupational fields (e.g., academe, business, medicine). Each panel in the series consists of four to five speakers, with every effort made to achieve diversity across race, ethnicity, and gender. People from a variety of professions and positions are invited to demonstrate that no career is closed to lesbian, gay, and bisexual people. We do, however, focus on those professions that data indicate are most often chosen by Penn students. Panelists with five or more years of experience are typically preferred because they can offer longer-term perspectives. Additionally, we seek to include at least one or two couples who can jointly address dual-career and work-family balance issues. As part of our efforts to secure diverse panelists, we try also to represent many points on the continuum of "out-ness" at work. Given that these panel discussions are held in public and are advertised very broadly to the campus community, it is harder to find people who are closeted and willing to speak publicly about being gay in the workplace. When reflecting upon their career histories, however, we do find that many panelists will address times when they were not as out as they may now be. Through this reflection, audience members get a sense of what it might be like to be closeted in the workplace. Panelists are asked to address not only degree of "out-ness" at work, but also how their orientation may have influenced career choices; what types of activities and experiences to include (or not) on a resume; whether or not and how to come out during a job interview; and what types of repercussions their identity has had on their careers and work life. The industry-specific panels provide further insight into the work cultures of various fields that are not always perceived as particularly gay-friendly and how things have changed over the years. The co-sponsorship between Career Services and the LGBT Center is essential to the success of this series. Panelists are invited from the personal and professional networks of the staff members organizing the series. Several meetings are held to brainstorm the types of people and careers offering the most effective and diverse perspectives. Marketing and publicity also benefit through collaborative efforts. The LGBT Center has more direct communication with the LGBT community on campus and throughout the city via mailing lists, an electronic newsletter, and day-to-day interaction with students. Career Services' involvement expands the reach of the program to all undergraduate and graduate/professional school students through E-mail distribution lists. Co-sponsorship includes co-funding of advertising, refreshments, and other associated costs (e.g., reimbursing panelists for parking and travel expenses), which makes providing a three-to-four session series more practical. This can be particularly true for student services offices that frequently operate on tight budgets. Finally, but not to be overlooked, is the value of collaborating with colleagues across your university to promote a broader sense of community in the delivery of student services. A number of resources and materials were developed to support "Out in the Workplace." Working as a team, the organizers split the responsibility for writing or developing correspondence, advertising materials, handouts, and Web resources. Invitation letters were drafted to provide panelists with a detailed overview of the goals, content, and structure of the program. The LGBT Center created flyers for newsletter distribution, advertisements for the campus newspaper, press releases to community publications with LGBT readership, and announcements for their electronic newsletter. Career Services sent announcements to all of their E-mail distribution lists and other career offices on campus. Career Services also developed handouts listing print and online resources that address career issues and sexual orientation, as well as an essay offering strategies for coming out on a resume and during a job interview. All of these resources were made available on a Web page for LGBT students and alumni, which was permanently added to the Career Services site. Both offices advertised the program on their Web sites. The most important elements of a program like "Out in the Workplace" are the benefits reaped by the students who attend. Students learn specific strategies for how and when to come out in the workplace or during the job search. They hear stories about many of the challenges, benefits and frustrations associated with being closeted or out on the job, which serve to normalize the anxieties that they might feel about coming out (e.g., "What if being out threatens my job?") as well as staying closeted (e.g., "I'll be miserable if I can't be open about who I am."). The industry-specific stories provided by the panelists help many students evaluate the likelihood that they will want to be out (e.g., an elementary school teacher might face more challenges being out than a writer for a gay magazine). Audience members learn about the types of GLBT employee groups that exist in various settings and how to become involved without necessarily outing oneself. The dual-career issues discussed during these panels are also very enlightening and rewarding to students, many of whom have not yet had to fully address the influence of committed relationships on career choices. Some job settings entail a great deal of socializing with other employees as well as clients and customers; panelists address what it is like to bring a partner to these functions or how to broach the issue the first time that it arises. On a recent panel, one couple with children talked about the need, at times, for one partner to take a less-demanding job in favor of being more of a primary caretaker for the children. Panelists also provide useful nuts-and-bolts advice on domestic partnership, financial, health insurance, and related issues, in terms of what benefits and resources their organizations do or do not provide. The cumulative benefit of this series is that participants hear "real-life" stories from LGBT individuals who have faced these issues throughout their careers and who can offer support, strategies, and empowerment to students about to embark on their own careers. In addition to benefiting current Penn students, "Out in the Workplace" has helped the LGBT Center and Career Services forge stronger links with the alumni who have been tapped as speakers over the years. Being asked to speak in this series has allowed these graduates to give back, and their feelings about the university are, we suspect, much more positive as a result. In all respects, "Out in the Workplace" is a program with a significantly positive impact. (Submitted by Becky Ross, career counselor at the University of Pennsylvania Career Services)

Chapter 16

The Lavender Leader: An *Inqueery* into Lesbian, Gay, Bisexual, and Transgender Student Leadership

Lesbian, gay, bisexual, and transgender (LGBT) students are found in nearly every organization on campus. Generally, openly LGBT students—that is, students who are forthcoming about their sexual and gender identities—are in LGBT-related student groups, but they are also in non-LGBT groups, and sometimes they are the leaders of those groups. Who are our LGBT student leaders? How do they learn about leadership, especially non-hierarchical leadership? This chapter explores the differences between students who learn leadership in their communities of origin, and students who find their way into the LGBT community—one based on nothing related to their communities of origin—and learn its leadership norms. It also discusses sexual identity development and leadership experiences of LGBT students and describes the importance of developing non-hierarchical leadership programs specifically geared to LGBT students. Finally, it offers a model of non-hierarchical leadership for LGBT students at a large public institution.

There is scant literature on leadership as it relates specifically to LGBT people, students, and campuses, yet some (Crist 1990; C. Gingrich, personal communication 1999; Sanlo 1998b; Shepard, Yeskel, & Outcalt 1995) agree that an LGBT person is a leader simply by acknowledging her or his sexual or gender identity. Porter (1998) reviewed literature relating to leadership programs in general and LGBT leadership programs specifically. He found that while campus leadership programs are "essential components of the mission of most colleges and universities" (p. 307), few institutions focus on more than the highly visible student leaders in the usual student organizations. A leadership model must be developed to meet the needs of all students, including those of ethnic minority, non-traditionally aged, differently abled, from those lower socio-economic backgrounds, and LGBT students. Such a model would send a message to the entire university community that these populations are important to the institution. According to Porter (1998, p. 308), such leadership programs would provide opportunities for all students to engage in the process of becoming visible as a campus community; help students see and understand the connectedness of similarities, differences, and oppressions of and with other minority students; and prepare LGBT students for the continuing challenges of fighting oppression and violence and for achieving equality and justice.

Porter (1998) merged the concepts of leadership and sexual identity development theory, while Mallory (1998) provided an overview of the types and roles of LGBT student organizations that exist on many campuses today. Ward (1998) discussed the role of the adviser—many of whom are not LGBT—for LGBT student organizations, while Shepard et al. (1995) wrote generically of leadership qualities as they relate to leaders of LGBT campus organizations. Outcalt (1998) described the obstacles that many LGBT student organizations experience. Several of those obstacles relate directly to LGBT leadership: underdeveloped leadership skills, leader burnout, and lack of continuity. By underdeveloped skills, Outcalt was referring to the failure to differentiate between a leader's personal goals and energies from those of the group so that the group's success is dependent solely upon the leader.

Outcalt (1998) defined burnout as "the tendency to work harder while accomplishing less and feeling worse...it can affect everyone in a group, but it might be most damaging to those who put the greatest amount of their energy into the group and its goals" (p. 331). He described lack of continuity as an outgrowth of burnout: "When leaders and group members have burned out and groups are forced to begin anew, the group finds itself reinventing the wheel and repeating the efforts of those of its predecessors. Student groups, with the turnover inherent in their membership, are particularly prone to this danger" (p. 332). Outcalt noted that administrators who are not interested in making the changes requested by students often rely on the fact that "today's activist students will leave campus relatively soon, often taking their agendas with them" (p. 332).

BUILDING COMMUNITY: LGBT STUDENTS ON CAMPUS

The American Council on Education (ACE) (1997) noted that predominantly white institutions "have isolated both minority students and the faculty and staff that work with them, thereby 'ghettoizing' their participants and contributing to their marginal status on campus" (p. 37). The same phenomenon happens to LGBT students as well. Even worse, Evans and Rankin (1998) noted that the "fear of discrimination, harassment, or violence leads many LGBT individuals to adopt a very low profile on campus" (p. 183), leaving them feeling isolated and disconnected there. Dreher (1996) wrote, "Without community, we're isolated individuals, separate pieces, unable to reach beyond our own ability" (p. 118).

LGBT people on campus may be isolated from one another as LGBT people, but they may belong to one or more communities that have nothing to do with their sexual or gender identities. Most people are born into a community based on their ethnic, racial, religious, economic, and/or geographic identities. They learn the norms of those communities—from their families, schools, media, religious institutions. As children grow, some may feel different at school or in their communities because of their race, ethnicity, or religion and may be taunted by their classmates. When they go home, they find a place of safety among people like themselves, that is, of the same race or ethnicity or religion. The family's norms, rules, expectations, and culture are learned from birth and practiced in the safe and welcoming environment of their homes.

Lesbian, gay, bisexual, and transgender people, however, are not born into an LGBT community. Once they identify their "difference," they eventually seek people like themselves and deliberately enter sexual/gender identity communities. They were not taught how to be LGBT in their homes or schools or religious institutions from their families. They did not learn about the norms, cultures, and expectations of LGBT communities. In fact, if they learned anything at all about being LGBT, it was probably uncomplimentary at best. If they spoke the words—that is, came out to others in their homes—about their sexual/gender identities, they likely found it as difficult and unsafe there as they did at school. For the sake of survival and for acceptance by others and/or to divert attention from their sexual/gender identities, LGBT young people often remain carefully closeted. Some drop out of school, some become involved in high-risk activities, and some become high- or over-achieving students, the class president, a brainy nerd, or an elite athlete.

It is not unusual, therefore, to find that many highly successful students on college campuses are also lesbian, gay, bisexual, or transgender. In many cases they have not felt safe enough to reveal their sexual or gender identities, but in some cases, in some institutions, they have done exactly that—come out openly on their campuses. The leaders of LGBT student groups, of course, are the most obvious. But many LGBT students—some open, some still closeted—are leaders in non-LGBT organizations: the sorority president, the quarterback, the ROTC officer, the Young Republicans' treasurer, the student government co-chair, or the fraternity membership chair may indeed be lesbian, gay, bisexual, or transgender.

Some campuses are large enough to have multiple LGBT groups where such group membership is based primarily on racial/ethnic identity. At UCLA, for example, not only are there identity-based LGBT groups—La Familia for Hispanic students, Mahu for Asian Pacific Islanders, and QAAR for African-Americans—but also LGBT student organizations within various schools or departments, such as the business school group, the law students' group, and the medical school students' group. Leaders in the campus LGBT community are as diverse as the campus itself. Many of these leaders struggle with whether they should devote their limited time, energy, and skills to their racial/ethnic identity group or to an LGBT group. The question—and the challenge—then becomes, How do these leaders guide their groups to work collaboratively to generate a cohesive LGBT campus community?

SEXUAL IDENTITY DEVELOPMENT AND LEADERSHIP

While there has been some research on gender and leadership, sexual identity development and leadership have not yet been clearly connected in the literature, but there appears to be a point at which leadership and sexual identity begin to intersect. Cass (1979) identified six stages of sexual identity development:

1.   identity confusion: an awareness of feeling different from the heterosexual norm; begins to personalize information about homosexuality; experiences inner turmoil; does not share her or his feelings with anyone.

2.   identify comparison: rationalization of feelings and behaviors; has strong feelings of isolation; may be actively anti-gay in word or deed.

3.   identity tolerance: seek contacts with the gay community; remains closeted to most people but looks for visible role models; says, "I may be gay."

4.   identity acceptance: immerses self in the gay community; is able to say, "I am gay."

5.   identity pride: becomes an activist; confronts and challenges closeted people; experiences a radical shift away from societal and family expectations; initiates classroom discussion; needs and seeks allies and role models.

6.   identity synthesis: experiences an integration of sexual, emotional, physical, and spiritual identities; anger becomes situational.

Fassinger (1998) noted several limitations of the Cass model, the most serious of which is that it ignores cultural and demographic factors that influence LGBT identity formation. Fassinger created a model that is "more inclusive of demographic and cultural influences and less reliant on identity disclosure as a marker of developmental maturity" (p. 16). Fassinger described a four-phase sequence of awareness, exploration, deepening/commitment, and internalization/synthesis. She stated that LGBT people, especially students, may find themselves in multiple stages of development. For example, a student may be in the exploration or the commitment stage while on campus but in the awareness stage when she or he goes home. Therefore, LGBT students may take on the added intense stress of juggling identity management in multiple locations in addition to all the other stresses that they experience simply by being college students.

As if sexual identity issues were not enough, LGBT students deal with their various cultural and ethnic identities as well. Integrating two or more central identities are important issues for LGBT people. Evans, Forney, and Guido-DiBrito (1998, pp. 101–102) described cultural differences in sexual identity discovery and development. They said that Latinas/os generally identify as bisexual rather than gay or lesbian because these concepts are considered to apply only to white people. In Black communities, "conformity to traditional gender roles is a significant pressure for men that often precludes their self-identification as gay" (pp. 101-102), but the African American community tends to be more tolerant of Black gay men "as long as they keep their identities quiet" (pp. 101-102). In both Hispanic and Black families, religious influences make coming out especially difficult.

Evans et al. (1998) noted that in Asian cultures "the idea of sexual identity beyond that familial expectation for procreation is nonexistent, and homosexuality can be expressed only if it doesn't interfere with the person's prescribed role within the family" (pp. 101-102). However, Native American cultures refer to homosexuals as two-spirited and value their contributions to the community. Evans et al. described conflict between ethnic identity and lesbian and gay identity as reported by Cuban women, African Americans, and Japanese Americans "who experience racial discrimination in the LGBT communities and homophobia and heterosexism in their respective racial or ethnic communities" (pp. 101-102).

LGBT students face a minority stress similar to that of racial or ethnic students: discrimination, stigmatization, and even violence are not uncommon, although such events may not be reported and are therefore kept invisible to the greater campus community. LGBT students tend to experience enormous amounts of stress as a result of living and going to school in a heterosexist and homophobic environment and tend to be tolerated only when they remain closeted (DiPlacido 1998).

It is most likely, then, that as LGBT students come out on our campuses, they search first for self, then seek community. It is also likely that as their racial, ethnic, and sexual identities intersect, they must decide where to place their extra- or co-curricular time. Some may find themselves in organizations that speak to their multiple identities of race or ethnicity and sexual orientation such as the groups described at UCLA. Interestingly, there is much crossover at UCLA; many students who are not of the primary ethnicity of most of the members of the organizations are welcomed in, and belong to, those organizations.

Within the context of their sexual identity development—and based on the Cass (1979) and Fassinger (1998) models described—LGBT students will likely seek community during one specific stage and rise to an identified leadership position in another. What is not known is in which community an LGBT student might establish connection and participation. In LGBT organizations, students may explore their sexual identities perhaps in conjunction with, or separate from, their racial, ethnic, or religious identities. Because students are often at different developmental stages, disagreement about activities and agendas is often prevalent in such organizations. Whether or not they acknowledge their sexual/gender identity openly, LGBT students on campus will find a community in which to participate, and they may rise to leadership positions within that community.

HOW CAN LGBT STUDENT LEADERS LEARN TO LEAD DIFFERENTLY?

Leadership skills are often learned by emulating leaders within one's communities of origin, as evidenced by student leaders.

As a Latina I have seen how my community has organized to fight against discrimination to bring equality. At home I learned the importance of fighting for what one believes in, how every little bit counts. At age 14 I attended my first conference on racism and street violence in inner-city communities. I guess I've inherited the activist gene from my grandmother. (Submitted by Maria Guerrero, UCLA undergraduate co-chair, La Familia)

I'm from a community I guess you would call white and privileged. I learned to be involved from my parents. Parents in my hometown were all involved with the school, working for issues that affected their children. They appeared to feel a real sense of stewardship for their kids. (Submitted by Sally Green, University of Michigan co-chair, graduate student network)

I come from Singapore, and things are slightly different there. Our racial/ethnic community groups tended to be self-help groups that helped less affluent members. The emphasis there was on personal/community/economic advancement as opposed to lobbying for the political interests of the ethnic groups. (Submitted by Siew Chye Phua, UCLA co-chair, Anderson Business School LGBT student group)

Similarly, when LGBT students seek out the LGBT community, they learn leadership by emulating their LGBT leaders—and that has been a problem historically. Stevens (1992) described the phenomenon. "The history of the gay and lesbian movement is punctuated with controversies that have rocked our organizations and that have caused our leaders to resign in rage and haste" (p. 33). Stevens noted that the LGBT community has suffered—and unfortunately modeled—several non-productive leadership habits: lack of inclusion of women, people of color, differently abled, poor, bisexual, and transgender people; hierarchical leadership that is individual or board-driven without the voices of those supposed to be served; and a kind of cannibalism where leaders are criticized without constructive feedback, embarrassed and demoralized, chewed up and spit out without a Plan B in mind.

Dreher (1996) noted that because of all the posturing, posing, and public relations, people often become cynical about their leaders. This seems to be the case in the LGBT community. In addition, Outcalt (1998) described a pattern typical of campus LGBT organizations:

The cycle is all too common: Men and women, full of enthusiasm, organize a lesbian, gay, bisexual, and transgender group on campus. The group flourishes for a year or two, attracting new members and racking up accomplishments. However, the group eventually withers as burnout and infighting set in. Finally, the group disbands, often leaving behind an impressive record but disaffected and unhappy former members. Indeed, this phenomenon is often a typical scenario with non-LGBT groups as well. (p. 329)

Leaders must possess integrity, good process skills, effective delegating skills, the ability to empower the team, and the vision and courage to move forward. Appropriate leadership skills should be modeled by campus leaders and taught to students—including LGBT students—so they may learn to lead with integrity and with love for community. Student leaders must be taught to lead through service, to build community rather than empires, and to be mindfully inclusive of those who identities may be invisible. Organization members must learn not to objectify their leaders but to share in a process of getting to know one another. All must learn to lead—and to follow—with love. This is non-hierarchical leadership in action.

LGBT LEADERSHIP ON CAMPUS

Leadership programs for all students must include the powerful components of heightened intercultural awareness as well as understanding and acceptance of differences (Zimmerman-Oster & Burkhardt 1999). LGBT students cross all borders of race, ethnicity, religion, socioeconomics, and ability; therefore, sexual orientation and gender identity issues must be included within the context of cultural awareness. Additionally, LGBT students should not be erroneously relegated to LGBT organizations when, in fact, assimilation of LGBT students—many of whom are still closeted—into predominantly non-LGBT campus organizations is the norm. This is precisely why, as stated previously, it is not unusual to find LGBT students in fraternities, on intercollegiate varsity teams, in student government, and elsewhere in typical campus organizations.

Students would benefit from campus leadership training programs that create experiences that increase self-awareness, solve problems, discover the meaning of leadership, and learn to help others through self-directed or community- or agency-initiated efforts. Kiechel (1992) noted that the principal aim of a leader is to take seriously the fulfillment of those being led. The leader listens to constituents, maintains a willingness to share in mistakes, allows herself or himself to be vulnerable, and sees herself or himself as a steward of the organization. Senge (1990, p. 12) noted that "leaders' sense of stewardship operates on two levels: stewardship for the people they lead and stewardship for the larger mission or purpose that underlies the enterprise."

THE UCLA MODEL OF LGBT LEADERSHIP: THE LGBT STUDENT LEADER ROUNDTABLE

"Leadership teams encourage flexibility. Instead of staying in the same role, one person may play many positions. The harmony of many people working together multiplies our power, with dramatic improvements in quality and productivity" (Dreher 1996, pp. 145–146).

The UCLA LGBT Student Leader Roundtable is a program that brings LGBT students together, establishes dialogue among the very diverse LGBT organizations, and fosters community and collaboration among these groups. For the first time, leaders of LGBT organizations as well as LGBT leaders from non-LGBT organizations are talking together, learning from one another, sharing their joys and their disappointments with one another, and building community.

The LGBT Student Leader Roundtable is patterned after the University of Michigan 2017 leadership program. A place is reserved on the roundtable for the leader of every LGBT organization on campus. In addition, any LGBT student who is the leader of a non-LGBT organization may participate. Finally, from the non-hierarchical perspective that everyone is a leader, any student who perceives herself or himself a leader, with or without organizational affiliation, may participate on the roundtable. All participants must commit to attend a fall retreat and monthly meetings throughout the academic year.

Appreciating All Participants

Leadership is taught experientially through active participation on the roundtable. There are four components to the process: (1) the identification of new leaders, whether or not in organizations, at the end of the spring quarter; (2) the fall retreat, where leadership becomes internalized; (3) the monthly meeting, where leadership is updated and validated; and (4) an end- of-the-year celebration event. This process is designed to promote communication, camaraderie, and understanding among the student leaders and, where appropriate, the organizations that they serve. It is a model designed to teach that such interaction among leaders and organizations is positive, that organizations in conflict with one another take away power and love from the greater good of the community, that communities are stronger when there is collaboration among organizations, and that most organizations have far more similarities than differences. As described by Komives, Lucas, and McMahon (1998, p. 19), everyone on the roundtable makes sure that "the environment is open to learning, making mistakes, and sharing knowledge." The LGBT student leaders build relationships with one another as leaders, paving the way for collaboration and community-building. From the roundtable experience, students model leadership behaviors, thereby teaching others to build community as they themselves are doing.

Spring Quarter

UCLA operates under the quarter system. Student leaders are encouraged to work with their organizations to identify, vote on, or somehow select new leaders for the coming academic year before the 5th week of the spring quarter. Once new leaders are identified, a meeting is scheduled with them during the 8th week so that they meet one another, learn about participation and responsibilities with the Roundtable, and initiate the strategic planning of their organizations if they are so affiliated.

Fall Retreat

The fall retreat occurs the weekend before the first quarter of the academic year. Woven throughout the weekend are leadership activities that share the values of non-hierarchical leadership. The LGBT student leaders spend Friday afternoon and evening learning about one another by sharing their coming-out stories. They spend individual and group time discovering the invisible identities that inform who they are and how they know and grow as leaders. On Saturday they explore personal visions for themselves and for their organizations. They also learn about the importance of a shared vision and mission by the stakeholders—the members—of their organizations and about leading through service to their communities. On Sunday they practice the non-hierarchical concepts of leading with love and with integrity.

Monthly Meetings

The LGBT Student Leader Roundtable meets once a month for two hours. During the first hour student leaders share calendars, issues, problems, and successes. They use one another as a support system to deal with issues at hand, although they are encouraged to meet with one another between meetings when organizational or campus issues arise. During the second hour they dialogue about leadership training and development and about theories of leadership with emphasis on the social change model. Occasionally, a guest speaker visits the group.

Spring Celebration

At the end of the spring quarter, the leaders meet for a celebration where they share their successes—and their disappointments—with one another. They receive encouragement to remain connected to one another both while they remain on campus and when they leave campus as future leaders in LGBT or other communities.

CREATING COMMUNITY

The purpose of community-building among LGBT student groups is not to make every LGBT group alike but to acknowledge and appreciate their differences. LGBT students must understand clearly the concepts of diversity within their common-ground realm of sexual/gender identity. McIntosh (1989) described the "difficulties and dangers surrounding the task of finding parallels." "Since racism, sexism, and heterosexism are not the same, the advantaging associated with them should not be seen as the same. In addition, it is hard to disentangle aspects of unearned advantage which rest more on social class, economic class, race, religion, sex, and ethnic identity than on other factors. Still, all of the oppressions are interlocking" (p. 12). As students learn about each other's organizations and communities, they also learn about the interlocking oppressions that they both experience and inflict. As they learn from one another, they also teach their members.

According to Taoist leadership theory (Dreher 1996, p. 119), a wise leader creates an environment that promotes community; sets agendas that open people up to participate; encourages members to take responsibility; and gets people to work together. The roundtable offers non-hierarchical leadership development for LGBT students and, as a result, also works to create a more supportive community for LGBT students in general.

"Leaders must have the courage to follow their vision, to believe in the invisible, to work for something that's still only a possibility" (Dreher 1996, p. 138). The LGBT Student Leader Roundtable encourages student leaders to develop and practice such courage so that when they leave UCLA, they are prepared to lead with integrity not only in their home communities but also in their local and national LGBT organizations.

CONSIDERATIONS WHEN PLANNING LGBT STUDENT LEADERSHIP TRAINING

Leadership training for LGBT student leaders is valuable in any college or university, but it is especially viable on campuses that have multiple LGBT student organizations. This has to do primarily with the number of potential trainees, the issues addressed, and the training methods utilized.

On small campuses or campuses with only one LGBT organization, training may be done informally or in brief meetings between center staff and student leaders. On campuses with many organizations, more formal sessions are required, utilizing more interactive training methods, such as structured experiences. One of the goals in the larger formats, after all, is to promote harmony and cooperation among organizations and student leaders.

Leaders on smaller or less progressive campuses need help in understanding ways of dealing with their isolation and with limited resources. They may need personal support as well as instruction in how to identify and forge alliances with potential allies, both on campus and in the community. Since they are able to draw upon a relatively small number of students, they may benefit from instruction about strategies designed to rank priorities and keep the number and scope of goals realistic.

On campuses that are larger, have multiple organizations, or are more progressive, resources are less likely to be limited. Student leaders in these circumstances still need to know how to plan and to be selective, but they also need to learn how to identify which of their goals are shared by other organizations, how to work collaboratively with them, and how to share valuable resources while doing so.

It is very important that LGBT student leaders are included in general leadership training activities sponsored by the student affairs operations on almost all college campuses. This provides a wonderful opportunity for all student leaders to be educated about the lives and concerns of LGBT people as well the importance of all kinds of diversity for student organizations. There may be LGBT students taking part in the training as representatives of other student organizations. This is valuable, too, especially if those students are comfortable self-identifying as LGBT during the training activities. But nothing substitutes in these circumstances for the presence of the leaders of clubs and organizations whose raison d'etre is education, service, social, and political activities in and about the LGBT community.

Several activities commonly found in general leadership training enterprises are equally useful, perhaps in some instances customized, in sessions aimed specifically at LGBT student leaders. These include group dynamics, personal style and management style (perhaps utilizing the Myers–Briggs Type Indicator or other similar measure with implications concerning leadership), and the uses and abuses of power. These instruments and ideas may be the most effective when students are sequestered at a retreat specifically to help build their leadership skills.

Case Study 16.1
The Generation Q Retreat at USC

In 1996, the University of Southern California Gay, Lesbian, Bi Student Service Advisory Board was reviewing the annual report from the previous year and discussing ways to further institutionalize the presence of a strong and visible GLB community on campus. Having a compilation of staff and student members from various disciplines, the idea of a retreat came up. A sub-committee was formed, and the work of brainstorming and coordinating a new program began.

Student leadership for both undergraduate and graduate programming had been inconsistent over the years. Staff support had been available but inconsistently utilized. Some student leaders possessed excellent organizational skills, while others brought more of a sense of inspiration than direction to the cause. The plan for a leadership retreat involved soliciting a commitment from both students and staff. The goals were to:

- facilitate self-development
- develop student leadership
- collect and build cohesion among a diverse group
- elicit a commitment for involvement in USC community/GLB community at large
- utilize facilitators who are committed to mentoring relationships with students
- access student funding for leadership programming
- have students pay a nominal fee for participation

Workshops were developed with gender balancing as much as possible. Evaluations of all aspects of the program were completed, and the feedback was strongly influential in the development of the Second Annual Generation Q Retreat. The Division of Student Affairs acknowledged and honored the Gen Q Committee with an award for one of the best and most innovative programs of the 1996–1997 academic year. Both staff and students were part of the previous year's retreat took part in the leadership. New members were invited, strengthening the graduate student and permanent staff base for this type of activity. The second retreat occurred with a heightened sense of camaraderie in the spring of 1998. The successful programming reflected the multicultural fabric of our community, and a talent show on Saturday night was a shining success in showcasing some of the many talents of the participants. (Submitted by Mary Andres and Elizabeth Davenport, USC)

Chapter 17

LGBT Peer Counselors

Christine Browning and Patricia Walsh

The human rights of lesbian, gay, and bisexual people and their families are the subject of debate in virtually all public and private institutions from government and education to religion, media, business, and families. This debate has a profound impact on the experience that students have living both in society and in their educational experiences. There is a need on university and college campuses to ensure that the quality of a student's education is not diminished because of his or her sexual orientation. Until recently there have been very few support services and/or educational programs designed to address some of these inequities. In this chapter, we discuss one program within a campus LGBT resource center that seeks to enhance the educational and quality of life experiences of lesbian, gay, or bisexual (LGB) students.

The University of California, Irvine (UCI) has had a lesbian, gay, and bisexual student group that provides regular meetings designed to encourage students to socialize and break down the isolation that many LGB students experience on campus. In reality, the student leaders of this group were often requested to serve in capacities beyond organizing and sustaining a student club. For example, student leaders were often sought by students to help them in dealing with coming-out issues and personal crises. They were asked to organize panels to talk about their life experiences for classes and residence halls. In addition, the students also wanted to produce educational programs for themselves to better understand issues that they were experiencing as young gay, lesbian, and bisexual adults. For a student group to serve the diverse needs of the LGB student body as well as educate the non-gay campus community was an overwhelming burden and often pushed the group to the brink of disaster. As a result, the student group often had difficulty sustaining itself. Although the campus Counseling Center offers individual counseling and support groups for LGB students, there are many students who are concerned about seeking psychological assistance in a professional setting. Cultural attitudes about mental health issues that sometimes prevent students from obtaining psychological services. The Counseling Center staff also provides educational programs to the campus community about LGB issues and heterosexism, but most of these requests come from staff, not student groups.

It was apparent that there was a need on campus for a program that would address the educational needs for the campus population as well as provide support for LGB and questioning students. Ideally, the program would be a direct link between the student population and campus and community resources. The UCI Peer Counseling/Education Program in Lesbian, Gay, and Bisexual Issues started in the 1994–1995 academic year, the same year that the campus created the LGBT Resource Center. The program is a collaborative effort between the UCI Counseling Center and the UCI LGBT Resource Center. The UCI Counseling Center provides the faculty for instruction and supervision, and the UCI LGBT Resource Center provides on-site supervision, peer office space, and administrative support.

CAMPUS CLIMATE FOR LGB STUDENTS

Campus life for the LGB student is often a lonely and alienating experience. A student's first exposure to university life is usually through campus orientation or residence hall programs that are typically geared toward meeting the needs of heterosexual students. On most campuses, there is little validation or recognition of students who are not heterosexual. For many students, coming to college presents an opportunity to explore their sexual orientation. LGB students are challenged with finding community support and resources to assist in their identity development.

Developing a healthy lesbian, gay, or bisexual identity within the context of a hostile campus climate can be stressful. Waldo (1998) reported that most LGB students perceive the academic climate as hostile. For example, LGB students are often the targets of anti-gay harassment and violence. D'Augelli (1992) found that 77% of LGB students had experienced verbal insults and that 27% were threatened with physical violence because of their sexual orientation. Actual physical assaults were experienced by 6% of LGB students, while property damage occurred to 13%. The perpetrators in these incidents were most frequently other students. Students do not generally report their experiences to authorities because they fear disclosure, have concerns about negative responses by police or other campus authorities, or lack information about how to report such incidents.

For many students, the coming-out process is very stressful. Among young people who have sought help, stress caused from verbal and physical abuse has been associated with academic problems, substance abuse, running away, high-risk sexual behaviors, and suicide among lesbian, gay, and bisexual youth (Savin-Williams 1994). More common responses to the coming-out process include feelings of alienation, loneliness, fear, anxiety, and depression.

LGB PEER COUNSELING/EDUCATION PROGRAM GOALS

The LGB Peer Counseling/Education Program reflects the mission of the LGBT Resource Center, which seeks to enhance the quality of campus life for LGB students by providing resources and support for individual student development. The peer program strives to minimize the stress related to coming out by providing support and educational programs designed to improve the campus climate by providing accurate information about the lives of LGB people.

The goals of the program are to reduce heterosexism through educational programs about LGB issues and to provide outreach and peer counseling support to students who are coming out, questioning their sexual orientation, or seeking to understand gay, lesbian, or bisexual friends or family members. Philosophically, the program recognizes the interconnections between all forms of discrimination and oppression, including sexism, racism, classism, ageism, anti-Semitism, and other prejudices. This understanding is embedded in peer training and delivery of services. Although peer counselors receive some training on transgender issues, the program does not currently address the unique needs of transgender students. Peer counselors are informed about resources available in the community that are better suited to meet the medical, psycho-social, and support needs of transgender students.

PEER SELECTION

Students are selected to be peers who reflect the diverse campus population in gender, sexual orientation, race and ethnicity, peer group affiliations, and academic interests. In addition, peer selection is based on the student's perceived approachability, willingness to learn, maturity, ability to take initiative, and communication skills. During their individual interviews, the applicants are asked questions about what they believe are pertinent issues faced by LGB college students as well as what concerns heterosexual students have about LGB issues. They are also asked about differences between LGB people based on culture and gender. Furthermore, previous experience in providing service to others and their interpersonal style in group interactions are assessed. Applicants are also provided information that might affect their desire to become peer counselors. For example, regardless of their sexual orientation, peers must be willing to be open about their identities when they are doing workshops or talking with students seeking help. For some, this might result in negative reactions from their friends, classmates, and sometimes family members who might learn about their sexual orientation because of their association with the program. By raising these issues, peers can make an informed choice about whether the program is right for them at this time in their lives.

Ten to 12 students are selected in the spring quarter for the following academic year. Students are required to make a commitment to the program for an academic year. They receive academic credit for each quarter and the classes are graded. This is an essential part of the program. By providing academic credit, students are rewarded for their contribution. The formal class structure also provides a method to ensure that all the peer counselors share the same basic knowledge. It also allows for a structured supervision process to monitor the delivery of counseling and educational services provided by the peer counselors.

A few aspects of the selection process that are especially important to note. The diversity of the peer group with respect to sexual orientation, gender, and ethnicity is critical. Typically, more heterosexual students apply to the program than LGB students. This may reflect that some LGB students have concerns about being open on campus as well as their developmental "readiness" to assist others when they may be in the midst of their own coming-out process. The heterosexual students are in an excellent position to model for other heterosexual students how to be allies to the LGB community. In addition, sometimes students who are in the early stages of coming out are afraid to speak to an LGB peer counselor for reasons related to their own internalized homophobia. Providing a positive experience with a heterosexual ally usually leads to the student's greater comfort in meeting with other LGB peer counselors or students.

Sexual orientation diversity within the class enriches the learning experience as well. Some of the negative experiences that LGB peer counselors have had with heterosexual friends and family may be mediated by being understood and accepted by the heterosexual peer counselors. Similarly, the presence of students from different ethnic and racial backgrounds allows the students to learn from each about the complex interaction of sexual orientation with race, ethnicity, and culture. Gender differences are also explored within the context of the student's sexual orientation as well as their gender-role socialization.

PEER TRAINING

Peers are trained in basic counseling, outreach and consultation skills, and issues related to boundaries and confidentiality. They also study LGB psychology and information from other academic disciplines (e.g., history, literature, and queer studies). Throughout the academic year, peer counselors learn about many topics, including: LGB identity models; gender and ethnicity influences on the coming-out process; the psychological impact of anti-gay violence and harassment; relationship and family issues; historical and contemporary theories about sexual orientation; religious issues; transgender issues; sexuality and safer-sex information; LGB health concerns; LGB history; career and employment issues; international perspectives; and mid-life and aging issues. Videos, guest speakers, class assignments, readings, and lectures are the primary methods of instruction.

Specific experiential exercises that focus on skill development are also required. For example, peer counselors attend off-campus community events to assess the appropriateness of these community resources for referrals. They interview students with sexual orientations different from their own about their coming-out process and compare this with what they have learned about the models of coming out. The peer counselors also interview LGB people at mid-life and older. Peer counselors participate in scavenger hunts in order to familiarize themselves with local resources and write social action letters to companies, politicians, or the media to respond to positive or negative actions directed toward the LGBT community. Peer counselors also learn how to design and implement educational workshops and to increase their knowledge of campus, local, and national resources. In the first quarter, peer counselors work in teams to develop a workshop that will be delivered to campus audiences in the winter and spring quarters. Members of the class provide feedback about their workshops.

Peer counselors also learn about workshop and public speaking by attending other campus workshops and noting the strength and weaknesses of these presentations. Peer counselors learn about peer counseling via lectures on communication skills, problem-solving techniques, and how to make effective referrals. The peer counselors participate in role-playing depicting situations that are commonly experienced by students, their friends, and families (e.g., coming out to roommates, learning that one's parent is gay, lesbian, or bisexual, coming out to self).

An important aspect of peer training is education about issues of confidentiality and boundaries between peer counselors and students. Since the openly LGB community tends to be small on campus, it is highly likely that a peer will interact with students in settings outside the peer counseling office. This requires that peer counselors be very careful about maintaining appropriate boundaries with those who have sought their help. Although the peer counselors are not professional counselors and not required to adhere to any professional standards, the peer counselors are expected to maintain a high degree of professionalism in how they approach their work.

It is important for peer counselors to understand the unique role that they play in a student's life and behave in a manner that protects the student's welfare. Clear boundaries must exist between the peer counselor and the student. For example, peer counselors are instructed never to meet with a student outside the LGBT Resource Center. When peers are providing counseling, it is in a designated, private space within the LGBT Resource Center. The peer counselors must not initiate or agree to meet a student socially. If a peer counselor sees a student at a social event, the peer must respect the student's confidentiality and not refer to their helping relationship or disclose to others information about the student obtained from their peer counseling relationship.

Students seeking help are generally in need and emotionally vulnerable; consequently, the relationship that they develop with a peer counselor is not equal. For example, because the peer counselor does not disclose his or her personal problems and seek consultation from the student, the peer counselor generally knows a great deal more about the student than the student knows about the peer. It might be easy for the peer counselor to inadvertently exploit the student's vulnerability by becoming romantically interested in the student and seek to get to know the student apart from the helping relationship. It is critical to the credibility of the peer counselor and the program that this does not occur. In addition, confidentiality is stressed in the supervision section of the class. When peer counselors are discussing their peer counseling interactions in supervision, the students' identities are not revealed. This is done in order to protect possible relationships that students might have with other peer counselors.

Another training component regarding confidentiality is helping peers to explain the confidentiality guidelines to students seeking help. Occasionally, students seeking help request that the peer counselors do not tell anyone about what they disclose. In a worst-case example, this could be information about a suicide plan or an intention to hurt someone. Obviously, the peer counselors cannot agree to keep secrets. The peer counselors must be prepared to explain to students that they work under supervision by a psychologist and that supervision is conducted in a group setting. In addition, just as in a professional setting, the peer counselor must help the student understand that the peer must discuss any information that a student might share that relates to possible harm to himself or herself or others. If the student does not agree to this, the peer counselor must refer the student to another helping resource. Although this situation does not occur frequently, it is prudent for the peer counselors to be prepared. In general, most students have expressed comfort in knowing that the peer counselors are being closely supervised.

Peer counselors are also encouraged to attend training opportunities offered by regional and national organizations. For example, peer counselors have attended the National Gay and Lesbian Task Force annual Creating Change conference and the University of California system-wide annual conference on LGBT issues. Local conferences sponsored by other colleges and universities, Parents and Friends of Lesbians and Gays (PFLAG), the Gay and Lesbian Alliance against Defamation (GLAAD), and the Gay Lesbian Straight Educators Network (GLSEN) are also sources of additional training. (See Appendix I) All of these opportunities help to broaden the peer counselors' understanding of the various activities that LGBT organizations emphasize and create occasions for networking with other LGBT activists.

Peer counselors begin providing services to the campus community in the winter quarter. In addition to continued training on LGB issues, the winter and spring quarter classes also include a supervision component on their work in providing peer counseling and educational programs. During the fall quarter, peer counselors from the previous years volunteer hours to provide peer counseling until the new peers are ready.

RELATIONSHIP BETWEEN THE LGBT RESOURCE CENTER AND THE PEER PROGRAM

The peer program is co-sponsored by the LGBT Resource Center and reflects the center's mission to foster a safe and supportive work and learning environment for all LGBT students, faculty, and staff; to increase LGBT student retention and graduation; and to decrease the harmful effects of discrimination based on sexual orientation and gender identity. The peer counselors work in collaboration with the other LGBT Resource Center staff, which consists of the center director, student interns, and volunteers. The interns and volunteers have various levels of expertise, experience and understanding about LGBT issues.

The fall quarter is a time when the peer counselors, interns, and volunteers are all learning about LGBT issues. The director facilitates the staff's basic understanding of the mission of the center. This includes understanding how heterosexism manifests within the university environment; university policy regarding sexual orientation; civil rights and barriers; and specific information about sexual orientation and gender identity. As a team, the peer counselors, interns, and volunteers work together to promote the center's mission and goals. For example, the staff must know how to assist students who report incidents of harassment or hate crimes within the university system.

One important dynamic within the LGBT Resource Center is how the peer counselors, interns, and volunteers provide support and learn from each other. The camaraderie that develops between the staff helps to create a welcoming environment within the LGBT Resource Center for visitors. Throughout the year, the peer counselors spend two hours per week providing office hours in the LGBT Resource Center. In the winter and spring quarter, the office hours also serve as the peer counselor's drop-in counseling hours. During the office hours, the peer counselors become familiar with the resources within the Resource Center, answer telephone calls, welcome students, and participate in projects.

The director works closely with peer counselors to supervise their on-site work. The Director meets with the peer counselors individually to determine their interests and match their interests and skills with specific Center needs or projects. For example, peer counselors have created resource manuals for specific LGBT issues or populations (e.g., Asian American AIDS resources; African American LGB support groups), organized the book and film library, created advertising materials for the Resource Center, and conducted a needs assessment for LGB students in housing.

One of the LGBT Resource Center's educational objectives is to assist academic departments, student organizations, and other campus groups to enhance and improve the campus climate for LGBT students, faculty, and staff. To this end, the director serves as a consultant to individuals or groups that request services, including diversity training. The director determines the level of intervention that is appropriate to the request. If the intervention is determined appropriate for peer counselor involvement (i.e., a workshop or panel presentation), then the director works with the peer counselors to develop an intervention.

SERVICES TO THE CAMPUS

The peers provide LGB-related workshops and panel discussions to campus organizations, classes, and residence halls. Often student groups request these workshops. Peer counselor may also develop their own workshop topics and present them on campus. Some of the common workshops are entitled, "Coming out Gay, Lesbian, or Bisexual on Campus"; "Ethnic Identity and Gay, Lesbian, Bisexual Issues"; "Friends and Family of Gay, Lesbian, Bisexual People"; and "Dismantling Myths and Stereotypes about Homosexuality and Bisexuality." Upon request, workshops can also be developed for a specific audience (e.g., LGB issues in the workplace, training for residence hall staff, LGB issues in the Athletics Department).

The peer counselors may also facilitate discussion and support groups. For example, the peer counselors have arranged an LGB film series and discussion and facilitated a lesbian and bisexual women's discussion group and an Asian queer support group. Peer counselors have participated in campus radio shows and written articles for the campus LGBT newspaper. Peer counselors have also been involved in programs that arise after a specific local or national event. For example, after Matthew Shepard's murder, peer counselors were involved in providing campus debriefing sessions and assisted in the planning for a campus-wide memorial service. Additionally, peer counselors have represented the LGBT Resource Center at diversity conferences at local high schools.

Peer counselors meet with students individually during their office hours. Typically, students seek peer counseling when they are in an early stage of the coming-out process. Students often have a lot of questions about whether or not they are gay, lesbian, or bisexual; how to disclose their sexual orientation to others; and how to become involved in the LGB community. Concerns about conflicts between religious and/or cultural values and their sexual orientation are common. Relationship difficulties or breakups may also cause a student to seek support from a peer counselor.

Occasionally, a student will be seeking information about how to "change" their sexual orientation. Heterosexual students may also seek support to better understand an LGB friend or family member who may have come out to them. The peer counselors are trained to know their limitations in providing counseling. They are informed about how to make referrals to the Counseling Center, Health Center, or other relevant resources. When a student is in crisis or is suicidal, the peer counselor helps the student by arranging an appointment at the Counseling Center.

There are various levels of supervision that a peer counselor can access in a crisis situation. The LGBT Resource Center director is the first line of support, followed by the Counseling Center staff. Peer counselors never meet with students when they are alone in the center. There is always another staff member available to assist.

The amount of actual peer counseling experience that peers have is directly related to the amount of visibility that the program has achieved through the workshop outreach programs and advertising efforts on campus. Another method to address the needs of individual students has been through the peer counselors' E-mail address. The mail received via this E-mail address is first screened by the program coordinator and then assigned to a peer counselor. The peer counselor usually requests that a student come to the center to discuss his or her concerns more thoroughly. If a student is uncomfortable meeting at the LGBT Resource Center because of fear of being seen by others, arrangements have been made to meet the student at the Center for Women and Gender Education. A peer counselor may not meet with a student at any other location. This is to ensure privacy, confidentiality, and safety for both the peer and the studeÏfthrough these methods the peer counselors have been able to reach thousands of students who might not have been exposed to sexual orientation issues. They also have been able to talk with students who may have been reluctant to seek professional counseling. After speaking with a peer, students are more likely to use other support systems. Lastly, participating in this experience enhances the peer counselors' personal growth. Those who identify as LGB benefit from being in a position to help others and to affirm their own identities. Their leadership role on the campus provides recognition that sexual orientation issues are valued within the university community. Peer counselors also feel empowered by their ability to make social change through education and through their interventions with individual students.

SUMMARY

Those who are interested in establishing a peer counseling/education program should consider what resources are available on their campuses to support the program. Campus size, availability of a staff office to support the program, and competent supervision and training of peer counselors are important considerations. This program may also be modified to work within a community agency serving an LGBT population. A few issues to consider when planning a program are whether or not to include transgender individuals and/or address transgender issues, whether or not to grant academic credit, the content of training, advertising strategies, selection criteria for peers, and liability issues regarding the conduct of the peer counselors. It is especially important that the peer counselors not represent themselves as therapists but rather as informed peers who are providing support, resources, and referrals.

The benefits of this type of program are significant. Beyond the obvious contribution that the peer counselors make, the structure of the program results in highly educated students capable and confident about addressing LGB issues in society. The personal growth that they experience by the end of the year is meaningful.

One of the closing activities that peers are asked to do each year is to write a letter to the other peer counselors dated five years into the future. In this letter they are asked to address how they will incorporate their experience as peer counselors into their lives. Invariably, all peer counselors regardless of their sexual orientation, are able to imagine how they will be able to further enhance society's understanding of LGB issues and individuals through their future careers. Whether their career goal is in the mental health field, teaching, ministry, medicine, government, or business, peer counselors are able to articulate how they will always communicate what they have learned to others. In this way, it is our hope that the LGB Peer Counseling/Education Program will make an ongoing contribution to the elimination of heterosexism in society.

Chapter 18

Lavender Graduation: Acknowledging the Lives and Achievements of LGBT College Students

For decades students at many colleges and universities around the country have been celebrating both their academic achievements and their cultural heritages at specialized commencement events (Weiss, 1998). Many of these events are student-initiated. They are "designed to provide a sense of community for minority students who, they say, often reel from culture shock" (Weiss 1998, p. A1). at their impersonalized institutions. For many it is the payoff for staying in school. Friends and families find the smaller, more ethnic ceremonies both meaningful and personal.

College students who are lesbian, gay, bisexual, and transgender (LGBT) often have a difficult time fitting into the mainstream of college life throughout their college careers. Even at the most liberal institutions, LGBT students are an invisible population, often forgotten at best and summarily rejected at worst (Sanlo 2000). Lavender Graduation is a cultural celebration designed to recognize LGBT students of all races and ethnicities and to acknowledge their achievements and contributions to the university as students who survived the college experience. Through such recognition LGBT students may leave the university with a positive last experience of the institution, thereby encouraging them to become involved mentors for current students as well as contributing alumni. In addition, Lavender Graduation was designed to support an institution's mission of excellent service to students that enhances their academic achievement. It tells LGBT students that they matter .

There are no data that describe a positive celebratory event in the lives of LGBT college students. Lavender Graduation is an event to which LGBT students look forward, where they not only share their hopes and dreams with one another but also are officially recognized by the institution for their leadership and their successes and achievements. An exhaustive review of the literature revealed no research regarding programs that addressed the achievements of LGBT students regardless of race or ethnicity. There are some data regarding the needs of LGBT college students (D'Emilio 1990; Evans & Wall 1991; McNaron 1991; Shepard, Yeskell, & Outcalt 1995; Sanlo 1998b), yet there is little research on LGBT issues among college students in general and nothing that specifically discovers or discusses achievement. Although Baxter Magolda (1992) and others have written about college students' ways of knowing, nothing has been written about the ways of knowing among LGBT students.

There is scant literature that describes celebratory experiences within LGBT culture. Indeed, there is little that describes LGBT culture at all. Most LGBT students experience the culture of their racial, ethnic, national, or religious backgrounds, but rarely experience a university-supported event directly associated with their college lives. The celebration event itself provides significant impact on the lives of students.

THE HISTORY

While working as the director of the LGBT Campus Resource Center at the University of Michigan, I realized that LGBT students needed and, in fact, deserved to be recognized not only for their achievements but for surviving their college years. As commencement activities were being planned for the spring of 1995, I saw an opportunity to include LGBT students in the celebration process. I noticed that many of the ethnic groups were hosting their own ceremonies, so why not something for LGBT students? I had heard from too many LGBT students that they simply didn't feel connected to the institution or to their various ethnic groups to want to participate in any commencement ceremony. Their journeys through college as out LGBT women and men had been painful enough, they said; they just wanted to quietly leave.

I happen to be a Jewish lesbian. I love rituals and celebrations. I was not invited to my own biological children's graduation celebrations because of my sexual orientation, so I felt a pain similar to that of my students and I wanted to ease it, however possible. With encouragement from Royster Harper, the then associate vice president for student affairs at Michigan, I designed a celebration just for LGBT students and called it Lavender Graduation. (Lavender is important to LGBT history because it is a combination of the color of the pink triangle that gay men were forced to wear in Nazi concentration camps and the black triangle that lesbians had to wear as they were raped in the Nazi Spring of Life homes. The LGBT civil rights movement took these symbols of hatred and combined them to make symbols and color of power and community.)

At the first Lavender Graduation at the University of Michigan in 1995 there were only 5 graduates and 3 attendees. Although it was a great idea, students said, it was just too frightening, too visible a ceremony for them to feel safe in attending. The 1996 event was a little larger. By 1997, there were 18 graduates, and nearly 100 people in attendance, including parents, and the speakers included both the vice president and associate vice president for student affairs. When I became the director of the UCLA LGBT Campus Resource Center in September 1997, I immediately developed the first UCLA Lavender

Graduation for the spring 1998 commencement. There were 27 graduates and nearly 300 people in attendance.

As chair of the National Consortium of Directors of LGBT Resources in Higher Education, I shared the development and process of Lavender Graduation with my colleagues around the country. By 1997 several other campuses had initiated their own Lavender Graduations, and by 1998 at least eight other institutions hosted such celebrations. It is my dream that Lavender Graduation will become an annual event at every major institution in the country, honoring the lives and achievements of our LGBT students. Since LGBT students cross all lines of race, nationality, ethnicity, gender, ability, and socioeconomics, this program provides unique multiple opportunities to present a truly multicultural event while acknowledging a population of students who often succumbed to the plight of invisibility on their campuses.

THE EVENT

Lavender Graduation, developed and presented by the UCLA Lesbian Gay Bisexual Transgender Campus Resource Center, provides a collaborative opportunity throughout the university community to bring people together to recognize LGBT students. For the 1998 ceremony at UCLA, volunteers from many ethnic backgrounds participated in the preparation of this project, especially as advertisements were developed, arrangements made, invitations created, and speakers, musicians, and dignitaries invited. Student affairs professionals were involved by advertising the event to their various units, departments, and students and by attending the event. The LGBT Studies Department presented the LGBT studies minor. The assistant vice chancellor for student and campus life, Dr. Robert Naples, extended official greetings from UCLA; the speaker of the California Assembly, Representative Sheila J. Keuhl, brought greetings from the state of California; and the executive director of the National Gay and Lesbian Task Force, Kerry Lobel, brought greetings from the national movement to the students and their families and friends. The 1999 ceremony had the added features of the music of Vox Femina, an all-women's chorus in Los Angeles, and Betty Degeneres as the keynote speaker. Mayor John Heilman brought greetings from the city of West Hollywood. At the celebration faculty and staff wear robes and proceed into the auditorium. Families and friends are seated as first faculty and staff, then graduating students proceed to their seats. Greetings and speeches are offered, and leadership awards are given. LGBT Studies minor graduates receive a certificate for the completion of the minor. All students receive a rainbow tassel and a Certificate of Distinction. (See Appendix N) A reception for the graduates, their families, friends, and guests follows.

At the 1998 event at UCLA, surveys were placed on each seat in the auditorium. Students were asked to complete the surveys while at the ceremony. They were asked about their expectations of Lavender Graduation and suggestions for future events. Their comments were quite poignant:

It was so inspiring and affirming. I loved it! Thanks for a wonderful memory.

It was like magic. Who would have thought that such an event would take place here as an official UCLA commencement?

I felt very honored to be part of the first Lavender Graduation.

It felt great being here. I felt like my work was worth it, that I finally counted here.

Non-graduating students also expressed their thoughts.

I'm here because I wanted to support and congratulate my friends.

This was so encouraging. I can't wait until my Lavender Graduation.

This was so fantastic! I got chills! I'll be there when I graduate.

Totally inspirational.

THE PROCESS

Lavender Graduation is designed to celebrate the lives and achievement of LGBT people who are graduating from an institution. It is not meant to take the place of the institution's primary commencement ceremonies but to augment the last experiences for a population of students who may have been less than valued in their institution. The purposes of Lavender Graduation are to support the institution's mission of excellent service to students that enhances their academic achievement; to offer a cultural celebration that recognizes LGBT students of all races and ethnicities; and to acknowledge LGBT students' achievements and contributions to the university. Its goal is that LGBT students leave the university with a positive last experience that encourages them to become involved as mentors for current students and become financially contributing alumni.

The following timeline for hosting a Lavender Graduation is based on a June graduation since Lavender Graduations are generally held the same weekend as the institution's commencement and other celebratory services:

October
>Connect with the campus commencement office
>Gather a committee
>Determine the budget

December
>Select date
>Select venue
>Invite speakers

February
>Get catering estimates
>Get photographer estimates
>Select music/musicians

March

Confirm speakers, music, photographer, caterer
Order food, flowers,
Order rainbow tassels (from David at www.goodcatch.com)
Order invitations

April

Call for graduates
Inform students, faculty, and staff of robe availability
First advertisement

May

Solicit Leadership Awards recipients

June

Order leadership plaques
Confirm food, flowers, photographer
Program to printers
Final advertisement
Make Certificates of Distinction
Write your speech!

Speakers for Lavender Graduation may come from many arenas. (See Appendix M). Other cost-effective ideas are:

chancellor/president, vice president/chancellor student affairs, deans, faculty senate chair, LGBT studies chair, faculty, students, alumni association

mayor, LGBT community center director, allies, PFLAG, local activist

Remember to have students speak, perform, or otherwise participate in whatever manner they wish within the time constraints of the event.

The certificate of distinction is not meant to replace one's diploma. It is an understanding that a student survived the university experience while acknowledging her or his sexual and/or gender identity. LGBT students are the strongest survivors, the greatest achievers, and the most gracious people. They deserve to be recognized for successfully enduring. For an example of a certificate see Appendix H. Along with the certificate, each student is given a rainbow tassel which may be obtained in bulk from www.goodcatch.com.

Lavender Graduation serves the special purpose on campus of telling graduating LGBT students that they made a difference. It offers non-graduating LGBT students something to which they may look forward. Each student knows that at UCLA she or he mattered.

Part IV

Maintaining Your Center

Chapter 19

Managing Ancillary Staff

Steven J. Leider

Cullen and Smart (1991) described three stages of being a gay or lesbian person in student affairs:

1. Gay professionals are newly out as lesbian or gay persons and are extremely conscious about their sexual identity. They make the decision to education the world, or at least the student affairs world. They become the people who initiate events, socials, and organizations such as staff groups. They are highly visible and seemingly of a single topic, so much that colleagues are threatened by their presence and begin to isolate them.

2. Gay professionals generally become tokens, people seen as the sole representatives of the gay community. Their ability to serve other parts of the campus community becomes minimized.

3. Gay professionals who are successful at integrating their sexual identity in the workplace and may or may not talk about their sexual orientation. However, they are fully out of the closet and are comfortable bringing their partner to staff social events.

There is one more stage that Cullen and Smart could not, in 1991, have identified within the context of student affairs: the gay-for-pay, according to Candace Gingrich (personal communication, August 1999), or, as Donna Redwing says, the homocrat (keynote speech, Something Queer is Bruin conference, UCLA, February 1998). This is the person who is employed on campus for the sole reason to provide services to the LGBT campus community. This is the LGBT campus resource center director, the person who is finally being paid to do work that she or he was probably fired for doing in other businesses. By virtue of working in an LGBT campus resource center, others, too, especially students, may be classified as gays for pay.

Ideally, an LGBT campus resource center has a full-time professional staff person and a full-time administrative assistant. Because the director is responsible for presenting campus training programs, attending student affairs staff meetings, and otherwise creating visibility for the LGBT campus community, the administrative assistant helps in keeping the consistency of hours and services that work-study students and volunteers may otherwise not be able to do.

Work-study students are wonderful assets for several reasons. First, they are often the voice and the experience of LGBT students on campus and are helpful in understanding what the true campus climate is like from their perspective. Work-study students who are students of color or students with disabilities provide a special mirror from which the faces of many are reflected in the center, creating a more welcoming environment to all.

According to Mitchell (1999), we have a responsibility to treat our work-study students—and all students—with dignity, respect, and equity, even if we strongly disagree on some issues and choices:

Our role is to help them develop skills: listening skills to hear other viewpoints; critical thinking skills to help them make informed choices; speaking and writing skills to help them more effectively engage in meaningful dialogue; human relations skills to help them more effectively interact with people from diverse perspectives and experiences. In this role, we can't afford to wear our own biases, prejudices, political persuasion, and values on our sleeves. (pp. 132-133)

Volunteers, especially those who are students, are a little harder to count on. They may offer their services as a means of connecting with community but are unable, due to school and work, to extend themselves much further. Alumni may be a great source for volunteers, especially as facilitators, development specialists, or advisory board members. The *NGLTF Campus Organizing Manual* (Shepard et al. 1995) suggests that volunteers, whether students or alumni, should be offered interesting tasks in addition to the often mundane chores of the center, and are expected to provide intelligence, initiative, and follow-through. Treat volunteers as equals rather than helpers.

Graduate assistants or graduate-level interns are excellent resources, especially in two issue areas: research projects and student affairs. Graduate students may decide that they wish to study a particular aspect of the LGBT community in the context of the center. With guidance form the director, they may write a grant proposal to a funding agency that would be interested in supporting their project. If the grant is successful, the intern receives the stipend that he or she wrote into the grant. In the context of student affairs, the graduate student may learn the practical, hands-on experience of directing an LGBT campus resource center. There is not yet curriculum developed that teaches a student affairs graduate student how to do the work required in an LGBT center. The graduate student may get the experience necessary to actually be hired by an institution to become its LGBT center director.

When I returned to college as a "non-traditional" student (older than the 18-24 age range of traditional college students), I never dreamed that I'd wind up doing what I now do. When I arrived as a transfer student at UCLA, I found a flyer about a campus office that helped lesbian, gay, bisexual, and transgender students to find both on-campus and off-campus resources that helped to make their lives easier. I thought this was really interesting because, back in the late 1970s when I came out, a number of friends who were undergraduates at UCLA complained of the utter lack of support for gay students. In fact, at the time, one could be dismissed from the university if it were discovered that one was gay or lesbian.

As a gay man who had been out for more than 20 years in Los Angeles and active in a wide variety of LGBT-identified social, cultural, political, and AIDS organizations, I was surprised when I discovered that, at the university, very little was known about these institutions, their purposes, programs, or activities. I realized that I could fill this void in services provided by the UCLA LGBT Campus Resource Center to the UCLA community. My longevity in the wider LGBT community of Los Angeles had equipped me with practical information about local social services and organizations, political organizations, health-care services and providers, cultural institutions, and business enterprises that could help UCLA students, faculty, and staff to lead happier, more productive lives as members of the LGBT community.

This is how I first came to be a volunteer as both an undergraduate and then a graduate student at UCLA. For once, the minutiae that I possessed about the Gay Men's Chorus, the Los Angeles Gay and Lesbian Center (LAGLC), Great Outdoors, and dozens of other organizations came in handy. I was able to help the students with whom I attended classes (and sometimes the professors and staff who taught them) find social organizations that fitted their interests, needs, and talents. Students wishing to perform community service or outreach were directed to Youth Services at LAGLC or Project 10 at L.A. Unified School District. Law students needing internships were directed to the Legal Services Department of LAGLC where I had been a volunteer myself. Those needing anonymous HIV or sexually transmitted diseases (STD) testing were sent to the Men's Clinic at the center, Minority AIDS Project, or AIDS Project L.A. Young men and women seeking social outlets other than bars, clubs, and raves were steered toward Great Outdoors, Los Angeles Tennis Association, Blades Hockey, BikeOut, Gay Men's Chorus of L.A., and countless others.

A STUDENT VOLUNTEER BECOMES A STAFF PERSON

When I started working as an official employee of the university, the change-over from working as a volunteer in the LGBT Campus Resource Center—doing whatever needed to be done whenever I could fit it into my own schedule—was pretty drastic. Suddenly, I was reined in by constraints that hadn't applied to me when I was a student—not being able to do programming (in our office that privilege is limited to students), showing up on a regular, fixed schedule, being treated as an employee instead of a volunteer. For a while it seemed as if I was less valued as an employee than I had been as a volunteer. My boss' busy schedule and the many demands made on her by many facets of the campus community made it all but impossible to find sufficient time to sit down and discuss the sudden changes, new expectations, and general duties that I was to fulfill. Of course, we eventually worked these out together, but my first few weeks were very uncomfortable. As an employee, the greatest difficulty I have in working in the office is the lack of space and equipment. Our office is small and has only one desk. Consequently, I share that desk with three work-study employees, the leaders of a number of student groups, and just about anyone else who wanders in and needs access to a computer. We all use the same computer to perform office work, check E-mail, write papers, do research, and participate in various student organizations and community service. This usually doesn't present a problem except during midterms and finals, when everyone's workload increases dramatically. Although everyone involved has managed to remain civil, tensions sometimes get pretty high. An upcoming move into new, larger quarters will help relieve this problem, as will the increase in the number of computers in the office as a result of donations and purchases. What I most love about working in the LGBT Campus Resource Center is working with the students. I appreciate the transformation that comes over them when they've come into the office seeking out information, or organizations, or a place of belonging, or even just a friendly gay face, and I'm able to help provide that for them. I always remember when I was their age and in their position and places like the LGBT Campus Resource Center didn't yet exist and what I would have given if they had. Remembering that, everything else I do during the day seems easy in comparison.

One of the most important issues with which center staff must be clear is the boundaries they must maintain with the students whom the center serves. Professional staff and graduate students are prohibited from intimate or sexual interaction with students. Undergraduate work-study students may date other students but not those seen as customers of the center. The line is very fine, but the concept of boundaries is excruciatingly important to prevent any sense of power abuse within the center.

When people direct LGBT centers, they both manage and lead. Hopefully, we manage from the heart so that our diverse staff obtain skills and competencies that encourage their growth. And hopefully, we lead with soul that breathes spirit and passion into our organization (Bolman & Deal 1995).

Chapter 20

Creating Visibility and Positive Public Relations

Regardless of how well you publicize your events, services, and existence, it is most likely that the LGBT Center is the best kept-secret on campus. Effective communication about your center increases participation by many populations, enhances the center's image, and generally increases support to, for, and by your center.

The ultimate goal of public relations (PR) is to anticipate change so the group can have programs in place when it comes. Groups that listen carefully to their constituencies can identify emerging trends and needs. At its best, PR is a means for engaging constituents in constructive dialogue (Smith 1994a, p. 198).

According to Smith (1994a, p. 168), public relations is not merely an image-building exercise but actually a two-way set of communications. It begins by listening to your constituents and by developing messages and initiatives that address their concerns. Through public relations, your center sets out to earn praise through good deeds, well-reasoned policies, careful work with the media, and outreach to valuable constituencies.

Research your campus to learn what people think about your center (if anything at all). Host focus groups and use quantitative surveys and qualitative interviews to discover people's thoughts and attitudes about the center. "The research you perform as the outset serves as a benchmark by which to gauge progress over the life of the PR program" (Smith 1994a, p. 172).

You may use many tools to communicate your center's activities, issues, services and programs, and general interest stories. First, use press releases to tell your story. News or press releases may tell your campus you're here, or you've expanded, or you're offering new services; announce accomplishments; report the number of people served or educated over a period of time; announce a large contribution or grant; provide a timely public service message such as asking people at Thanksgiving to host LGBT students; present the center's position on an issue; describe the history of the center when it reaches a milestone; describe a moving story; announce the elections of new officers in student groups; announce the establishment of an advisory council; let your campus know when the center receives an award or recognition or when a staff member is honored or recognized by another group; honor generous donors, volunteers, or allies or outstanding student leaders; advertise a major event; share new survey findings; and present annual progress and goals for the next academic year. The *National Gay and Lesbian Task Force Campus Organizing Manual* (Shepard et al. 1995) is an excellent source for samples of effective press releases.

Second, publish an annual report with photos, charts, and financial information. Use it to document accomplishments and new programs. Share it with your supervisor and with other deans, directors, and department chairs on campus. Be sure your development office has several copies as they solicit LGBT alumni for donations.

Third, speak publicly. The more information you get out about the services of the center, the more often you'll be invited to speak in a variety of on- and off-campus venues. When possible, use videos or slides of your programs and services to enhance your presentation. Obtain student permission to include their photos as well. After you deliver a major speech, broaden the impact by sending a copy of it to the campus paper as well as to alumni and faculty/staff magazines.

Fourth, work with your campus media. When a reporter calls, ask about the topic, ask for time to reflect, call back when you say you will. Respect reporters' deadlines. Make campus media your friends. Be sure you stick with your field of expertise. Resist the temptation to speak on subjects outside of the Center's purview. It's perfectly fine—and sometimes desired since most campus reporters have a three-source rule—to refer the reporter to others.

Fifth, maintain strong community relations. Participate in on- and off-campus information fairs, local walk/run events, community fund-raising events such as an annual AIDS walk, and, of course, the local gay pride parade.

Sixth, be prepared for crisis communications. When a local or national story breaks that affects your students, you need to determine whether and when to talk with the media. It's best to initiate media contact yourself so that you control the flow of information. Communication in a crisis should be limited to verified facts. Speculation is never a good idea; especially not in a crises. You should also inform all constituents in a timely manner. Once the crisis has subsided, meet with the campus crisis team or even your center's advisory board or crisis team to review the experience, consider the need for follow-up, and to thank individuals who were especially helpful. Regarding adverse publicity, criticism is bound to happen from time to time. Give your side of the story without the drama. If charges are made, address them immediately.

When considering whether or how to answer an adverse report, you have to weigh several factors. First, your response may keep in the news an issue that you'd rather have disappear. Dignified silence is often the best course for matters of secondary importance. Second, you could limit the response to correcting factual errors in the spirit of setting the record straight. This approach is wise if the issue is likely to rise again. An aggressive response should be reserved for matters that threaten the integrity of the organization or its constituency. In all cases, the response should be built on facts and reason; emotions tend to be counterproductive (Smith 1994a, p. 194).

Finally, communicate with constituents. College and university students are becoming increasingly skilled in computer use (Barnett & Sanlo 1998). E-mail listservs and newsletters are replacing hard-copy newsletters on campuses. Brochures, flyers, and posters, however, are still useful and usable visual aids in residence halls, commuter buses, and information fairs. Be sure you have a Web site that is easily accessible for students who do not have the fastest modems or state-of-the-art hardware and software. Also be sure that your Web site has information regarding coming out, how to report hate crimes on campus, a calendar of events, a list of student groups and support groups and their locations, and where to find the center.

Chapter 21

Funding and Development

The primary source of funding for campus LGBT centers has been, will most likely continue to be, and, given the nature of these organizations, probably should be the institution's central administrative funds. As the higher education realm becomes more competitive and more corporate, and the related right-sizing and belt-tightening are implemented, obtaining dollars from this source may be considerably more difficult. LGBT centers are not generally or extensively revenue-generating units. That increases the financial responsibility of the central administration. This becomes particularly challenging at institutions that implement responsibility-center budget systems, in which each office or department needs to pay for its own expenses, including compensation to other institutional entities that provide services. With little revenue generated and with dependence on other units for basic services, LGBT centers must have an institutional funding stream.

An additional, substantial problem has resulted from challenges regarding the use of student activity fees (which are separate from tuition). Litigation, for example, brought by conservative students at the University of Wisconsin, a public institution, contended that students should not be required to pay that part of their student fees that supported activities with which they disagree. They claim that students should be allowed to decide how their dollars are deployed. Predictably, LGBT student organizations and LGBT programs were a primary target of the students' wrath. The case, *Southworth v. University of Wisconsin* (Lambda Legal Defense and Education Network, http://www.lambdalegal.org, 2001) was upheld by the U.S. Supreme Court.

Many LGBT centers are heavily dependent on student activity fees. Since most centers are located in their institution's student services operations, which are usually funded almost entirely by student activity fees, upholding the litigants' contention could be disastrous for LGBT groups and centers, at least in institutions supported by public funds.

Objection to the use of public funds for LGBT activities has a long history. Many administrators at state-funded colleges and universities have had to hide or disguise funding LGBT groups in order to avoid the enmity of state legislators who control the institutions' overall budgets. In one particularly contentious battle, a state university chancellor had to locate private funds for his institution's LGBT resource center because legislators threatened to scuttle the entire university budget if that one item remained in it. The legislators were prepared to risk their state university's solvency for a budget item that was a mere fraction of the total. The funding that the chancellor ultimately provided that year was widely believed to come from his own pocket.

Tight funds and disapproval from some quarters are not reasons for LGBT centers to pull back. On the contrary, it is under such circumstances the sponsoring institution's mettle will be tested. In these instances that LGBT center staff and LGBT campus community leaders and allies need to organize and demand reasonable funding. Clearly, apart from guaranteeing ongoing provision of services and programs, continued funding expresses the institution's commitment to equity.

Institutional funding for LGBT centers has rarely, if ever, been luxurious and will almost certainly always be modest at best. Therefore, the center staff and its consumers and community must be energetic in finding supplemental funds that will enhance the basic operation and support programs and services that, otherwise, would not be possible. There are two primary potential sources for such funding: grants and gifts.

GRANTS

Center directors need to spend some time identifying sources for grant opportunities and writing proposals. Center directors would do well to develop or hone their proposal-writing skills. Courses addressing such skills are sometimes provided by the institution's training or development operations and are also offered by many foundations. These are activities that could be delegated to others, but they need to be monitored carefully by the director. No grant proposal should be submitted without the director's review and approval.

Guides to funding sources are made available by institutions' administrations, by foundations, and by organizations that assist non-profit organizations. For example, the Working Group on Funding Lesbian and Gay Issues— www.workinggroup.org—publishes a list of foundations and other organizations that fund LGBT organizations and activities.

Foundations have specific guidelines regarding which programs they will or will not fund. Reviewing these guidelines narrows considerably the organizations to which campus LGBT centers should submit proposals. For example, the Gill Foundation primarily supports activities that have national, rather than local, scope, with the exception of organizations in its home state of Colorado.

A problem frequently encountered is that several foundations that fund LGBT activities aim to support "grass-roots" organizations. Definitions of "grass-roots" vary but almost always involve an upper limit for budgets, say $250,000 a year. While the annual budgets of virtually all campus LGBT centers fall below this limit, the annual budgets of the institutions within which these centers are housed are well above this amount. Funders note that centers are using the tax-exempt status of the sponsoring college or university. In addition, they sometimes express the view that the sponsoring institutions should be providing greater funding, leaving the foundations' dollars for organizations that have no other sources to tap. It is understandable that foundations reason in this way, but, at the same time, most centers are already at the upper limit of what they will ever receive from their institutions' budgets.

One possible strategy is seeking tax-exempt status (501c3), separate from that of the university. This may be difficult and time-consuming to achieve and will involve some legal fees, and institutional administration may frown upon the practice. What's most important, though, is that it may be seen as a fairly transparent strategy though which potential funders may see and disregard.

Many foundations are interested in funding specific programs or activities, especially new initiatives, rather than providing money for continuing administrative expenditures. Therefore, they are more likely to overlook the center's affiliation with a large-budget institution when the proposed program is innovative and unlikely to be funded by the college or university administration. Even more appealing are programs that reach beyond the institution's walls to serve the surrounding area and, as a result, bring the campus and the community closer together.

Some colleges and universities have internal funding made available through a proposal process. Some alumni make contributions to provide funding for particular purposes. In these instances, the alumni relations office may seek proposals and distribute the gifts. Still other funding may be made available by the central administration in the interest of fulfilling certain institution-wide goals. Especially when the goals pertain to multiculturalism or diversity within the institution, campus LGBT centers are prime contenders for the offered funds.

GIFTS

Gifts from individuals are a fertile, though largely untapped, resource for campus LGBT centers. Primary among potential givers are alumni. A secondary possibility is donors from the community in which the college or university is located.

Alumni have always been seen as a valuable resource by institutions of higher education. Their involvement in campus life and institutional projects is aggressively solicited. Such involvement has inherent value but is also a means through which financial contributions from alumni are encouraged. Loyalty to alma mater is cultivated while future alumni are still students. The whereabouts of alumni are carefully tracked, and campaigns—both annual giving and support for special projects—are vigorously mounted and managed, often by a large development staff. LGBT alumni have only recently begun to be seen as an important funding category.

While the validity of research suggesting that most lesbian and gay people have greater disposable income than their heterosexual counterparts has been questioned, this segment of the general population does merit more attention as donors than has been given to it previously. In 1997, a famous writer and gay community activist offered to bequeath the bulk of his estate to his alma mater. The bequest was rumored to be worth several million dollars. The conditions that the donor placed on the proposed gift were stringent, ones that the university administration ultimately either could not or would not meet. The prospective donor cried homophobia. University officials claimed that they would be happy to accept the gift and use it to serve LGBT students if the alumnus would be more flexible in his specifications. A compromise was finally reached.

The situation generated a lot of attention, including prominent articles in The New York Times and several other major publications. This coverage was partly a result of the donor's media savvy but also due to the growing interest in LGBT people as donors to universities and other organizations and even as major philanthropists.

An interesting aspect of the story of the proposed bequest was contained in a statement made by the prospective donor at the time of his offer. He indicated that when he was a college student in the 1950s, he was aware of his homosexuality, convinced that he was the only gay person on campus at the time, and simply miserable. He asserted that conversations with current students at his alma mater led him to believe that they were not much better off than he had been 40 years before. He thought that his gift might help change the situation.

Recent LGBT alumni gifts—both substantial and modest—to institutions of higher education have been given with very different tone and intent. These gifts are from younger alumni who have given the gifts in appreciation for the support and services provided to them when they were college students questioning their sexual orientation and coming out on campus. Their donations are intended to solidify and expand programs and services for current LGBT students. These gifts reaffirm the value of such activities and, in a sense, reward institutions for having made them available. Younger alumni are more likely sources of gifts not only because their experiences have been more positive but also because they are more likely than their older counterparts to have been out as LGBT while still in school. By no means should older alumni be ignored, however. Many whose years at the institution preceded the provision of services and programs designed for LGBT people or who were not out at the time they were in college have come out since they left school, and a significant number of them have become active in and supportive of the LGBT community where they live.

LGBT alumni organizations are an important route for reaching potential donors. LGBT centers should begin early to communicate with current students regarding their future as alumni, encouraging them to provide contact information before they graduate and to keep in touch regarding their whereabouts. Understandably, some students cannot or do not wish to use their parents' mailing addresses as a temporary means to reach them. Many institutions are providing life-long E-mail addresses administered on campus. These will facilitate communication with alumni wherever they may land and guarantee the confidentiality that they require.

Though it may sound mercenary, LGBT center personnel need to regard all current students as potential alumni donors. Staff members need to behave in a courteous manner under all circumstances, and programs and services need to be designed and provided in a timely, effective, and helpful fashion because these are in accordance with professional standards. But bearing in mind that current consumers may be future funders may reinforce the importance of these standards.

Raising money from alumni should be done in close collaboration with the institution's development officers. Most colleges and universities have rigorous procedures that need to be followed in making contact with prospective donors. If a development officer has targeted a gay alumnus for a gift to fund a scholarship or an academic program, and the LGBT center director then independently approaches that prospect for a donation, contention will ensue. Aside from the value of avoiding conflict, good working relationships with development officers may provide prospect contacts as well as useful pointers about soliciting gifts.

LGBT center directors would be wise to find lead donors, individuals who can assist in fund-raising, such as signing letters or making calls to fellow alumni, and whose own initial gifts can underwrite fund-raising efforts. Depending on the resources available to these donors, they might be prevailed upon to provide matching dollars as an incentive for other alumni.

Fund-raising from alumni may occur in several ways, singly or in combination. The first is an annual giving campaign. In this approach, alumni are asked for gifts every year at the same time. Gifts may be modest—$50 or $100 a year. What's important here is that alumni, even very soon after graduation, get in the habit of giving and, through their gifts, keep in touch with the center. A second method is a one-time campaign, a solicitation for a particular program or project. Though this approach may yield a reasonably high return, particularly if the activity benefiting from the gifts is especially appealing in some way, there are no longer-term advantages to this kind of endeavor. Alumni who respond may feel that their one-time gift is all they can or will do.

Capital campaigns, which need to be managed by development professionals, yield the most significant amount of money with the greatest impact in the long term. These campaigns need to be carefully orchestrated, offering several levels of giving and naming a number of specific programs or activities as recipients of the funds raised. This approach is expensive. Aside from the time of professionals involved, attractive materials outlining the campaign and its beneficiaries need to be prepared. Gifts have to be carefully tracked and timely acknowledgments provided to donors. In light of the time and expenses involved, capital campaigns should be undertaken only when the center has identified major outcomes, such as a long-term endowment or new building.

In addition to alumni, center personnel should consider seeking gifts from individuals in the LGBT community in the city or area surrounding the campus. Depending on how extensive the resources are in the area, some community members may frequently attend events on campus. LGBT students may belong to community groups or volunteer in community organizations. All of these activities familiarize community members with the work being done by the campus center or program, some of which directly benefits them. In that context gifts can be solicited from individuals in the community.

Prospects can be identified by looking through sign-up lists from campus programs and by combing through the lists of benefactors that are usually provided at community fund-raising events benefiting other organizations. Such individuals can first be placed on the center's mailing list to receive announcements of upcoming programs or the center's newsletter. When they have become familiar with the center's programs and services, a letter can be sent or an in-person contact made requesting funds to support the center activities that benefit not only the campus but also the neighboring community. It is possible that this approach may be more effective in areas that have fewer LGBT organizations competing for donations.

Chapter 22

Grass-Roots Activism versus the Ivory Tower

Institutions of higher education are frequently called "ivory towers," which Webster's *New World Dictionary* defines as "places of mental withdrawal from reality and action." Life on campus is often regarded as both more protected and more rarefied than life in "the real world." References are made to students' preparing themselves for life after college, as if what happens to them during their college years merely comprises a rehearsal. The perceptions of those in the so-called ivory tower are, of course, contrary those viewing it from outside.

Views of LGBT centers and the activities in which they engage are similarly divergent. Indeed, community organizing and activism on a college or university campus are different in some respects from those endeavors in other locations. Many of these are described throughout this book. But the disparate perceptions of organizing and activism themselves present challenges and may cause conflict between campus and community LGBT activists.

Community activists sometimes subscribe to the belief that what happens on college campuses is inconsequential compared to the rest of the world. These activists see what campus organizers are doing as trivial compared to the important work that they themselves are undertaking. Many campus LGBT center personnel have had experiences working in the world outside higher education. As a result, either they may see the perceptions of community activists as inaccurate, even insulting, or, at some level, they may share community activists' views and feel guilty that they have left "real" community activism behind.

Full-time college or university faculty members are even more frequently the targets of enmity from community activists. They are disparaged for studying issues and conflicts in the "real world" but not really engaging in them. Academics respond to such disdain by asserting that their scholarship makes a significant—and genuine—contribution to addressing issues and resolving conflicts.

In turn, some faculty and staff members may see community activists as strident and ineffectual. They think that the activists are "spinning their wheels" or "tilting at windmills." Some activists are seen as having unreasonable demands or expectations and some as protesting merely because they need to be fighting about something.

The dichotomy is not as absolute as it is usually considered. Some university faculty and staff members use actual community situations as case examples in the courses that they teach and invite participants in those situations to their classes. Many faculty and staff members also work as volunteers for community organizations and causes. Some bring the principles and practices that they use in those endeavors—past and present—to their work on campus. Some community activists work regularly with academic counterparts, seeking clarity about situations that may be difficult to understand while in the midst of them.

The tension between "town" and "gown" has many incarnations. This particular form can be damaging to all involved. Community publications may ignore campus programs and activities. Community activists may unfairly target the institution as the source of broader problems and worthy of protest. Those in the community may stay away from campus, missing out on the many rich opportunities that it offers. Faculty and staff may withdraw from the community and retreat to campus, thus reinforcing the image of the institution as remote and out of touch.

Students are also he victims of the tension. If they are scorned by community members as privileged or out of touch, they may shun the community, which might already have a tarnished reputation on campus. They could withhold valuable volunteer efforts and other forms of involvement in the community. This risks establishing an unfortunate model for their later lives.

These circumstances present particular challenges to LGBT center personnel. Of course, the situation represents a much larger set of issues, deeply entrenched and long-standing, so what center personnel can do needs to be modest and tailored to the particular version of the tension between campus and community that they are encountering.

The approach generally involves center personnel's spearheading building bridges of some kind. Students, staff, and faculty cannot wait for community members to reach out to them. They must be proactive. First steps will be small but important: volunteering to help with community projects or raising money to support it; providing a presence at rallies or protests in the community; visiting community organizations and initiating discussion of shared concerns; and inviting community activists to speak at a campus-wide program or in the classroom.

Many other such steps that can contribute to the construction of bridges between grass-roots community organizing and activism of college campuses. Though they may seem elementary, they are, in fact, important building blocks. They may provide the foundation first for mutual understanding and respect and, ultimately, for collaborative efforts that benefit both the campus and the community.

Part V

Appendices

Appendix A: Directory of the National Consortium of Directors of LGBT Resources in Higher Education

As of January 2002

American University
Mindy Michels, Coordinator
Gay, Lesbian, Bisexual, Transgender and Ally Resource Center
226 Mary Graydon Center,
4400 Massachusetts Ave., NW, Washington, D.C. 20016
E-mail: glbta@american.edu
phone: (202) 885-3347
fax: (202) 885-3396
http://www.american.edu/glbta/

Brown University
Liaison for LGBT Concerns
James Stascavage, Assistant Dean
Office of Student Life, Box P
Brown University, Providence, RI 02912
E-mail: James_Stascavage@Brown.EDU
phone: (401) 863-3800
fax: (401) 863-1999

Bucknell University
Lesbian Gay Bisexual Concerns Office
Fran McDaniel, Coordinator
Roberts Hall
Bucknell University 100, Lewisburg, PA 17837
E-mail: lgb@bucknell.edu
phone: (570)577-1609
fax: (570) 577-3163
http://www.bucknell.edu/departments/lgb/

California State Polytechnic University, Pomona
Pride Center (Gay, Lesbian, Bisexual, and Transgender Student Center)
Jonnie Owens, Coordinator
3801 W. Temple Avenue, Bldg. 1, Room 206
Pomona, CA 91768
E-mail: jjowens@csupomona.edu
phone: (909) 869-3064
http://www.csupomona.edu/~pride_center

Carleton College
Kaaren Williamsen, LGBT Student Adviser
1 North College Street, Northfield MN 55057
E-mail: kwilliam@acs.carleton.edu
phone: (507) 646-5222
fax: (507) 646-7473
http://www.carleton.edu/campus/community/pride/

Central Michigan University
Office of Gay & Lesbian Programs
Dr. Michael L. Stemmeler, Director
130 Sloan Hall, Mt. Pleasant, MI 48859-0001
E-mail: michael.l.stemmeler@cmich.edu
phone: (517) 774-3637
fax: (517) 774-2723
http://www.cmich.edu/DIV_GLP.HTML

Colorado State University
Gay, Lesbian, Bisexual, and Transgender Student Services
Randy McCrillis, Director
Lory Student Center (lower level)
Fort Collins, CO 80523
E-mail: randym@lamar.colostate.edu
phone: (970) 491-4342
http://www.colostate.edu/Depts/glbtss/

Community College of Denver
(program also serves University of Colorado at Denver
and Metropolitan State College of Denver)
Gay Lesbian Bisexual Trans Student Services at Aurora
Karen Bensen, LCSW, Director
CB 74, P.O. Box 173362, Denver, CO 80217-3362
E-mail: BensenK@mscd.edu
phone: (303) 556-6333
fax: (303) 556-3896
http://clem.mscd.edu/~glbtss/

Cornell University
Lesbian Gay Bisexual Transgender Resource Center
Gwendolyn Alden Dean, Coordinator
135 White Hall, Ithaca, NY 14853
E-mail: lgbtrc@cornell.edu
phone: (607) 254-4987
fax: (607) 255-7793
http://www.lgbtrc.cornell.edu

Dartmouth College
Gay, Lesbian, Bisexual, Transgender Advocacy & Programming
Pamela Misener, Assistant Dean of Student Life and Advisor to LGBT Students
Collis Center, HB 6217, Hanover, NH 03755
E-mail: GLB.Programming@dartmouth.edu
phone: (603) 646-3635
fax: (603) 646-1386
http://www.dartmouth.edu/~glbprog

DePauw University
Office of Multicultural Affairs
Jeannette Johnson-Licon, Director
Program Coordinator, LGBT Services
302 Harrison Hall, Greencastle, IN 46135
E-mail: JJLICON@depauw.edu
phone: (765) 658-4027
fax: (765) 658-4021

Duke University
Center for Lesbian, Gay, Bisexual & Transgender Life
Karen Krahulik, Director
Kerry John Poynter, Program Coordinator
202 Flowers, Box 90958, Durham, NC 27708-0958
E-mail: lgbcenter@acpub.duke.edu
phone: (919) 684-6607
fax: (919) 681-7873
http://lgbt.stuaff.duke.edu/homepage.html

Eastern Michigan University
Lesbian, Gay, Bisexual, Transgendered Resource Center
Kathleen Russell
209 King Hall, Ypsilanti, Michigan 48197
E-mail: lgbtrc@emich.edu
phone: (734) 487-4149
fax: (734) 487-6910

Emerson College
Office of Gay, Lesbian, Bisexual and Transgender Student Life
Curtis W. Hoover, Coordinator
100 Beacon Street, Boston, MA 02116
E-mail: choover@emerson.edu
phone: (617) 824-8087
fax: 617-824-8937
http://www.emerson.edu/student_life/glbt/index.html

Emory University
Office of Lesbian/Gay/Bisexual/Transgender Life
Dr. Saralyn Chesnut, Director
Dobbs University Center, Room 246E
P.O. Box 24075, Atlanta, GA 30322
E-mail: schesnu@emory.edu
phone: (404) 727-2136
fax: (404) 727-4774
http://www.emory.edu/LGBOFFICE/

Framingham State College
Office of Social Issues and Wellness
Julie Bell-Elkins
509 College Center, Framingham, MA 01701
E-mail: jbellel@frc.mass.edu

Georgia Southern University
GLBT Resource Center
Multicultural and International Student Center
Rosenwald Building, Room 2034
P.O.Box 8068, Statesboro, GA 30460
E-mail: glbtres@gsaix2.cc.gasou.edu
phone: (912) 681-5409
fax: (912) 486-7437
http://www2.gasou.edu/sta/multiprog/gays_lesbians.htm

Grinnell College
Stonewall Resource Center
Nicholas Myers, Director
Box B-1, Grinnell, IA 50113
E-mail: srcenter@ac.grin.edu
phone: (515) 236-3327
http://www.grinnell.edu/studentaffairs/StudentAffairs/src.html

Guilford College
Gay Lesbian Bisexual Resource Center
Travis Compton

5800 West Friendly Avenue, Greensboro, NC   27410
E-mail: chenok@netmcr.com
phone: (336) 316-2374
http://www.guilford.edu/original/glbta/Rc.html

Indiana University
Gay, Lesbian, Bisexual & Transgender Student Support Services
Doug Bauder , Coordinator
Carol Fischer, OSAS
Office of Student Ethics and Anti-Harassment Programs
Campus Life Division
705 E. Seventh Street, Bloomington, IN 47408-3809
E-mail: glbtserv@indiana.edu
phone: (812) 855-4252
fax: (812) 855-4465
http://www.indiana.edu/~glbtserv/office.htm

Iowa State University
Lesbian, Gay, Bisexual & Transgender Student Services
Johnny Rogers, LGBT Student Services Coordinator
224 Dean of Students Office
Ames, IA 50011
E-mail: lgbtss@iastate.edu
phone: (515) 294-5433
fax: (515) 294-5670
http://www.public.iastate.edu/~lgbtss/homepage.html

Ithaca College
LGBT Education, Outreach, and Services
Lisa Maurer, Coordinator
150 Hammond Health Center, Ithaca NY 14850-7116
Lmaurer@ithaca.edu

Marshall University
Lesbian Gay Bisexual Outreach
Raymie White, Co-Coordinator
Jimel Beckett, Co-Coordinator
Prichard Hall 137, Huntington, WV 25755
E-mail: lgbo@marshall.edu
phone: (304) 696-6623
http://www.marshall.edu/lgbo/

Massachusetts Institute of Technology
Ricky A. Gresh, Program Administrator
Dania Palanker, Graduate Assistant
W20-549

77 Massachusetts Avenue, Cambridge, MA 02139
E-mail:lbgt@mit.edu
phone: 617-253-4158
fax: 617-253-8391
http://web.mit.edu/lbgt/

Metropolitan State College of Denver
(the program also serves the University of Colorado at Denver
and the Community College of Denver at Aurora)
Gay Lesbian Bisexual Trans Student Services at Aurora
Karen Bensen, LCSW, Director
CB 74, P.O. Box 173362, Denver, CO 80217-3362
E-mail: BensenK@mscd.edu
phone: (303) 556-6333
fax: (303) 556-3896
http://clem.mscd.edu/~glbtss/

Michigan State University
Brent Bilodeau, Assistant for LBGT Concerns
101 Student Services
East Lansing, MI 48823
E-mail: bilodeau@pilot.msu.edu
phone: (517) 355-8296
fax: (517) 535-5495
http://www.msu.edu/user/alliance/

Minnesota State University, Mankato
Lesbian, Gay, Bisexual Center
c/o program advisor
CSU 242
Minnesota State University, Mankato, MN 56001
E-mail: mankato_lgbc@hotmail.com
phone: (507) 389-5131
http://www.csu.mnsu.edu/lgbc/

Morningside College
Dr. Gail Dooley , LGB Student Adviser
1501 Morningside Ave., Sioux City, IA 51106
E-mail: bgd001@morningside.edu
phone: (712) 274-5208
fax: (712) 274-5101

New York University
Office of Lesbian, Gay, Bisexual & Transgender Student Services
Todd M. Smith, Coordinator
244 Greene Street, New York, NY 10003-6612

E-mail: lgbt.office@nyu.edu
phone: (212) 998-4424
fax: (212) 995-4796
http://www.nyu.edu/lgbt/

Northern Illinois University
Margaret M. "Margie" Cook, Program Coordinator for Lesbian, Gay, Bisexual
Transgender Programs
University Programming and Activities
Campus Life Building 150, DeKalb, Il 60115
E-mail: mcook@niu.edu
phone: (815) 753-2235
fax: (815) 753-2905
http://www.niu.edu/lgbt/

Oberlin College
Gay/Lesbian/Bisexual/Transgender Multicultural Resource Center
Michael Hartwyk, Coordinator
Wilder 208, Oberlin, OH 44074
E-mail: michael.hartwyk@oberlin.edu
phone: (440) 775-8802
fax: (440) 775-6848

Ohio State University, The
Student Gender and Sexuality Services
Willa Young, Director
Gay, Lesbian, Bisexual, Transgender Student Services
Brett Beemyn, Coordinator
464 Ohio Union
1739 North High Street, Columbus, OH 43210
E-mail: young.58@osu.edu, beemyn.1@osu.edu
phone: (614) 688-4898 or (614) 292-6200
fax: (614) 292-4462

Ohio University
GLBT Student Programs
Laura Harrison, Coordinator
314 Baker Center, Athens, OH 45701
E-mail: harrisol@ohio.edu
phone:(740) 593-0239
fax: (740) 593-0825
http://www.ohiou.edu/glbt/

Oregon State University
Queer Resource Center/Women's Center
Katja Pettinen

Benton Annex
Corvallis, OR 97331-2503 USA
phone: (541) 737-3186
E-mail: Fattire@angelfire.com
http://www.oregonstate.edu/dept/women/

Pennsylvania State University, The
The LGBTA Resource Room
Office of the Vice Provost for Educational Equity
Sue Rankin
313 Grange Building, University Park, PA 16802
E-mail: sxr2@psu.edu
phone: (814) 863-8415
fax: (814) 863-8218
http://www.lions.psu.edu/lgbt/

Princeton University
Office of the Dean of Student Life
Debbie Bazarsky, Coordinator
313 West College, Princeton, NJ 08544
E-mail: bazarsky@princeton.edu
phone: (609) 258-1353
fax: (609) 258-3831
http://www.princeton.edu/~pride/

Rutgers, the State University of New Jersey
The Office of Diverse Community Affairs and Lesbian-Gay Concerns
Cheryl Clarke, Director
Bishop House, Room 105
115 College Avenue, New Brunswick, NJ 08901-8544
 E-mail: divcoaff@rci.rutgers.edu
phone: (732) 932-1711
fax: (732) 932-8160
http://www-rci.rutgers.edu/~divcoaff/

St. Cloud State University
Sheri Atkinson, GLBT Services Coordinator
16 Atwood Memorial Center
720 4th Avenue South, Cloud, Minnesota 56301-4498
E-mail: satkinson@stcloudstate.edu
phone: (320) 654-5166
fax: (320) 654-5190
http://www.stcloudstate.edu/~glbt/

Stanford University
Lesbian, Gay, and Bisexual Community Center

Benjamin Davidson, Director
Tresidder Union
PO Box 8265, Stanford, CA 94305
E-mail: LGBCC@forsythe.stanford.edu
phone: (650) 723-5851
fax: (650) 725-6227
http://www.stanford.edu/group/QR/lgbcc.html

Texas A&M University
Office of Gender Issues Education Services
Lesbian, Gay, Bisexual Education & Support
Beatriz Armillas Coordinator
Department of Student Life
College Station, Texas 77843-1257
E-mail: gies@stulife2.tamu.edu
phone: (409) 845-1107
fax: (409) 845-6138
http://studentlife.tamu.edu/gies/

Tufts University
Lesbian, Gay, Bisexual Transgender Center
Judith Brown, Director
226 College Avenue
Tufts University, Medford, MA 02155
E-mail: lgbt@tufts.edu
phone: (617) 627-3770
fax: (617) 627-3579
http://ase.tufts.edu/lgbt/

Tulane University
Lesbian, Gay & Bisexual Life at Tulane
Christopher Daigle, Director
Warren, Basement, New Orleans, LA
E-mail: cdaigle@mailhost.tcs.tulane.edu
phone: (504) 865-5763
fax: (504) 865-5784

University of California, Berkeley
LGBT Services
Billy Curtis, Coordinator
250 César Chávez Student Center #2440
Berkeley CA 94720-2440
E-mail: lgbt@uclink.berkeley.edu
phone: (510) 643-5728
fax: (510) 642-4788
http://www.uga.berkeley.edu/sas/lgbt/

University of California, Davis
LGBT Resource Center
University House Annex
One Shields Ave., Davis, CA 95616
phone: (916) 752-2452
http://lgbcenter.ucdavis.edu/

University of California, Irvine
LGBT Resource Center
Pat Walsh, Director
106 Gateway Commons, Irvine, CA 92697
E-mail: lgbtrc@uci.edu
phone: (949) 824-3277
fax: (949) 824-3412
http://www.lgbtrc.uci.edu/

University of California, Los Angeles
LGBT Campus Resource Center
Dr. Ronni Sanlo, Director
220 Kinsey Hall, Los Angeles, CA 90095-1579
E-mail: lgbt@ucla.edu
phone: (310) 206-3628
fax: (310) 206-8191
http://www.saonet.ucla.edu/lgbt/

University of California, Riverside
LGBT Resource Center
Nancy Tubbs, Director
250 Costo Hall
University Commons, Riverside, CA 92521
E-mail: lgbtrc@ucrac1.ucr.edu
phone: (909)787-2267
fax: (909) 787-2439
http://lgbtrc.ucr.edu/

University of California, San Diego
LGBT Resource Office
Shawn Travers, Coordinator
9500 Gilman Drive, MC 0023
La Jolla, CA 92093-0023
E-mail: rainbow@ucsd.edu
phone: (858) 822-3493
fax: (858) 822-3494

University of California, San Francisco
LGBT Resources

Shane Snowdon, Coordinator
Center for Gender Equity
Woods Building, Ground Floor
100 Medical Center Way, San Francisco, CA 94143-0909
E-mail: ssnowdon@genderequity.ucsf.edu
phone:(415) 502-5593
fax: (415) 476-4849
http://www.ucsf.edu/cge/lgbtr/

University of California, Santa Barbara
Center for Sexual and Gender Diversity
Stacey Shears, Director
University Center, Room 3137
Cen Road, Santa Barbara, California 93106
E-mail: shears-s@sa.ucsb.edu
phone: (805) 893-5846
http://www.sa.ucsb.edu/women'scenter/qrc/

University of California, Santa Cruz
GLBT Resource Center
Deb Abbott, Director
1156 High Street, Santa Cruz, CA 95064
E-mail: dabbott@cats.ucsc.edu
phone: (831) 459-4385
fax: (831) 459-4387
http://www2.ucsc.edu/glbtcenter/

University of Colorado at Boulder
GLBT Resource Center
Bruce E. Smail, Director
Campus Box 103, 227 Willard Hall, Boulder, Colorado 80309-0103
E-mail: glbrc@stripe.colorado.edu
phone: (303) 492-1377
fax: (303) 735-3572
http://www.Colorado.edu/GLBTRC/

University of Colorado at Denver
(the program also serves Metropolitan State College and
the Community College of Denver at Aurora)
Gay Lesbian Bisexual Trans Student Services at Aurora
Karen Bensen, LCSW, Director
CB 74, P.O. Box 173362, Denver, CO 80217-3362
E-mail: BensenK@mscd.edu
phone: (303) 556-6333
fax: (303) 556-3896
http://clem.mscd.edu/~glbtss/

University of Connecticut
Rainbow Center
1315 Storrs Rd, U-96, Storrs, CT 06269-4096
E-mail: rnbwdir@uconnvm.uconn.edu
phone: (860) 486-5821
fax: (860) 486-6674
http://www.rainbowcenter.uconn.edu/

University of Delaware
LGBT Community Office
Greg Weight and Tessa Bye, Coordinators
305 Hullihen Hall, Newark, DE 19716
E-mail: gweight@udel.edu
phone: (302) 831-8703
fax: (302) 831-4110

University of Illinois at Chicago
Office of GLBT Concerns
Patrick Finnessy, Director
OGLBTC (M/C 369)
1007 W Harrison St 1180 BSB, Chicago, IL 60607
E-mail: oglbc-1@uic.edu
phone: (312) 413-8619
fax: (312) 996-4688
http://www.uic.edu/depts/quic/oglbc/

University of Illinois at Urbana-Champaign
Office of LGBT Concerns
Curt McKay and Pat Morey, Co-Directors
322A Illini Union
1401 West Green Street, Urbana, IL 61801
E-mail: curtb@uiuc.edu and p-morey@uiuc.edu
phone: (217) 244-8863
http://www.odos.uiuc.edu/lgbt/

University of Maryland
LGBT Student Involvement and Advocacy
Wallace Eddy, Coordinator
1135 Stamp Student Union, College Park, MD 20742
E-mail: weddy@wam.umd.edu
University of Maryland, College Park
Office of LGBT Equity
Dr. Luke Jensen, Coordinator
2105 Computer & Space Sciences Bldg
College Park, Maryland 20742-5031
E-mail: ljensen@deans.umd.edu

phone: (301) 405-8721
fax: (301) 405-8722
http://www.inform.umd.edu/LGBT/

University of Massachusetts, Amherst
The Stonewall Center: A LGBT Educational Resource Center
Dr. Felice Yeskel, Director
Crampton House/SW
Box 3-1799, UMass, Amherst, MA 01003
E-mail: stonewall@stuaf.umass.edu
phone: (413) 545-4824
fax: (413)545-6667
http://www.umass.edu/stonewall/

University of Michigan, Ann Arbor
Office of LGBT Affairs
E. Frederick Dennis, Director
3200 Michigan Union, Ann Arbor, MI 48109-1349
E-mail: lgbta@umich.edu
phone: (734) 763-4186
fax: (734) 647-4133
http://www.umich.edu/~inqueery/

University of Michigan, Flint
LGB Center
Nikki Mann, LGB Center Advocate
365 UCEN
U-M Flint, Flint, MI 48502
E-mail: mmann@flint.umich.edu
phone: (810) 766-6606
fax: (810) 762-3023
http://www.flint.umich.edu/Departments/STLIFE/

University of Minnesota
GLBT Programs Office
Office of Multicultural Affairs
Beth Zemsky, Director
340 Coffman Memorial Union
300 Washington Avenue, S.E., Minneapolis MN 55455
E-mail: glbt@tc.umn.edu
phone: (612) 626-2324
fax: (612) 626-0909
http://www.umn.edu/glbt/

University of Minnesota-Duluth
Gay, Lesbian, Bisexual, Transgender Services

Angela C. Nichols, Director
Campus Center 66
10 University Drive, Duluth, MN 55812
E-mail: anichols@D.UMN.EDU
phone: (218) 726-7300
fax: (218) 726-6244

University of Missouri-Columbia
LGBT Resource Center
230 Brady Commons
University of Missouri-Columbia, Columbia, MO 65203
phone: (573) 884-7750
fax: (573) 884-5780
http://web.missouri.edu/~stulife/GLB/

University of Nebraska at Lincoln
GLBT Resource Center
Maria Carrasco, Director
Room 234, Nebraska Union
Lincoln, NE 68588-0455
E-mail: mcarrasc@unlserve.unl.edu
phone: (402) 472-5644
http://www.unl.edu/lambda/

University of New England
Anne Coyle, Resource Coordinator for GLBTQ Students
E-mail: acoyle@une.edu

University of New Hampshire
Office of Multicultural Student Affairs
Bob Coffey, GLBT Coordinator
12034 Granite Square Station, Durham, NH 03824
E-mail: GLBT@unh.edu
phone: (603) 862-2050
fax: (603) 862-2660

University of Northern Colorado
GLBT Resource Office
Linda Beeler, Coordinator
Turner Hall, Greeley, CO 80639
E-mail: lmbeele@bentley.unco.edu
phone: (970) 351-2906

University of Oregon
LGBT Educational & Support Services Program
Chicora Martin, Director

Office of Student Life
164 Oregon Hall
5216 University of Oregon, Eugene OR 97403-5216
E-mail: program@darkwing.uoregon.edu
phone: (541) 346-1134
fax: (541) 346-5811
http://darkwing.uoregon.edu/~program/

University of Pennsylvania
LGBT Center
Robert Schoenberg, Director
3537 Locust Walk, Third Floor, Philadelphia, PA 19104-6225
E-mail: bobs@pobox.upenn.edu
phone: (215) 898-5044
fax: (215) 573-5751
events line: (215) 898-8888
http://dolphin.upenn.edu/~center/

University of Southern California
GLBT Student Support
Elizabeth Davenport, Director
USC STU-202, Los Angeles, CA 90089-0890
E-mail: ejld@usc.edu
phone: (213) 740-4900
fax: (213) 740-7646
http://www.usc.edu/student-affairs/glbss/

University of Southern Maine
Sarah Holmes, GLBTQA Resources Coordinator
Portland Student Life
Woodbury Campus Center, USM
P.O. Box 9300, Portland, Maine 04104
e-mail: sholmes@usm.maine.edu
phone: (207) 228-8235
fax: (207) 780-4463
http://www.usm.maine.edu/glbtqa

University of Toronto
Lesbian, Gay, Bisexual, Transgender, Queer Resources and Programs
Jude Tate, Coordinator
Koffler Student Services Centre, Room #07
214 College Street, Toronto, ON M5T 2Z9, Canada
E-mail: lgbtq.resources@utoronto.ca
phone: (416) 946-5624
fax: (416) 971-2037
http://lgbtq.sa.utoronto.ca/

University of Vermont
Center for Cultural Pluralism
Dorothea Brauer, Lesbian, Gay, Bisexual, Transgender Services Coordinator
461 Main Street, Allen House
Burlington, Vermont 05405
E-mail: dbrauer@zoo.uvm.edu
phone: (802) 656-8637
fax: (802) 656-3348
http://www.uvm.edu/~lgbtqa

University of Washington
GLBT Commission of the ASUW
Brian Thurston, Director
Box 352238 / SAO 09, Seattle, WA 98105-2238
E-mail: asuwgblc@u.washington.edu
phone: (206) 685-GBLC (4252)
fax: (206)543-9285
http://depts.washington.edu/asuwgblc/

University of Wisconsin La Crosse
Diversity Resource Center
Kim F. Elderbrook, LGBTQ Issues Director
E-mail: lgbtq@unitedcouncil.net
phone: (608) 263-3422

University of Wisconsin Madison
Dean of Students Office
Sara Hinkel, LGBT Issues Coordinator
75 Bascom Hall
500 Lincoln Drive, Madison, WI, 53706-1314

Washington State University
Gay, Lesbian, Bisexuals, and Allies Program
Melynda Huskey, Director
Compton Union Building B-19
P.O.Box 647204, Pullman, WA 99164-7204
E-mail: melyndah@mail.wsu.edu
phone: (509) 335-6428
fax (509) 335-4178
http://www.wsu.edu/glbap/

Washington University
Social Justice Center
515 Wydown Blvd. Box 1250, St. Louis, MO 63105
E-mail: sjc@rescomp.wustl.edu
phone: (314) 935-8293

fax: (314) 935-4001
http://www.rescomp.wustl.edu/~sjc/

Wayne State University
Lesbian Gay Bisexual Transgender Services
Dr. Steven Schoeberlein, Coordinator
1001 Faculty Administration Building, Detroit, MI 48202
E-mail: s.schoeberlein@wayne.edu
phone: (313) 577-3398
fax: (313) 577-4995
http://www.stuaffrs.wayne.edu/about/ucps.html

Wellesley College
Programs and Services for Lesbian, Bisexual & Transgender Students
Katya Salkever, Director
Green Hall 441, Wellesley, MA 02181
E-mail: Ksalkever@Wellesley.edu
phone: (617) 283-2389
fax: (617) 283-3674

Western Michigan University
Lesbian, Bisexual, and Gay Student Services
Wanda Viento, MSW, ACSW, Coordinator
A327 Ellsworth Hall, Kalamazoo MI 49008
E-mail: SALP_LBG@wmich.edu
phone: (616) 387-2123
fax: (616) 387-4222
http://www.salp.wmich.edu/lbg/

Williams College
Stephen D. Collingsworth, Queer Issues Coordinator
and Assistant Director of the Multi Cultural Center
Jeness House, POB 315, Williamstown, MA 01267
E-mail: stephen.d.collingsworth@williams.edu
phone: (413) 597-3353

Source: National Consortium of Directors of LGBT Resources in Higher Education, www.lgbtcampus.org

Appendix B: Campus Climate Report: Three Meta-Analysis Themes

1. Invisibility/Ostracism. Institutionalized heterosexism on college campuses creates an oppressive situation for queer people. The university environment negates their existence, thereby promoting further invisibility. The fear of rejection has a tremendous impact on the way that these individuals lead their lives: "What has to be the most painful to me is the invisibility I have had to face as a gay student. I have often felt unwelcome in the place that is my home. What I can say is that except for the university gay community, I have not participated in campus life. It may be an unwritten rule, but it is clear that gays are not welcome in fraternities or on athletic teams" (undergraduate student, University of Minnesota, 1993). "At work, I am not a human being. At 5:00, that's when I can be who I am. I remember thinking about finishing school and starting work as being a freeing experience. Now I know better; it makes me bitter at the University and the world" (queer staff, University of Colorado, Boulder, 1991).

2. Isolation/Self-Concealment. In order to prevent what they anticipate will be rejection by their colleagues/peers, many queer members of the academic community choose to conceal their sexual orientation. To protect themselves from discrimination, LGBT individuals do a lot of lying. The university climate communicates the message that being honest about one's sexual orientation may have direct negative effects on salary, tenure, promotion, and emotional well-being, so they chose to remain "in the closet," where it is safe: "An untenured faculty member has been afraid to attend meetings of the Faculty/Staff Lesbian, Gay, Bisexual Caucus for fear that senior colleagues might hear about it" (Tufts University, 1993). "I completed your survey at home so no one would see me" (queer staff member, University of Colorado, Boulder, 1991).

3. University Consequences. The university suffers from its own heterosexism. Talented LGBT students, faculty, and staff feel "forced" to leave the university, and students (both LGBT and heterosexual) are deprived of role models and

academic growth: "I'd be scared to be an advisor to the lesbian, gay, and bisexual student association because that is being too obvious. I am close to tenure, and I don't want them to find a reason not to give it to me" (faculty member, Pennsylvania State University, 1994). "A heterosexual athlete told his advisor that he wanted to drop a dance course because he was afraid that his Tufts teammates might think he was gay" (Tufts University, 1993).

Appendix C: Summary of Recommendations for Change

I.   Structural Transformation

Create an office for LGBT concerns
Create and identify a designated safe, social meeting place
Integrate LGBT presence in university documents/publications
       (grievance procedures, housing guidelines, application materials)
Actively recruit and retain LGBT persons and allies
Create an LGBT alumni group within the existing alumni organization
Create a documentation form reporting hate crimes against LGBT persons
Create a standing LGBT advisory committee

II. Policy Inclusion

Include sexual orientation/gender identity in the institution's nondiscrimination
       policy
Extend employee spousal benefits to domestic partners (health insurance, tuition
       remission, sick/bereavement leave, use of campus facilities, child-care
       services, comparable retirement plans)
Provide safe housing for same-sex partners

III. Curricular Integration

Create an LGBT studies center/department
Provide release time for LGBT course development
Expand LGBT library holdings
Integrate LGBT issues into existing courses
Use inclusive language in the classroom (e.g., create a pamphlet with examples
       of heterosexist assumptions and language with suggested alternatives)
Obtain inclusive audiovisual materials that introduces LGBT materials

IV. Education

Develop workshops/programs to address the Greek community
Develop workshops/programs to address residence life
Include sexual orientation/gender identity issues in student orientation programs
Include sexual orientation issues in new faculty/staff orientations
Sponsor lectures, concerts, symposia, and other activities to increase queer
    aware-ness on campus
Provide course credit to LGBT students for peer education initiatives
Provide training for campus health care professionals regarding the special
    health needs of LGBT individuals
Provide training sessions for public safety officers on violence against LGBT
    persons

Appendix D: Example of Structure

I.   Direction /Philosophy

What is the purpose of the LGBT presence on campus? (create a mission statement)

Given the context within which one has to work, what is the best way to meet that mission?

Is the office/center an autonomous unit (advisory board, paid staff, bylaws and constitution, office, etc.) or under the auspices of another unit (shared staff, resources, etc.)?

II.   Organizational Structure

Creation of organizational chart (dependent on vision)
Proposal One: semi-independent unit
    Staff (director, administrative assistants, office manager, volunteers, interns)
    Advisory board
    Constitution
    Bylaw
    Office space, location
Proposal Two: under auspices of another unit
    Seat on Executive Committee of lead unit
    Resource sharing (staff, funds, etc.)
    Working groups? (Policy, Structure and Process, Education and Advocacy, Communication and Visibility, etc.)

III.   Relationships with Other Organizations on Campus

Meeting with allies
Meeting with other related organization representatives
How and when should this happen?
Who is at the table?

What is the current relationship with each group?
What is the proposal for future relationships with these groups?
With what other groups should the office cultivate relationships in order to
    realize the vision?

IV.   Action Plans

Articulate structure and process for relationships with other groups on campus
Cultivate communications (e.g. Web site, regional forums, listservs, etc.)
Create a corporate identification program (logo, letterhead, visibility)
Develop quick response kits for "hot" issues (list contact persons)

Appendix E: Center Director
Position Description

The Lesbian Gay Bisexual and Transgender (LGBT) Resource Center, a unit within the division of Student and Campus Life (S&CL), provides a broad array of services and information to the campus and community on LGBT related issues. The Director plans, directs, and implements campus student affairs programs to, for, and about the LGBT campus community. Specific programmatic responsibilities include functional areas such as outreach, recruitment, and retention; campus and university relations; advising; crisis counseling; and training and education of the campus community related to LGBT issues. The Director also provides support to the LGBT Studies program and sits on the program's Faculty Advisory Committee. Under the general direction of the Assistant Vice Chancellor (AVC) of Student & Campus Life, the Director operates with considerable independence within the context of the Student Affairs mission and planning statements, S&CL goals, and department objectives.

A. General Services and Programming

A1. Establish working relationships with offices and entities serving the LGBT community, on and off campus, in order to make appropriate and effective referrals. Identify, compile and maintain an inventory of services and opportunities available from offices, agencies, and organizations on and off campus.

A2. Develop and maintain a library of informational, reference, and source materials (e.g., books, periodicals, tapes) on LGBT related topics not typically available from other campus offices, libraries, or bookstores.

A3. Plan and coordinate events of interest to individuals, organizations and departments, including but not limited to workshops, support groups, colloquia, inservice training, and presentations intended to raise campus awareness regarding LGBT issues. Respond to requests for lecturers, panels, and resources on LGBT issues. Coordinate or insure participation in annual campus events including Lavender Graduation Ceremonies, National Coming Out Week, Faculty/Staff

Reception, New Student Orientation, Lambda Alumni Reception, and Open House.

A4. Train facilitators for support/discussion groups.

A5. Develop, train, and supervise LGBT Speaker's Bureau.

A6. Provide general assistance and counseling to students, faculty, staff, and campus organizations on LGBT issues, topics, and concerns, including sexual orientation, gender identity, and multiple/invisible identity.

A7. Advise student groups including LGBT graduate student group, Gay and Lesbian Alliance, Delta Lambda Phi fraternity, *Ten Percent* news magazine, La Familia, and Mahu.

A8. Facilitate leadership programs and projects including students' attendance at NGLTF Creating Change Leadership Conference, and the LGBT Student Leader Roundtable.

B. Institutional Liaison and Support Activities

B1. Act as a liaison between LGBT focused services and opportunities on campus and potential users and interested parties.

B2. Serve on major campus and UC-wide committees, including the Lesbian Gay and Bisexual Studies program Faculty Advisory Committee, Chancellor's Advisory Committee on Gay and Lesbian Issues, Steering Committee for LGBT Faculty/Staff Network, and Steering Committee for UC LGBT Association.

B3. Facilitate networking and coalition building among existing campus groups serving the LGBT community.

B4. Monitor the needs and quality of life for LGBT students, faculty, and staff and convey the findings to campus officials, departments, and leaders.

B5. Act as a contact point and consultation resource to the campus on matters of policy development, service assessment, dispute resolution and advocacy of LGBT concerns. Serve as a resource for campus administrators on policy and procedural matters regarding the LGBT community.

B6. Identify and assist in developing extramural internships with service opportunities for students seeking placements with off campus agencies and organizations working with the LGBT community.

C. Management and Administration

C1. Determine the scope and nature of the Center's services. Develop departmental strategic plan, and conduct periodic evaluations of effectiveness, making necessary modifications to respond to changing campus needs.

C2. Establish service delivery methods and operating procedures appropriate to the university environment and campus users.

C3. Establish and utilize an Advisory Board.

C4. Establish protocols for access and lending of source and reference materials in the Center's library.

C5. Recruit, select, train, supervise and evaluate LGBT office staff and volunteers. Supervise graduate level interns.

C6. Project annual budget and administer allocated funds, including authorizing and monitoring expenditures, making adjustments as needed. Prepare periodic status reports. Search and write grant proposals.

C7. Design and implement or coordinate implementation of publicity and outreach activities to raise campus awareness of the Center's services and resources, including selection of appropriate mechanisms, editing content, and crafting "targeting" strategies. Oversee production of flyers, posters, brochures, newsletters, and website.

C8. Maintain data on program activities and compile administrative reports. Write reports and correspondence as requested or necessary, including publication of scholarly articles or books as appropriate.

D. Other

D1. Represent S&CL on non-LGBT committees as assigned.

D2. Act as a sponsor of (self-selected) S&CL Visions Teams.

D3. Participate in professional organizations such as the National Coalition of Directors of LGBT Resources in Higher Education, NASPA, ACPA, the Southern California LGBT CRC Directors' Organization, and National Gay and Lesbian Task Force.

D4. Special projects as assigned.

Qualifications

Working knowledge of fundamental principles of student development.

Working knowledge of fundamental principles of education and human development theory, especially regarding adolescents in a college setting.

Working knowledge of fundamental principals of sociology, psychology, and community development, especially in college residence halls.

Demonstrated detailed knowledge and understanding of LGBT issues and needs and the intersection of race, class, gender, and sexual orientation.

Experience and working knowledge of the role of student services in a large, public research university.

Ability to communicate and establish effective working relationships with students, faculty, staff, and community members of diverse cultural, social, political, and religious backgrounds and varied age, gender, and sexual orientation.

Strong verbal communication skills including listening skills. Strong written communication skills including ability to compose clear, grammatically correct, well-constructed correspondence, reports, and informational materials.

Ability to counsel students, faculty, and staff in a sensitive and supportive manner.

Ability to establish and maintain cooperative working relationships with faculty, staff, students, and members of the community to produce quality group work.

Ability to facilitate resolution of disputes between individuals/groups.

Skill in supervising staff and directing supervisors.

Outstanding organizational skills, including ability to prioritize and carry out multiple assignments in a timely fashion with minimal direction.

Ability to effectively plan, administer, coordinate, and present a variety of concurrent and ongoing activities and educational and informational programs appropriate to a diverse university-wide audience, including extensive working knowledge of conference and event planning and coordination, including ability to identify, organize, and execute multiple event planning tasks simultaneously.

Skill in organizing information, human, and financial resources, including working knowledge of basic accounting principles and financial record keeping.

Outstanding analytical and problem-solving skills, including ability to analyze data, evaluate programs and procedures, and interpret information.

Working knowledge of effective publicity strategies and materials.
Working knowledge of microcomputer applications in a local area network, including word-processing, spreadsheet, presentation, database, and electronic mail applications, as well as the ability to create and maintain websites.

Advanced degree in Educational Leadership, Counseling, Social Psychology, or related field preferred.

Appendix F: Pennsylvania State University's LGBT Resource Room Goals and Actions

Goal 1: To create and maintain an open, safe, and welcoming space for lesbian, gay, bisexual, and transgender students, faculty, and staff, as individuals and as groups.

Actions:
1. maintain database prototype for recording space utilization and resource requests

2. coordinate orientation workshops and act as a contact for incoming students, faculty, and staff

3. provide crisis intervention and referrals for students, faculty, and staff

4. coordinate the administration of assessment tools to evaluate the campus climate for LGBT students, faculty, and staff

5. form alliances with other diversity/equity-focused groups on campus

Goal 2: To provide services, information, and referral to lesbian, gay, bisexual, and transgender students, faculty, and staff to enhance their educational experiences as well as to address their concerns.

Actions:
1. update resource notebooks

2. create, publish, and distribute LGBT newsletter four times a year (both on-line and in hard copy)

3. develop, update, and distribute relevant brochures and printed media

4. maintain LGBT Resource Web Page

5. collaborate with appropriate faculty, students, and staff organizations to develop programs and activities for events of particular interest to LGBT persons (e.g., LGBT History Month, National Coming out Day, Pride Week, etc.)

6. assist LGBT Support Network Committee in expanding , maintaining, and assessing the LGBT Support Network

7. create faculty/staff advisory board

8. develop "Reference Guide to the LGBTA Resource Room" for dissemination (specifically to the new USG Department of LGBT Affairs)

Goal 3: To provide programs and opportunities that will encourage and enhance community leadership, role modeling, and peer education training for lesbian, gay, bisexual, and transgender students.

Actions:
1. update teaching manuals for Straight Talk class

2. coordinate Straight Talks for the Penn State community

3. provide opportunities (e.g., brown-bag colloquia) for LGBT graduate students to discuss issues and concerns in a safe and supportive environment

4. provide support for LGBT student groups (Coalition of LGBT Graduate Students, ALLIES, Lambda Delta Lambda, Delta Lambda Phi)

5. provide support for the Rainbow Alliance

6. develop LGBT mentoring program

7. develop and implement Queer Leadership Retreat for LGBT student leaders

Goal 4: To establish, maintain, and promote an open and supportive campus environment whereby any sexual orientation/ gender identity is experienced as a positive aspect of individual identity.

Actions:
1. assist with policy development and implementation

2. expand/maintain LGBT library/ resource center

3. serve as a link and a resource for State College/Center County community regarding LGBT issues and concerns

4. promote LGBT resources (e.g., resource room) to university community through various media outlets (e.g., Web page, showcase displays, articles in *Intercom* and *Collegian*, etc.)

5. provide resources and act as a contact point for other PSU locations in regard to LGBT issues and concerns

6. support the coordination of efforts regarding university policy changes or enhancements for the LGBT community

Goal 5: To develop and maintain the Penn State community's understanding of lesbian, gay, bisexual, and transgender equity through sponsorship and support of specific educational programming.

Actions:
1. assist with current educational efforts regarding LGBT issues and concerns (e.g., education salons, book group, etc.)

2. provide assistance with the development of new educational programming aimed at specific constituencies within the Penn State community

3. collect and disseminate information on LGBT educational programs to faculty, staff, and students

4. assist the Education and Curriculum Integration committees in coordinating educational initiatives

5. coordinate Straight Talk class including training for peer educators providing publicity and maintaining database

6. develop and support monthly brown-bag colloquiums for LGBT students examining LGBT issues and concerns

Appendix G: Inventory of Questions for Service Providers

Counselors

1. In what ways are the counselors at Student Psychological Services (SPS) comfortable with providing services for LGBT students?

2. In what ways are the counselors trained to provide appropriate service to LGBT students?

3. Are there specific counselors designated to provide service to LGBT students? If so, please list their names and phone number. May students contact them directly?

Provider Environment

1. Are there brochures and other information pieces about LGBT students and issues in your waiting room?

2. Are there LGBT-related magazines in your waiting room?

3. Are your intake forms inclusive for LGBT students and their various presentation issues?

4. Would you like to have your intake forms reviewed for inclusion? If so, who would we call to make these arrangements?

Provider Training

1. Do you have a person on staff who is responsible for in-house training about issues affecting students? If so, please list the name and phone number.

2. Would you like to have an all-staff presentation on LGBT people and issues? If so, when?

Note: Be sure to always ask for the name of the person completing the form, their position, and the date.

Appendix H: Referral Letter, Resource Guide Referral Form, and Survey of Community Practitioners

A. Referral Letter

Elletsville Dental Center
5915 W Hwy 46
Elletsville, IN, 47429

Dear Elletsville Dental Center:

The Gay, Lesbian, Bisexual and Transgender Student Support Office opened at Indiana University five years ago. During that time our society has undergone dramatic change in its understanding of GLBT issues and has seen dramatic events that have underscored how far we still need to progress.

The GLBT Office has undertaken a project to provide all its constituents, students and non-students alike, with a comprehensive list of health care professionals currently practicing in Bloomington and the surrounding area. We wish to recognize these professionals as both sensitive to these social changes and willing to meet the needs of a gay, lesbian, and bisexual clientele.

If you would like to be listed, please fill out the referral form included in this mailing or on the Web at http://www.indiana.edu/~glbtserv/dentists.htm. You can also view the guide in progress at the same address. If you have any questions or concerns about the GLBT Health Resource Guide or the GLBT Office, please contact Carol Fischer at cafische@indiana.edu or call the GLBT Office at 812-855-4252.

We believe this guide will benefit our local community and you. Thank you for your participation!

Sincerely,

Carol Fischer
GLBT Assistant
Indiana University

B. Resource Guide Referral Form

Thank you for taking the time to complete our referral form. If there is any information on the form you would like to be kept confidential from referred clients, please indicate that on the form itself. If you need more space to answer any of the questions, please attach additional sheets to this form. We understand that our allies in the fight against discrimination have a variety of sexual orientations, gay and non-gay, as well as varying degrees of comfort publicly revealing them. We do not require that you indicate your sexual orientation on this form.

Name:
Business Name:
Address:
Phone: Fax:
Email: Web Site:

Areas of specialty:

Would you feel comfortable arranging travel for gay, lesbian, bisexual, or transgender persons or their partners?

Do you offer travel arrangements specifically for LGBT individuals or those in a committed relationship?

Would you like to receive a copy of the LGBT Travel Agent's Resource guide?

The LGBT Travel Agent's Guide is in the process of being compiled by the GLBT Student Support Services Office at Indiana University. If you have any questions, comments, or concerns regarding the Resource Guide or the Office, please contact Carol Fischer at cafische@ indiana.edu or call the GLBT Office at (812) 855-4252.

Thank you for your cooperation in this endeavor. Please fold in half and tape shut to mail postage-free.

Thank you!

C. Survey of Community Practitioners

Your name
Address
Telephone   email   website

What type of service do you provide?

Do you provide services for lesbian, gay, bisexual, and/or transgender people?

What is the nature of the service?

What is the cost of the service?

What type of insurance do you accept?

Do you provide service on a sliding scale

May we call to ask further questions about the services you provide?

May we add you to our service referral list?

Questions or comments you may have:

Appendix I: National Organizations

Higher Education Organizations

American Association of University Women
http://www.aauw.org/home.html

American College Health Association
http://www.acha.org/

American College Personnel Association (ACPA)
www.acpa.org

American Education Research Association
http://www.aera.net/

Association of American Colleges and Universities
http://www.aacu-edu.org/

Association of College Unions International
http://www.indiana.edu/~acui/

Association on Higher Education and Disability
http://www.ahead.org/

Council for the Advancement of Standards in Higher Education (CAS)
http://www.cas.edu/

National Association of Student Personnel Administrators (NASPA)
www.naspa.org

National Collegiate Athletics Association
http://www.ncaa.org/

National Consortium of Directors of LGBT Resources in Higher Education
http://www.lgbtcampus.org

National Orientation Directors Association
http://www.indiana.edu/~noda1/

Lesbian, Gay, Bisexual, and Transgender National Organizations

Bisexual Resources
http://www.biresource.org/

Gay and Lesbian Advocates and Defenders
http://www.glad.org/

Gay and Lesbian National Hotline
toll-free number 1-888-THE-GLNH (1-888-843-4564)
http://www.glnh.org/

Gay Lesbian Straight Educators Network (GLSEN)
http://www.glsen.org/

Human Rights Campaign (HRC)
http://www.hrcusa.org/

International Gay and Lesbian Human Rights Commission
http://www.iglhrc.org/

Intersex Society of North America
http://www.isna.org/

Lambda Legal Defense and Education
http://www.lambdalegal.org/

Llego: The National Latina/o Lesbian, Gay, Bisexual, & Transgender
Organization
http://www.llego.org/Encuentro.htm

National Black Lesbian and Gay Leadership Forum
http://www.nblglf.org/

National Center for Lesbian Rights
http://www.nclrights.org/

National Consortium of Directors of LGBT Resources in Higher Education.
http://www.lgbtcampus.org

National Gay and Lesbian Task Force (NGLTF)
www.ngltf.org

OutProud
http://www.outproud.org/

Parents and Friends of Lesbians and Gays (PFLAG)
http://www.pflag.org/

P.E.R.S.O.N. Project
http://www.youth.org/loco/PERSONProject/

Pride Collective Events
http://www.pridecollaborative.org/

The Transgender Guide
www.tgguide.com

Transgender Resources
http://www.lava.net/~dewilson/gender/resources.html

Appendix J: Resources for LGBT Centers, Services, Programs, and Libraries

Instructional Guides and Curricula

Advanced Antihomophobia Training.
Gay, Lesbian, Straight Education Network
10 Cannon Ridge Drive, Watertown, CT 06795-2445
phone: (212) 727- 0135
E-mail: Glsen@Glsen.Org
http://www.Glsen.Org

Affording Equal Opportunity to Gay and Lesbian Students Through Teaching and Counseling: A Training Handbook for Educators. National Education Association Human And Civil Rights Division, 1201 16th Street NW, Washington, DC 20036, phone: (202) 2328777.

Besner, H. F., & Spungin, C.1. (1995). *Gay and Lesbian Students: Understanding Their Needs.* Washington, DC: Taylor & Francis. Includes a detailed outline for a six-hour faculty workshop on homophobia.

Blumenfeld, W. (1992). *Homophobia: How We All Pay the Price.* Boston: Beacon.

Crosier, L., & Bassett, P., (Eds.). (1994). *Looking Ahead: Independent Schools Issues and Answers.* Washington, DC: Avocus.

Gallos, J., Ramsey, V. J., & Associates. (1997). *Teaching Diversity: Listening to the Soul, Speaking from the Heart (Educators Speak about the Joys and Complexities of the Work).* San Francisco: Jossey-Bass.

Jennings, K. (1994). *Becoming Visible: A Reader in Gay and Lesbian History for High School and College Students.* Boston: Alyson.

Lipkin, A. (N.D.). *A Staff Development Manual for Antihomophobia Education in the Secondary Schools.* Harvard Graduate School of Education, 210 Longfellow Hall, Cambridge, MA 02138, Phone: (617) 495-3441.

McNaught, B. (1993). *Gay Issues in the Workplace.* New York: St. Martin's.

Mitchell, L. (Ed.). (1998). *Tackling Gay Issues in School.* Gay, Lesbian, Straight Education Network, 10 Cannon Ridge Drive, Watertown, CT 0679-52445 Phone: (212) 727-0135, E-mail: Glsen@Glsen.Org, http://Www. Glsen.Org.

Riddle, D. (1994). *Alone No More: Developing a School Support System for Gay, Lesbian and Bisexual Youth* (Appendix A). Report from Minnesota Department of Education, 550 Cedar St., St. Paul, MN 55101, Phone: (612) 296-5833.

Sears, J., & Williams, W. (Eds.). (1997). *Overcoming Heterosexism and Homophobia: Strategies That Work!* New York: Columbia University Press.

Stewart, C. (1992, rev. 1995). *Training for Law Enforcement: Gay and Lesbian Cultural Awareness.* Los Angeles Gay and Lesbian Police Advisory Task Force, P.O. Box 931135, Los Angeles, CA 90093.

Stewart, C. (1995). *The Efficacy of Sexual Orientation Training in Law Enforcement Agencies.* University of Southern California.

Stewart, C. (1997). Sexual Orientation Training in Law Enforcement Agencies: A Preliminary Review of What Works. In J. Sears and W. Williams (Eds.), *Overcoming Heterosexism and Homophobia: Strategies That Work!* New York: Columbia University Press.

Textbooks and Content Resources

Listed are books that are exemplary in their fields and can be used as specialized textbooks in the classroom and college settings.

Adelman, J., et al. (1993). *Lambda Gray: A Practical Emotional and Spiritual Guide for Gays and Lesbians Who Are Growing Older.* North Hollywood, CA: Newcastle.

Arnup, K. (1995). *Lesbian Parenting: Living with Pride and Prejudice.* Charlottetown, Canada: Gynergy.

Balka, C., & Rose, A. (Eds.). (1989). *Twice Blessed: On Being Lesbian or Gay and Jewish.* Boston: Beacon.

Barnett, D. C., & Sanlo, R. L. (1998). The Lavender Web: LGBT Resources on the Internet. In R. Sanlo (Ed.) *Working with Lesbian, Gay, Bisexual, and Transgender College Students: A Handbook for Faculty and Administrators.* Westport, CT: Greenwood Press.

Barret, R., & Robinson, B. (1990). *Gay Fathers.* Lexington, MA: Lexington.

Benokraitis, N. V. (Ed.). (1997). *Subtle Sexism.* Thousand Oaks, CA: Sage.

Blumenfeld, W. (1992). *Homophobia: How We All Pay the Price.* Boston: Beacon.

Blumenfeld, W., & Raymond, D. (1993). *Looking at Gay and Lesbian Life.* Rev. ed. Boston: Beacon.

Borhek, M. V. (1983). *Coming Out to Parents.* New York: Pilgrim.

Bowker, L. H. (Ed.). (1997). *Masculinities and Violence.* Thousand Oaks, CA: Sage.

Cabaj, R. P., & Purcell, D. W. (Eds.). (1998). *On the Road to Same-Sex Marriage: A Supportive Guide to Psychological, Political, and Legal Issues.* San Francisco: Jossey-Bass.

Cabaj, R. P., & Stein, T. S. (1996). *Textbook of Homosexuality and Mental Health.* Washington, DC: American Psychiatric Press, pp. 154–156.

Cohen, S., & Cohen, D. (1989). *When Someone You Know is Gay.* New York: M. Evans.

Cohn, M. (1995). *Do What I Say: Ms. Behavior's Guide to Gay and Lesbian Etiquette.* Boston: Houghton Mifflin.

Corvino, 1. (Ed.). (1997). *Same Sex: Debating the Ethics, Science, and Culture of Homosexuality.* Lanham, MD: Rowman & Littlefield.

Davis, D. M., Yarber, W. L., Bauserman, R., Schreer, G., & Davis, S. L. (1998). *Handbook of Sexuality-Related Measures.* Thousand Oaks, CA: Sage.

DeCrescenzo, T. (Ed.). (1994). Helping *Gay and Lesbian Youth: New Policies, New Programs, New Practice.* New York: Haworth/Harrington Park.

DeCrescenzo, T. (1997). *Gay and Lesbian Professionals in the Closet: Who's In, Who's Out, and Why.* New York: Harrington Park.

Drucker, J. (1998). *Families of Value: Gay and Lesbian Parents and Their Children Speak Out*. New York: Plenum.

Duberman, M., Vicinus, M., & Chauncey, G., Jr. (Eds.). (1990). *Hidden from History: Reclaiming the Gay and Lesbian Past*. New York: Meridian.

Eisenback, H. (1996). *Lesbianism Made Easy*. New York: Crown.

Eisler, R. (1995). *Sacred Pleasure: Sex, Myth, and the Politics of the Body*. San Francisco: Harper.

Eskeridge, W. N., Jr. (1996). *The Case for Same-Sex Marriage: From Sexual Liberty to Civilized Commitment*. New York: Free Press.

Evans, N. J., & Wall, V. A. (Eds.). (1991). *Beyond Tolerance: Gays, Lesbians and Bisexuals on Campus*. Alexandria, VA: American College Personnel Association.

Faderman, L. (1981). *Odd Girls and Twilight Lovers: A History of Lesbian Life in Twentieth Century America*. New York: Penguin.

Fairchild, B., & Hayward, N. (1989). *Now That You Know: What Every Parent Should Know about Homosexuality*. New York: Harcourt.

Fanning, P., & Mckay, M. (1993). *Being a Man: A Guide to the New Masculinity*. Oakland, CA: New Harbinger.

Farmer, H. S., & Associates. (1997). *Diversity and Women's Career Development*. Thousand Oaks, CA: Sage.

Firestein, B. A. (Ed.). (1996). *Bisexuality: The Psychology and Politics of an Invisible Minority*. Thousand Oaks, CA: Sage.

Ford, M. T. (1996). *The World Out There: Becoming a Part of the Lesbian and Gay Community*. New York: New Press.

Garnets, L. D., & Kimmel, D. C. (Eds.). (1993). *Psychological Perspectives on Lesbian and Gay Male Experiences*. New York: Columbia University Press.

Green, B., & Herek, G. M. (Eds.). (1994). *Lesbian and Gay Psychology: Theory, Research, and Clinical Applications*. Thousand Oaks, CA: Sage.

Greenberg, D. (1988). *The Construction of Homosexuality*. Chicago: University of Chicago Press.

Greene, B. (Ed.). (1997). *Ethnic and Cultural Diversity among Lesbians and Gay Men*. Thousand Oaks, CA: Sage.

Groff, D. (Ed.). (1997). *Out Facts: Just about Every Thing You Need to Know about Gay and Lesbian Life*. Out Magazine. New York: Universe.

Gruskin, E. P. (1998). *The Care and Treatment of Lesbian and Bisexual Women: A Guide for Health Professionals*. Thousand Oaks, CA: Sage.

Hanes, K. (1994). *The Gay Guy's Guide to Life: 463 Maxims, Manners, and Mottoes for the Gay Nineties*. New York: Simon & Schuster.

Harris, D. (1997). *Rise and Fall of Gay Culture*. New York: Hyperion.

Hemphill, E. (1991). *Brother to Brother: New Writings by Black Gay Men*. Boston: Alyson.

Herek, G. M. (Ed.). (1998). *Stigma and Sexual Orientation: Understanding Prejudice against Lesbians, Gay Men, and Bisexuals*. Thousand Oaks, CA: Sage.

Herek, G. M., & Berrill, K. (Eds.). (1992). *Hate Crimes: Confronting Violence against Lesbians and Gay Men*. Newbury Park, CA: Sage.

Herek, G. M., & Greene, B. (Eds.). (1995). *AIDS, Identity and Community: The HIV Epidemic and Lesbians and Gay Men*. Thousand Oaks, CA: Sage.

Hogan, S., & Hudson, L. (1998). *Completely Queer: Gay and Lesbian Encyclopedia*. New York: Holt.

Hunter, N. D., Michaelson, S. E., & Stoddard, T B. (1992). *The Rights of Lesbians and Gay Men: The Basic ACLU Guide to a Gay Person's Rights*. Carbondale: Southern Illinois University Press.

Kaiser, C. (1997). *The Gay Metropolis, 1940–1996*. Boston: Houghton Mifflin.

Kominars, S. B., & Kominars, K. D. (1996). *Accepting Ourselves and Others: A Journey into Recovery from Addiction and Compulsive Behavior for Gays, Lesbians, and Bisexuals*. Center City, MN: Hazelden.

Landrine, H., & Klonoff, E. A. (1997). *Discrimination against Women: Prevalence, Consequences, Remedies*. Thousand Oaks, CA: Sage.

Lowenthal, M. (Ed.). (1997). *Gay Men at the Millennium: Sex, Spirit, Community*. New York: Jeremy P. Videos Tarcher/Putnam.

Lucier, A. (1998). Technology: A Potential Ally for Lesbian, Gay, Bisexual, and Transgender Students. In R. Sanlo (Ed.), *Working with Lesbian, Gay, Bisexual, and Transgender College Students: A Handbook for Faculty and Administrators*. Westport, CT: Greenwood Press.

Lutes, M. A., & Montgomery, M. S. (1998). Out in the Stacks: Opening Academic Library Collections to Lesbian, Gay, Bisexual, and Transgender Students. In R. Sanlo (Ed.), *Working with Lesbian, Gay, Bisexual, and Transgender College Students: A Handbook for Faculty and Administrators*. Westport, CT: Greenwood Press.

Marcus, E. (1993). *Is It a Choice? Answers to 300 of the Most Frequently Asked Questions about Gays and Lesbians*. San Francisco: HarperCollins.

Mark, R., & Portugal, B. (1996). *Victories of the Heart: Inside Story of a Pioneer Men's Group (How Men Help Each Other Change Their Lives)*. Rockport, MA: Element.

Martin, S. E., & Jurik, N. C. (1996). *Doing Justice, Doing Gender: Women in Law and Criminal Justice Occupations*. Thousand Oaks, CA: Sage.

Miller, D. A. (1993). *Coping When a Parent Is Gay*. New York: Rosen.

Mitchell, M., & Leavitt, D. (Eds.). (1997). *Pages Passed from Hand to Hand: The Hidden Tradition of Homosexual Literature in English from 1748 to 1914*. Boston: Houghton Mifflin.

The National Consortium f Directors of LGBT Resources in Higher Education. http://www.lgbtcampus.org

The National Gay and Lesbian Task Force (NGLTF). *Campus Organizing Manual*. Available on the NGLTF Web site at Ngltf@Ngltf.Org

Our Bodies, Ourselves for the New Century: A Book by and for Women. The Boston Women's Health Book Collective. (1998). New York: Simon & Schuster.

Outcalt, C. (1998). The Life Cycle of Campus LGBT Organizations: Finding Ways to Sustain Involvement and Effectiveness. In R. Sanlo (Ed.), *Working with Lesbian, Gay, Bisexual, and Transgender College Students: A Handbook for Faculty and Administrators*. Westport, CT: Greenwood Press.

Penn, R. (1997). *Gay Men's Wellness Guide: The Natural Lesbian and Gay Health Association's Complete Book of Physical, Emotional and Mental Health and Well-being for Every Gay Male*. New York: Holt.

Petersen, A. (1998). *Unmasking the Masculine: "Men" and "Identity" in a Skeptical Age.* Thousand Oaks, CA: Sage.

Pharr, S. (1988). *Homophobia: A Weapon of Sexism.* Little Rock, AR: Chardon Press.

Real, T. (1997). *I Don't Want to Talk About It: Overcoming the Secret Legacy of Male Depression.* New York: Scribner.

Reed, R. (1997). *Growing Up Gay: Sorrows and Joys of Gay and Lesbian Adolescents.* New York: Norton.

Sabo, D., & Gordon, D. (Eds.). (1995). *Men's Health and Illness.* Thousand Oaks, CA: Sage.

Sanlo, R. (1999). *Unheard Voices: The Effects of Silence on Lesbian and Gay Educators.* Westport, CT: Greenwood Press.

Sanlo, R. (Ed.). (1998). *Working with Lesbian, Gay, Bisexual, and Transgender College Students: A Handbook for Faculty and Administrators.* Westport, CT: Greenwood Press.

Shilts, R. (1993). *Conduct Unbecoming: Lesbians and Gays in the U.S. Military.* New York: St. Martin's.

Smith, B. (1997). *Openly Bob/Bob Smith.* New York: Rob Weisbach.

Strock, C. (1998). *Married Women Who Love Women.* New York: Doubleday.

Tierney, W. G. (1997). *Academic Outlaw: Queer Theory and Cultural Studies in the Academy.* Thousand Oaks, CA: Sage.

Wall, V., & Evans, N. (Eds.). (2000). *Toward Acceptance: Sexual Orientation Issues on Campus.* University Press of America

Ward, A. (1998). Advising Student Organizations: Opportunities for Student Development. In R. Sanlo (Ed.), *Working with Lesbian, Gay, Bisexual, and Transgender College Students: A Handbook for Faculty and Administrators.* Westport, CT: Greenwood Press.

White, J., & Martinez, C. (Eds.). (1997). *The Lesbian Health Book: Caring for Ourselves.* Seattle: Seal.

White, M. (1994). *Stranger at the Gate: To Be Gay and Christian in America.* New York: Simon & Schuster.

Williams, W. L. (1992). *The Spirit and the Flesh: Sexual Diversity in American Indian Culture*. Boston: Beacon.

Videos

After Stonewall. A sequel to Before Stonewall, this film documents gay and lesbian life following landmark New York riots of 1969.

All God's Children (25 min.) 1986. Celebration of black churches as they embrace and acknowledge the spiritual value of their gay and lesbian members. Women Vision Library, 22D Hollywood Ave., Hohokus, NJ 07423 phone: (800) 343-5540.

Always My Kid: A Family Guide to Understanding Homosexuality (74 min.) 1994. Parents and children of Parents and Friends of Lesbians and Gays (PFLAG) tell their experiences. Triangle Video Productions, 550 Westcott, Suite 400, Houston, TX 77007, phone: (713) 869-4477.

Anti-Gay Hate Crimes. This video takes a guided tour through the Christian Right's anti-gay factions. Watch hatemonger Reverend Fred Phelps and his followers angrily picket Matthew Shepard's funeral and see shocking footage of the re-enactment of Shepard's murder. Finally, go inside the headquarters of the Family Research Council, the largest and most powerful anti-gay organization in the nation. As gays come out of the closet, those intolerant of homosexuality may also be stepping out to force an entire segment of society back into hiding—or face deadly consequences. Part of A&E's Investigative Reports series and can be ordered from the A&E on-line store.

Ballot Measure 9. This film covers the story of a measure for Oregon's 1992 ballot that would have denied civil rights to lesbian and gay people. It interviews representatives from both sides and offers a chilling reminder of the anger and violence in which some anti-gay activists engage in their challenges to a more inclusive world.

Beautiful Thing (90 min.). A crowd-pleasing heartfelt drama of young love with an irrepressible sound track by Mama Cass. The accents of the main characters are hard to understand for some at first, but the film is well worth the time to learn to understand the remarkable characters that it portrays.

Before Stonewall: The Making of Gay and Lesbian Community. This film examines the background to this sudden burst of political energy-from the social experimentation of the Roaring Twenties and the discovery of the size of the gay population during World War II, to the scapegoating of homosexuals during the McCarthy era and the development of the early homophile rights movement (winner of two Emmy Awards).

Both of My Moms' Names Are Judy (10 min.) 1994. Powerful and moving series of interviews with children (ages 6-11) who have gay or lesbian parents. Training materials for Overcoming Homophobia in the Elementary Classroom are also available from the Lesbian and Gay Parents Association, P.O. Box 52, 519 Castro St., San Francisco, CA 94114-2577, phone: (415) 522-8773 E-mail: lgpasf @ aol.com.

The Castro. Uplifting edification about the gay mecca. *The Castro* recounts the evolution of San Francisco's gay community as it tells the story of this former German/Irish immigrant neighborhood. This exceptionally touching documentary is full of rare archival footage and features interviews with such luminaries as Del Martin and Phyllis Lyon (founders of the first lesbian organization, the Daughters of Bilitis), gay historian Allan Bérubé, and former Pomo Afro Homo, Brian Freeman.

The Celluloid Closet. Lily Tomlin narrates this assembly of footage from 120 films that illustrate the changing face of cinema sexuality from cruel stereotypes, to covert love, to the activist triumph of the 1990s.

Changing Our Minds: The Story of Dr. Evelyn Hooker. During the repressive 1950s, Dr. Evelyn Hooker undertook groundbreaking research that led to a radical discovery: homosexuals were not, by definition, "sick." Her finding sent shock waves through the psychiatric community and culminated in a major victory for gay rights. In 1974 the weight of her studies, along with gay activism, forced the American Psychiatric Association to remove homosexuality from its official manual of mental disorders. Startling archival footage of medical procedures used to "cure" homosexuality, images from the underground gay world of the McCarthy era, and "home movies" of literary icon Christopher Isherwood bring to life history that we must never forget. Dr. Hooker's insights into "gay marriage" and the "gay community" (a term that she coined) make this documentary education at its most exciting and enjoyable. This film was nominated for an Academy Award.

Coming Out under Fire (71 min.) 1994. Powerful documentary profiling the experiences of nine gay and lesbian veterans, documented by Director Arthur Dong. He combined rare archival footage, declassified documents, interviews, and photographs. Witness the persecution of these brave men and women who volunteered to fight for their country, only to be the targets of witch-hunts to find the "undesirables" in the service. Wolfe Video, P.O. Box 64, New Almaden, CA 95042, phone: (800) 438-9653 or (800) 642-5247, fax: (408) 268-9449, http://www.wolfevideo.com.

Common Threads: Stories from the Quilt (73 min.) 1992. Academy Award-winning film uses powerful stories from the Names Project AIDS Quilt to recount the tumultuous history of the first decade of the AIDS epidemic in America. Telling Pictures, 121 Ninth St., San Francisco, CA 94103, phone: (415) 864-6714, http://www.tellingpix.com.

Doña Herlinda and Her Son. Mexican comedy-of-manners feature film recounts story of a gay surgeon and his somewhat manipulative, but good-hearted, mother. This is lightweight, optimistic, sexy entertainment.

For Better of Worse: Same-Sex Marriages in America (1997) video examines the landmark Hawaii case that is rewriting marriage laws nationwide and offers interviews with leading activists on both sides of this divisive issue. This is part of the Investigative Reports series on A&E and is available via the A&E Web site.

Forbidden Love. This fun and fascinating documentary explores lesbian sexuality and survival during the sexual dark ages of the 1950s and 1960s. The film uses a backdrop of book covers, tabloid headlines, archival photographs, and film clips. It features interviews with writers and readers of campy lesbian pulp novels of that time period and includes a fictional drama re-enacting a young woman's coming out and erotic seduction.

Gay Cops (15 min.) 1992. Produced by Lowell Bergman, this 60 Minutes video highlights the conflict between being gay and working as a law enforcement officer. Excerpts from the Los Angeles Police Department, Mitch Grobeson case, San Francisco Police Department, and the FBI. Item CSM20913A. CBS Video, PO. Box 2284, S. Burlington, VT 05407, phone: (800) 848-3256.

Gay Issues in the Workplace (25 min.) 1993. A cross-section of gay, lesbian, and bisexual workers speak for themselves in this engaging and enlightening discussion hosted by Brian McNaught. TRB Production, P.O. Box 2014, Provincetown, MA 02657, phone: (508) 487-3700, http://www.brianmcnaught.com.

Gay Lives and Culture Wars (27 min.) 1994. Gay youths tell their stories against the backdrop of antigay propaganda used in Oregon's Ballot Measure 9. Democracy Media, P.O. Box 82777, Portland, OR 97282, phone: (503) 235-5036.

Gay Youth (40 min.) 1993. Poignant stories of two adolescents: one who committed suicide, the other openly gay in high school. With classroom guide. Wolfe Video, P .O. Box 64, New Almaden, CA 95042, phone: (800) 438-9653, (800) 642-5247, fax: (408) 268-9449, http://www.wolfevideo.com.

Growing Up Gay and Lesbian (57 min.) 1993. Wonderful presentation by Brian McNaught about what it is like to grow up gay in a heterosexist society. He a powerful face on the issue with this non-threatening, but highly effective, presentation on the isolation and alienation of growing up gay. In the same gentle manner with which he has made allies of heterosexual audiences in the past 20 years, McNaught explains what it is like growing up with a secret that you don't understand and are afraid to tell for the fear of losing people's love and respect. It also received the highest rating from the American Library Association. Available from TRB Productions. TRB Production, P.O. Box 2014, Provincetown, MA 02657, phone: (508) 487-3700, http://www.brianmcnaught.com.

Hate, Homophobia and Schools (60 min.) 1995. Discussions between gay and antihomosexual youths and adults about what it is like to grow up gay in this society. NEWIST/ CESA 7, IS 1040, UWGreen Bay, Green Bay, WI 54311 phone: (920) 465-2599, (800) 633-7445, http://www.uwgb.edu/newist E-mail: newist@uwgb.edu.

Hermaphrodites Speak! Before 1997, virtually the only pictures of intersex people available were pathologizing and dehumanizing photos in medical texts. In 1996, for the first time, intersex people came together for a weekend retreat to discuss their lives and their pain and to heal together. This film documents the incredible spirit that grew during that weekend. Eight of the retreat-goers sit together and speak simply, forcefully, and articulately about themselves and about their passion to change social and medical treatment of people who are born different. Because this tape was produced as a home video, the image quality is poor, but the sound is quite good. Available from the Intersex Society of North America., http://www.isna.org

Homo Promo. Take a crash course about lesbian and gay movie history with this look at the best and worst of Hollywood hard-sells of this "subject matter." It features trailers for virtually every major mainstream gay and lesbian film produced between 1956 and 1976.

Homophobia in the Workplace. Brian McNaught explains why companies need to address issues of concern to gay, lesbian, and bisexual employees and how to do so effectively. This video received the highest rating from the American Library Association. Available from TRB Productions, P.O. Box 2014, Provincetown, MA 02657, phone: (508) 487-3700, http://www.brianmcnaught.com.

It's Elementary: Talking about Gay Issues in School (78 min. or shorter 37-min. version) 1997. A feature-length documentary film shot in schools across the United States, it makes a compelling case for including gay issues in multicultural education. Produced by Women's Educational Media, 2180 Bryant St., Suite 203, San Francisco, CA 94110, phone: (415) 641-4616

Last Call at Maud's. This is a fascinating look at the life and times of the world's longest-running lesbian bar, San Francisco's Maud's. Opened in 1966, Maud's was a thriving and popular meeting place for a "secret sorority" until it closed its doors in 1989. Interwoven are rare archives of the gay bar scene of the 1940s, vice raids of the 1950s, and the counterculture of the 1960s with personal stories of coming out, sexual politics, and humorous adventures.

License to Kill (80 min.) 1997. The film premiered at the 1997 Sundance Film Festival and was awarded honors for Best Documentary Director and the Film-maker's Trophy Award. This film explores the relationship between internalized homophobia and maleness through a series of interviews with men convicted of homophobic murders. These men are not demonized but rather are studied to see how societal hatred of gay men and lesbians brought them to be capable of such terrible actions. A study guide is available for this film. Deep Focus Production, 4506 Palmero Drive, Los Angeles, CA 90065-4237, phone: (213) 254-7072, fax: (213) 254-7112, E-mail: adongla@aol.com http://filmmag.com/ community/adong

The Life and Times of Harvey Milk (50 min.) 1984. By Robert Epstein and Rich-ard Schmiechen. Gay politics of San Francisco during the 1970s and 1980s, par-ticularly surrounding the events of Supervisor Harvey Milk's assassination. Tell-ing Pictures, 121 Ninth Street, San Francisco, CA 94103, phone: (415) 864-6714 http://www.tellingpix.com.

A Little Respect (30 min.) 1991. Helps college students combat homophobia. Rutgers University, Department of Health Education, University Heights, 249 University Ave., Newark, NJ 07102, phone: (973) 353-1236

Live to Tell (30 min.) 1995. A touching, brave account of the first gay and les-bian senior prom ever. *Live to Tell* captures these students' stories as they affirm their self-respect by joining together to realize a collective dream—their very own high school prom, attended by over 200 gay and lesbian students Wolfe Video, P.O. Box 64, New Almaden, CA 95042, phone: (800) 438-9653, (800) 642-5247, fax: (408) 268-9449, http://www.wolfevideo.com.

Looking for Langston (1988). Film by Isaac Julien is a meditation on the life and work of Langston Hughes and brings the Harlem Renaissance out of the closet.

Ma Vie en Rose (My Life in Pink). In this dramatic feature film, six-year-old Ludovic believes that he was meant to be a girl and awaits a miracle: the correc-tion of that mistake. Instead, he finds rejection, isolation, and guilt and has to cope with the intense reactions of family, friends, and neighbors. Winner of the Golden Globe for Best Foreign Language Film, this unique work delivers magic of the rarest sort through a story of difference, rejection, and childlike faith in miracles.

Nitrate Kisses. This film explores eroded emulsions and images for lost vestiges of lesbian and gay culture. Archival footage from the first gay film in the United States, *Lot of Sodom* (1933), and footage from German documentary and narra-tive films of the 1930s are interwoven with current images of desire in this sexy and haunting documentary.

Not All Parents Are Straight. The film examines the dynamics of the parent–child relationship within several different households where children are being raised by gay and lesbian parents. Through open and honest interviews with the children and their parents, the film explores emotional conflicts within the family, legal custody problems, and the social discrimination that these families face.

On Being Gay (57 min.) 1994. In this highly praised, two-part presentation, Brian McNaught explains the unique aspects of growing up gay. Addresses often cited, but erroneously interpreted, biblical quotes. Can be used in 20-minute segments. TRB Production, P.O. Box 2014, Provincetown, MA 02657, phone: (508) 487-3700, http://www.brianmcnaught.com.

One Nation under God (50 min.) 1994. This film explores the variety of funny, bizarre, and often terrifying methods that have been used over the decades in attempts to "cure" gay men and lesbians of their homosexuality. It visits "ex-gay" ministries and focuses on the former leaders of one such ministry who happened to fall in love. Video Finder (for Public Television), 425 E. Colorado St., #B10, Glendale, CA 91205, phone: (800) 328-7271.

Oranges are Not the Only Fruit. Profile of young lesbian girl grappling with fundamentalist parents and eccentric friends. This BBC production is a masterful re-creation of this cult novel and stars Cathryn Bradshaw and Charlotte Coleman.

Out at Work: America Undercover (60 min.) 1998. The best documentary detailing people who experienced job discrimination for being lesbian or gay. Includes the Cracker Barrel case. HBO Consumer Affairs, 1100 Avenue of the Americas, New York, NY 10036, phone: (212) 512-1000.

Out for a Change: Addressing Homophobia in Women's Sports (27 min.) 1996. Women Vision Library, 22D Hollywood Ave., Hohokus, NJ 07423, phone: (800) 343-5540.

Out in Suburbia (28 min.) 1994. A wide range of lesbians tell about their families, friends, and loves. Wolfe Video, P.O. Box 64, New Almaden, CA 95042 phone: (800) 438-9653, (800) 642-5247, fax: (408) 2689449 http://www.wolfevideo.com.

Out of the Past: The Struggle for Gay and Lesbian Rights in America. This excellent film reviews the stories of civil rights activists (including Henry Gerber, Bayard Rustin, and more) through the eyes of Kelli Peterson, a 17-year-old high school student in Salt Lake City, http://www.glsen.org.

Positive Image (30 min.) 1995. Parents of lesbians and gays speak out. Produced and directed by Gerry Allers, Federation of Parents and Friends of Lesbians and Gays, P.O. Box 4087, Hollywood, CA 91617, phone: (626) 914-1421 http:// www.pflag.org.

The Question of Equality. A provocative, enlightening, and highly entertaining series from public television documents the struggle for lesbian and gay equality. (Usually sold as a boxed set with all four parts)

   Part 1: Out Rage '69. Covers the Mattachine Society demonstrations, the Stonewall riots , the emergence of a new generation of gay activists in the early 1970s, and Anita Bryant's 1977 Dade County "Save Our Children" campaign (the first orchestrated attempt to squelch lesbian and gay civil rights).

   Part 2: Culture Wars. Examines antigay violence by focusing on the brutal murder of Julio Rivera and the organized protest that followed. It also covers the conservative attack on public arts funding and the religious rights efforts to mount Oregon's Ballot Measure 9 to deny equal protection to lesbians and gay men.

   Part 3: Hollow Liberty. Includes the history of the U.S. military's discriminatory policies (including a 1980 attempt to discharge 24 women sailors accused of being lesbians). Also focuses on the 1986 Supreme Court decision in Bowers v. Hardwick, which upheld Georgia's sodomy statute.

   Part 4: Generation Q. Includes segments on students at the EAGLE Center (a gay alternative high school in Los Angeles), interviews with members of Albuquerque's Under 21 lesbian and gay youth group, and a story on actions by students in Massachusetts to write, file, and lobby on behalf of legislation to outlaw discrimination against lesbian and gay students.

The Rhetoric of Intolerance (30 min.) 1996. Dr. Mel White was once a ghost-writer for leaders of the religious right. He later came out as gay. In this video, he addresses intolerance spread by the religious Right. The Justice Report, 1280 Bison, Suite B9431, Newport Beach, CA 92660, phone: (714) 224-9392.

The Right to Marry (72 min.) 1996. Interviews with Dr. Mel White, Phyllis Burke, Richard Mohr, and Kevin Cathcart discussing the issues around lesbians' and gay men's right to marry. Partners Task Force for Gay & Lesbian Couples, Box 9685, Seattle, WA 981090685, phone: (206) 935-1206, E-mail: demian@buddybuddy.com.

The Sexual Brain (50 min.) 1987. Looks for causes of human sexuality through brain research. This was a KCET Public Television (Los Angeles) production. Contact: Film for the Humanities and Sciences, P.O. Box 2053, Princeton, NJ 085432053, phone: (800) 257-5126, E-mail: custserv@films.com http://www.films.com.

Sexual Orientation: Reading Between the Labels (30 min.) 1993. Discussions between gay and antihomosexual youths and adults about what it is like to grow up gay in this society. NEWIST/ CESA 7, IS 1040, UWGreen Bay, Green Bay, WI 54311, phone: (920) 465-2599, http://www.uwgb.edu/newist E-mail: newist@uwgb.edu

Silent Pioneers (30 min.) 1984. Produced by Patricia Ginger Synder. Contrary to popular myth, gay men and lesbians do grow old. Through profiles of eight men and women, *Silent Pioneers* tells us their stories, how they have lived and loved, and how, despite harmful societal prejudices about gay people, they have led meaningful lives. *Silent Pioneers* is a film about struggle and silence and the emergence from both. Filmsmaker Library, 133 East 58th Street, New York, NY 10022, phone: (212) 3556545.

Silver Lake Life (99 min.) 1994. Winner of over 10 international awards, including the grand jury prize at the Sundance Film festival, *Silver Lake Life* is the extraordinary video diary of living with AIDS. This film documents the love and dedication of longtime companions Tom Joslin and Mark Massi and their incredible journey that is ultimately a celebration of strength of the human spirit. Wolfe Video, P .O. Box 64, New Almaden, CA 95042, phone: (800) 438-9653 http://www.wolfevideo.com

The Silver Screen: Color Me Lavender. Mark Rapport takes us on a hilarious and provocative romp through the hidden and not-so-hidden gay undercurrent of Hollywood's golden years. Dan Butler acts as the tour guide as the film uncovers efforts to launder American cinema of even the faintest of gay influences.

Speaking for Ourselves: Portraits of Gay and Lesbian Youth (27 min.) 1994. Presents the lives of five lesbian and gay youths. Intermedia, 1700 Westlake Ave. N., Suite 724, Seattle, WA 98109, phone: (800) 553-8336 http://www.intermediaine.com.

Stolen Moments. Canadian documentary presents a sweeping chronicle of lesbian history. Social history buffs and those interested in queer culture will appreciate this film's balanced, well-informed, often celebratory approach.

Straight from the Heart (24 min.) 1995. Moving accounts of parents' struggles with homophobia on learning that their child is lesbian or gay. Women Vision Library, 22D Hollywood Ave., Hohokus, NJ 07423, (800) 343-5540.

Teaching Respect for All (52 min.) 1996. A project of the Gay, Lesbian, & Straight Teachers Network. This is a "Homophobia 101" workshop. GLSTN, 122 W. 26th Street, Suite 1100, New York, NY 10001, phone: (212) 727-0135 http://www.glstn.org.

Tongues Untied: Black Men Loving Black Men. This is the acclaimed account of Black gay life by Emmy Award-winning director Marlon Riggs. Using poetry, personal testimony, rap, and performance, Tongues Untied describes the homophobia and racism that confront Black gay men. Some of the tales are troublesome: the man refused entry to a gay bar because of his color; the college student left bleeding on the sidewalk after a gay-bashing; the loneliness and isolation of the drag queen. Yet Riggs also presents the rich flavor of the Black gay male experience, from protest marches and smoky bars, to the language of the "snap diva" and Vogue dancer. A benchmark film that speaks for itself.

Transgender Revolution. This video attempts to venture beyond damaging stereotypes for an intimate, uncensored look at America's growing transgender communities. This is part of the Investigative Reports series on A&E and is available from the A&E Web site.

Transsexual Menace. Director Rosa Von Praunheim shows the enormous range of mind-sets and physical types that exist in the trans community. Von Praunheim intercuts medical footage with little-known facts and interviews with transsexuals and the health care professionals who help them and the casualties in the process.

Trevor (18 min.) 1995. Academy Award-winning movie tells the story of a 13-year-old boy, his emerging sexuality, and his realization that he is gay. Intermedia, 1700 Westlake Ave. N., Suite 724, Seattle, WA 98109, phone: (800) 553-8336, http://www.intermediainc.com.

We Were Marked with a Big "A." This intimate interview with three gay Holocaust survivors reveals a story hidden for years from the public. Shown at the U.S. Holocaust Museum in 1993, it tells how these men were labeled with an "A," which they were forced to wear around their legs before the pink triangle was instituted as the mark of a homosexual.

What If I'm Gay (55 min.) 1987. Dramatizes the problems faced because of coming out gay while an adolescent. CBS After School Special. Coronet/Phoenix Film & Video, 2349 Chaffee Drive, St. Louis, MO 63146 phone: (800) 777-8100

Who's Afraid of Project 10? (23 min.) 1989. Video interview with Virginia Uribe, founder of Project 10; gay and lesbian students; political and religious opponents to the program; and the mother of a teen who committed suicide over being gay. Friends of Project 10, 7850 Melrose Ave., Los Angeles, CA 90046 phone: (213) 651-5200, http://www.project10.org

Your Mom's a Lesbian, Here's Your Lunch: Have a Good Day at School; Eve's Daughters; Maybe We're Talking about a Different God (1996). Three videos look at spirituality and homophobia in the church. Leonardo's Children, Inc., 26 Newport Bridge Road, Warwick, NY 10990, phone: (914) 986-6888

Internet Sources

The World Wide Web is a significant source for information on lesbian, gay, transgender, transsexual, and intersex issues. For educators, one of the better sources is Gregory M. Herek, Ph.D., Sexual Orientation: Science, Education, and Policy, under the auspices of University of California at Davis. Most universities and Internet service providers (ISPs) also have active queer sites that can be springboards to other sites on the Web. Probably the most comprehensive site is the Queer Resource Directory. It contains over 14,000 connections to virtually everything related to this topic.

Queer Resource Directory
www.qrd.com

Bisexual Resource Center
www.qrd.conVqrd/orgs/BRC

Hawaii Equal Rights Marriage Project
www.qrd.com/qrd/orgs/HERMP

Lesbian, gay, and bisexual organizations
www.qrd.com/qrdlorgs

Religious organizations
www.qrd.com/qrd/religion/orgs

BiNet USA
www.binetusa.org/)

FTM International! (female-to-male transvestites and transsexuals)
www.ftmintl.org

Gay & Lesbian Alliance Against Defamation
www.glaad.org/glaad

Gay, Lesbian, & Straight Educators Network
www.glsen.org

Intersex Society of North America
www.isna.org

Kinsey Institute for Research in Sex, Gender, and Reproduction
www.indiana.edu/kinsey

Law Enforcement Gays and Lesbians International
users.aol.com/legalmn2/LegalI.html

ONE Institute/International Gay and Lesbian Archives
www.edu/isd/archives/oneigia

Parents and Friends of Lesbians and Gays
www.pflag.org

Queer America (national database of LGBT resources)
www.queer.com

Sexual orientation science, education, and policy
http://psychology.ucdavis.edulrainbow

Studies on gay and lesbian language
www.hng.nwu.edu/ward/gaybib.htrnl

Transgender Forum
www.transgender.org

Veterans for Human Rights
www.solnlogic.com/ VFHR2

Youth Assistance Organization
www.youth.org

Rainbow Tassels to be used at Lavender Graduation events
www.goodcatch.com

Anti-LGBT Web Sites

These are Web sites that provide direct evidence of the hatred and discrimination perpetrated by anti-LGBT proponents. Although we abhor having them in our book, we believe it's important for you to know who they are:

American Family Association, Inc.
www.afa.net

Antigay religious organizations (listing)
www.qrd.org/ qrd/religion/anti

Death Penalty for Homosexuals Is Prescribed in the Bible
www.identity.org/files/homo.htznl

Pastor Peter J. Peters
www.identity.org/pjp.htmi

The Pink Swastika: Homosexuality in the Nazi Party
http://home.earthlink.netAively/pscont.htm

Westboro Baptist Church (Fred Phelps)
www.godhatesfags.com

Appendix K: Announcement of the Safe Zones Program to Student and Campus Life Staff

We would like to explain a new and exciting program that has been developed for the UCLA community. The program, which is called "Safe Zones," has been instituted on many campuses throughout the country, and we are pleased to unveil it at UCLA. The purpose of this program is to identify spaces on campus in which those who occupy the space are understanding, non-judgmental and knowledgeable of lesbian, gay, bisexual and transgender (LGBT) people's needs and concerns. The display of a "safe zones" sticker is a symbol of willingness and commitment to provide an atmosphere of acceptance and inclusion. In order to obtain a safe zones sticker, one must attend a 90-minute Safe Zone Training Workshop. These workshops are offered several times throughout the year, with the next being offered on February 10th. The purpose of this workshop is to provide a detailed explanation of the program to ensure that the participants understand the responsibilities associated with displaying a safe zones sticker. During the workshop, presenters also provide a wealth of information related to being LGBT here at UCLA. Safe zone workshop participants receive a literature packet that includes valuable information and resources related to sexual orientation. This packet is a helpful tool for increasing knowledge of the LGBT community. It is our sincerest hope that one day every office, lab, classroom, and residence hall room will display a safe zone sticker. These stickers are a visible reminder to all students, staff, and faculty that UCLA is striving to become welcoming and inclusive of all members of the community. We strongly encourage you to consider attending one of these workshops. If you have any questions about these workshops, or if you would like more information, please contact Safezones@orl.ucla.edu

Appendix L: Testimony to the Regents of the University of California

My name is Dr. Rose Maly. I have been assistant professor of Family Medicine at the UCLA School of Medicine since July of 1994. Within 3 weeks of beginning work in this position, my life partner of 11 years, Sally Ann Armstrong, was diagnosed with breast cancer that had spread to her liver. What proceeded for us was the most nightmarish 2 years imaginable, including multiple courses of chemotherapy and radiation, emergency brain surgery, and a bone marrow transplant.

After waging many tremendous battles with grace and dignity, Sally died at home with me beside her last August 7th. I do not have the words to tell you how much I loved her, how horrifying it was to watch her go through that hell, and how terribly, terribly much I miss her.

Let me tell you how the University of California's current policy on domestic partner benefits contributed to this agony. After her bone marrow transplant, Sally was completely exhausted after having nearly died of septic shock and heart and kidney failure. But because of the critical need to maintain her health insurance, she was forced to go back to work well before she was ready. Sally spent what was to be the last good 8 months of her life commuting in LA traffic and working in a highly stressful job, for the sole reason of keeping her health insurance.

Had we been a heterosexual couple, health insurance would have been available to her through my employment at UCLA, and Sally would have been able to spend those last good months of her life doing the things she really liked and wanted to accomplish.

I cannot state strongly enough how upset I am about the effect this inequity had on the most precious person in my life. It particularly distresses me that a heterosexual colleague of mine was able to obtain health insurance for his spouse immediately after marrying a woman he had known for only a few months, while I could not, despite being in a long term and deeply committed relationship with my partner.

Let me tell you what the consequences of this discrimination could be for the University of California. The position I hold is a tenure-track faculty position designated for a family physician with proficiency in geriatric medicine research. Because of the rarity of such a combination, this position was held open for 8 years at UCLA before the appropriate person was found and recruited. I was also heavily recruited by a number of other major universities, before accepting the position at UCLA. And I have not let the University of California down. Last year I received national recognition for my research in geriatric medicine by winning the American Geriatrics Society New Investigator Award.

I have greatly enjoyed my work at UCLA, but I can tell you that if this inequity persists in the future when I enter into another committed relationship, I am likely to give consideration to a position with one of the many other major universities that offer domestic partner benefits. As a result, a position at the UCLA School of Medicine that took 8 years to fill may go empty.

It is simply not ethical nor just for a major university to continue to stand for discrimination against its employees based solely on sexual orientation. Nor is it in the University's hest interest to discriminate in this way, if it wants to attract and retain the best and brightest faculty and staff.

The Academic Senates of all UC campuses have voted unanimously to recommend that domestic partner benefits be offered by the University of California, as do other major universities, including Stanford, Harvard, Yale, Princeton, Dartmouth, and many others. I strongly urge you to carefully consider the terrible impact that UC's current discriminatory policy has had on this one faculty member, much less on the many other gay and lesbian employees of the University of California, and do whatever is in your power to bring this university in line with the other great universities of this nation as quickly as possible.

Thank you.
Rose C. Maly, M.D., M.S.P.H
Assistant Professor of Family Medicine
UCLA School of Medicine

Source: http://www2.ucsc.edu/uclgbta/dpb/health/press.html

Appendix M: Associations and Agents that Provide Speakers and Entertainers

National Association of Campus Activities (NACA)
http://www.naca.org/
NACA is a member-based, not-for-profit association composed of colleges and universities, talent firms and artists/performers, student programmers and leaders, and professional campus activities staff. It is a clearinghouse and catalyst for information, ideas, and programs promoting a variety of college and university activities, from leadership development to student programming.

Association of College Unions International
http://www.indiana.edu/~acui/
The resources page includes a list of film distributors should you want to bring LGBT films to your campus.

GLAMA: Gay & Lesbian American Music Awards
http://www.glama.com/
The first national music awards program to celebrate the work of openly queer recording artists. The lists of winners and nominees may help you consider whom you want to try to bring to campus.

Specific LGBT/Multicultural Speakers/Agency Resources

Damon Brooks Associates
DBA specializes in disability issues but has a new Gender Studies roster as well.
phone: (323) 465-3400
E-mail: info@damonbrooks.com
http://www.DamonBrooks.com/

Lambda 10: Fraternity & Sorority Speakers on LGBT Issues

Lambda 10 provides a list of names and E-mail addresses for individuals to consider bringing to your campus for lectures and educational presentations on the topic of sexual orientation issues within the college Greek community.
http://www.indiana.edu/~lambda10/speakers_lectures.htm

OUTmedia
OUTmedia seeks to increase the positive visibility of LGBT people through the arts by promoting diversity within mainstream and queer culture. It features out LGBT and queer-affirmative artists (musicians, comics and theatrical performers) and speakers, many rooted in African American, Latino, Jewish, and women's traditions.
285 5th Ave. Suite 446, Brooklyn, NY 11215
phone: (718) 789-1776
E-mail: outmedia@msn.com
http://www.geocities.com/~OUTmedia/index.html

OUTMusic
OUTMusic is part of a nonprofit arts organization called All Out Arts, formerly the Community Lesbian and Gay Resource Institute. It features a variety of up-and-coming gay and lesbian musicians.
http://outmusic.com/

OutRIGHT Speakers & Talent Bureau
OutRIGHT's roster offers comedy, lecture, multicultural programs, theater/Broadway, as well as training/development experts.
Craig Dean
phone: (800) 294-3309
E-mail: outtalent@aol.com

Speak Out
Speak Out, a project of the Institute for Democratic Education and Culture, is the United State's only national not-for-profit speakers and artists agency. It is committed to political, economic, cultural, and social justice. P.O. Box 99096, Emeryville, CA 94662
phone: (510) 601-0182
E-mail: speakout@igc.org
http://www.vida.com/speakout/

Source: This list created by David Barnett and Shane L. Windmeyer for the National Consortium website, www.lgbtcampus.org.

Appendix N: Lavender Graduation Certificate of Distinction

*O*n the occasion of the 5th Lavender Graduation ceremony,
the UCLA Lesbian Gay Bisexual Transgender Campus Resource Center
awards this

Certificate of Distinction

for outstanding contributions to our community as a scholar
and a person of pride, integrity, and honor

to

Casey Gay Bruin

On this 16th day of June, 2001

Ronni L. Sanlo, Ed.D.
Director

References

Allen, W. (1986). *Gender and Campus Race Differences in Black Student Academic Performance, Racial Attitudes and College Satisfaction.* Atlanta: Southern Education Foundation.

American Council on Education. (1997). *Minorities on Campus: A Handbook for Enhancing Diversity.* Washington, DC: American Council on Education.

Andreas, R. E. (1993). Program Planning. In M. J. Barr (Ed)., *The Handbook of Student Affairs Administrators.* San Francisco: Jossey-Bass, 199–215.

Astin, A. W. (1982). *Minorities in American Higher Education: Recent Trends, Current Prospects, and Recommendations.* San Francisco: Jossey-Bass.

Astin, A. W., Tsui, L., & Avalos, J. (1996). *Degree Attainment Rates at American Colleges and Universities: Differences by Race, Gender, and Institutional Type.* Los Angeles: Higher Education Research Institute, University of California.

Barnett, D., & Sanlo, R. (1998). The Lavender Web: LGBT Resources on the Internet. In R. Sanlo (Ed.), *Working with Lesbian, Gay, Bisexual, and Transgender College Students: A Handbook for Faculty and Administrators.* Westport, CT: Greenwood Press, 403–412.

Barr, M. J. (1993). Becoming Successful Student Affairs Administrators. In M. J. Barr (Ed.), *The Handbook of Student Affairs Administration.* San Francisco: Jossey-Bass, 522–529.

Bauder, D. (1998). Establishing a Visible Presence on Campus. In R. Sanlo (Ed.), *Working with Lesbian, Gay, Bisexual, and Transgender College Students: A Handbook for Faculty and Administrators.* Westport, CT: Greenwood Press, 95–114.

Baxter Magolda, M. (1992). *Knowing and Reasoning in College: Gender-Related Patterns in Students' Intellectual Development.* San Francisco: Jossey-Bass.

Berrill, K. (1989). *Anti-Gay Violence, Victimization, and Defamation in 1988.* Washington, DC: National Gay and Lesbian Task Force.

———. (1990). Anti-gay violence and victimization in the United States. *Journal of Interpersonal Violence, 5,* 274–294.

————. (1992). Anti-gay violence and victimization in the United States: An Overview. In G. Herek & K. Berrill (Eds.), *Hate Crimes: Confronting Violence against Lesbians and Gay Men.* Newbury Park, CA: Sage, 19–45.

Bolman, L. G., & Deal, T. E. (1995). *Leading with Soul: An Uncommon Journey of the Spirit.* San Francisco: Jossey-Bass.

Bryan, W. A., & Mullendore, R. H. (1993). Applying professional standards in student affairs programs. In M. J. Barr (Ed.), *The Handbook of Student Affairs Administration.* San Francisco: Jossey-Bass. 509–521.

Cass, V. (1979). Homosexual Identity Formation: A Theoretical Model. *Journal of Homosexuality, 4,* 219–235.

Chickering, A. W., & Reisser, L. (1993). *Education and Identity* (2nd ed.). San Francisco: Jossey-Bass.

Cimons, M. (2000, January 14). Minorities' AIDS Toll Exceeds Whites. *Los Angeles Times,* A13.

Council for the Advancement of Standards in Higher Education (CAS). http://www.cas.edu/

Crist, S. (1990). *Out on Campus.* Bloomington, IN: Association of College Unions-International.

Cullen, M., & Smart, J. (1991).Issues of Gay, Lesbian, and Bisexual Student Affairs Professionals. In N. J. Evans & V. A. Wall (Eds.), *Beyond Tolerance: Gays, Lesbians, and Bisexuals on Campus.* Alexandra, VA: American College Personnel Association, 179–194.

D'Augelli, A. R. (1989). Lesbians' and Gay Men's Experiences of Discrimination and Harassment in a University Community. *Journal of Community Psychology, 17:*317–321.

D'Augelli, A. R. (1992). Lesbian and Gay Male Undergraduates' Experience of Harassment and Fear on Campus. *Journal of Interpersonal Violence, 7*(3), 383–395.

Delworth, U., & Hanson, G. R. (1996). Foreword. In S. R. Komives & D. B. Woodard (Eds.), *Student Services: A Handbook for the Profession* (3rd ed.). San Francisco: Jossey-Bass, xiii–xvi.

D'Emilio, J. (1990). The Campus Environment for Gay and Lesbian Life. *Academe, 76*(1), 16–19.

DePree, M. (1997). *Leading without Power: Finding Hope in Serving Community.* San Francisco: Jossey-Bass.

DiPlacido, J. (1998). Minority Stress among Lesbians, Gay Men, and Bisexuals: A Consequence of Heterosexism, Homophobia, and Stigmatization. In G. Herek (Ed.), *Psychological Perspectives on Lesbian and Gay Issues: Vol. 4. Stigma and Sexual Orientation:*

Understanding Prejudice against Lesbians, Gay Men, and Bisexuals. Thousand Oaks, CA: Sage, 138–159.

Dolence, M. G., Rowlet, D. J., & Lujan, H. D. (1997). *Working toward Strategic Change.* San Francisco: Jossey-Bass.

Dreher, D. (1996). *The Tao of Personal Leadership.* New York: HarperCollins.

Evans, N. J., Forney, D., & Guido-DiBrito, F. (1998). *Student Development in College: Theory, Research, and Practice.* San Francisco: Jossey-Bass.

Evans, N. J., & Rankin, S. (1998). Heterosexism and Campus Violence: Assessment and Intervention Strategies. In A. M. Hoffman, J. H. Schuh, & R. H. Fenske (Eds.), *Violence on Campus: Defining the Problems, Strategies for Action.* Gaithersburg, MD: Aspen, 169–86.

Fassinger, R. (1998). Lesbian, Gay, Bisexual Identity and Student Development Theory. In R. Sanlo (Ed.), *Working with LGBT College Students: A Handbook for Faculty and Administrators.* Westport, CT: Greenwood Press, 13–22.

Fayol, H. (1993). Planning. In M. T. Matteson & J. M. Ivancevich (Eds.), *Management and Organizational Behavior Classics.* Boston: Irwin.

Gaumnitz, L. (1996, July 10). Profs Wary of Gay Safe Zone Stickers: They Don't Want to Send the Wrong Message. *Bellingham (Washington) Herald.* http://personal.ecu.edu/luciera/article1.html

Gose, B. (February 1, 1996). The Politics and Images of Gay Students. *Chronicle of Higher Education, 42*(22), A33–A34.

Harbeck, K. (1997). *Gay and Lesbian Educators: Personal Freedoms, Public Constraints.* Malden, MA: Amethyst Press.

Hothem, K. C., & Keene, C. D. (1998). Creating a Safe Zone Project at a Small Private College: How Hate Galvanized a Community. In R. L. Sanlo (Ed.), *Working with Lesbian, Gay, Bisexual, and Transgender College Students: A Handbook for Faculty and Administrators.* Westport, CT: Greenwood, 363–368.

Human Rights Campaign
www.hrc.org

Iowa State University Safe Zones Web site (1999).
http://www.public.iastate.edu/~clund/safezones/research.html

Jensen, L. (1996). *Embracing Diversity: Lesbian, Gay, and Bisexual Students, Faculty, and Staff at the University of Maryland at College Park.* http://www.inform.umd.edu/LGSF/.index/diverse.html.

Kiechel, W. (1992, May). The Leader as Servant. *Fortune Magazine,* May 4, 1992, pp. 121–122.

Kinsey, A. C., Pomeroy, W. B., & Martin, C. E. (1948). *Sexual Behavior in the Human Male*. Philadelphia: W. B. Saunders.

Kinsey, A. C., Pomeroy, W. B., Martin, C. E., & Gebhard, P. H. (1953). *Sexual Behavior in the Human Female*. Philadelphia: W. B. Saunders.

Klein, F., Sepekoff, B., & Wolf T. J. (1985). Sexual Orientation: A Multi-variable Dynamic Process. *Journal of Homosexuality, 11*(1/2), 35–49.

Komives, S. R., Lucas, N., & McMahon, T. R. (1998). *Exploring Leadership: For College Students Who Want to Make a Difference*. San Francisco: Jossey-Bass.

Komives, S. R., & Woodard, D. B. (Eds.). (1996). *Student Services: A Handbook for the Profession* (3rd ed.). San Francisco: Jossey-Bass.

Kuh, G. D. (1993). Assessing Campus Environments. In M. J. Barr (Ed.), *The Handbook of Student Affairs Administration*. San Francisco: Jossey-Bass, 30–48.

Kuh, G., & Whitt, E. J. (1988). *The Invisible Tapestry: Culture in American Colleges and Universities*. ASHE-ERIC Higher Education Report No. 1. Washington, DC: Association for the Study of Higher Education.

Lark, J. S. (1998). Lesbian, Gay, and Bisexual Concerns in Student Affairs: Themes and Transitions in the Development of the Professional Literature. *NASPA Journal, 25*(2), 157–168.

Lorde, A. (1984). *Sister Outsider*. Freedom, CA: Crossing Press.

Mallory, S. L. (1998). Lesbian, Gay, Bisexual, and Transgender Student Organizations: An Overview. In R. Sanlo, (Ed.), *Working with LGBT College Students: A Handbook for Faculty and Administrators*. Westport, CT: Greenwood, 321–328.

Manago, C. (1999, October 3). Why What Worked for White Gays Won't Work for Blacks. *Los Angeles Times*, M5.

Marcus, E. (1993). *Is It a Choice? Answers to 300 of the Most Frequently Asked Questions about Gays and Lesbians*. San Francisco: Harper.

Markowitz, L. (1998). Invisible Violence. *All in the Family*, 15–21.

Matteson, M. T., & Ivancevich, J. (1993). *Management and Organizational Behaviors Classics*. (5th Ed.) Boston: Irwin.

McIntosh, P. (1989, July/August). White Privilege: Unpacking the Invisible Knapsack. *Journal of Peace and Freedom* (July/August), 10–12.

McNaron, T. (1991). Making Life More Livable for Gays and Lesbians on Campus: Sightings from the Field. *Educational Record, 72*(1), 19-22.

Michael, R., Gagnon, J., Laumann, E., & Kolata, G. (1994). *Sex in America: A Definitive Survey*. Boston: Little, Brown.

Miller, R (2000). Bibliography: Campus Climate Reports. www.lgbtcampus.org

Mitchell, R. L. (1999). *Fables, Labels, and Folding Tables: Reflections on the Student Affairs Profession*. Madison, WI: Atwood.

National Consortium of Directors of LGBT Resources in Higher Education http://www.lgbtcampus.org

National Gay and Lesbian Task Force (NGLTF). (1997). *The Importance of Hate Crime Laws*. Washington, DC: National Gay and Lesbian Task Force.

Nora, A., & Cabrera, A. (1996). The Role and Perceptions in Prejudice and Discrimination and the Adjustment of Minority Students to College. *Journal of Higher Education, 62*(2), 119–148.

Nuss. E. M. (1996). The Development of Student Affairs. In S. R. Komives & D. B. Woodard (Eds.), *Student Services: A Handbook for the Profession* (3rd ed.). San Francisco: Jossey-Bass, 22–42.

Outcalt, C. (1995). Establishing a LGBT Resource Center. In C. F. Shepard, F. Yeskel, & C. Outcalt (Eds.), *Lesbian, Gay, Bisexual, and Transgender Campus Organizing: A Comprehensive Manual*. Washington, DC: National Gay and Lesbian Task Force, 213–268.

———. (1998). The Life Cycle of Campus LGBT Organizations: Finding Ways to Sustain Involvement and Effectiveness. In R. Sanlo (Ed.), *Working with LGBT College Students: A Handbook for Faculty and Administrators*. Westport, CT: Greenwood Press, 329–337.

Peterson, M., & Spencer, M. (1990). Understanding Academic Culture and Climate. In W. Tierney (Ed.), *Assessing Academic Climates and Cultures*. San Francisco: Jossey-Bass.

Porter, J. D. (1998). Leadership Development for Lesbian, Gay, Bisexual, and Transgender Student Organizations. In R. Sanlo (Ed.). *Working with LGBT College Students: A Handbook for Faulty and Administrators*. Westport, CT: Greenwood Press, 307–319.

Puch, D. (2000, January 21). Policies to Keep Gays Safe Urged. *Champaign (Illinois) News-Gazette*. http://www.glsen.org/templates/news/record.html?section=12&record=99.

Rankin, S. (1994). The Perceptions of Heterosexual Faculty and Administrators toward Gay Men and Lesbians. Diss., Pennsylvania State University.

———. (1998). The Campus Climate Report: Assessment and Intervention Strategies. In R. Sanlo (Ed.), *Working With Lesbian, Gay, Bisexual, and Transgender College Students: A Handbook for Faculty and Administrators*. Westport, CT: Greenwood, 277–284.

Rich, A. (1980). *Invisibility in Academe*. New York: W.W. Norton.

Sanlo, R. (1998a, April). Creating a Safe Campus for Gay, Lesbian, Bisexual, and Transgender Students and Student Affairs Professionals: Practical Ideas after Convention Theories. *NASPA Forum, 19*(9).

———. (Ed.). (1998b). *Working with Lesbian, Gay, Bisexual, and Transgender College Students: A Handbook for Faculty and Administrators.* Westport, CT: Greenwood.

———. (2000a, Spring). The LGBT Campus Resource Center Director: The New Profession in Student Affairs. *NASPA (National Association of Student Personnel Administrators) Journal, 37*(3), 485–495.

———. (2000b, November/December). Lavender Graduation: Acknowledging the Lives and Achievements of LGBT College Students. Journal of College Student Development. *Journal of College Student Development, 41*(6).

Savin-Williams, R. C. (1994). Verbal and Physical Abuse as Stressors an the Lives of Lesbian, Gay Male, and Bisexual Youths: Associations with School Problems, Running Away, Substance Abuse, Prostitution, and Suicide. *Journal of Consulting and Clinical Psychology, 62,* 261–269.

Sax, L. G., Astin, A. W., Korn, W. S., & Mahoney, K. M. (1998). *The American Freshman: National Norms for Fall 1998.* Los Angeles: Higher Education Research Institute, UCLA.

Senge, P. (1990, Fall). Learning Organizations. *Sloan Management Review,* (Fall), 10–19.

Shepard, C., Yeskel, F., & Outcalt, C. (1995). *Lesbian, Gay, Bisexual, and Transgender Campus Organizing: A Comprehensive Manual.* Washington, D C: National Gay and Lesbian Task Force. www.ngltf.org

Smith, G. B. (1998, February 20). Breaking Out of the College Closet. *Frontiers Magazine.*

Smith, T. W. (1994a, May). Changes in American Sexual Behavior. Paper presented to the American Association for Public Opinion Research, Danvers, MA.

Smith, W. E. (1994b). *The Complete Guide to Nonprofit Management.* New York: John Wiley & Sons.

Spears, L. (1991, May-June). Servant-Leadership and Experiential Education. *Experiential Education,* 5–6.

Stevens, R. (1992, August 13). Eating Our Own. *The Advocate,* 609, 33–41.

Tierney, W. G. (Ed.). (1990). *Assessing Academic Climates and Cultures.* San Francisco: Jossey-Bass.

Tierney, W. G., & Dilley, P. (1999). Constructing Knowledge: Educational Research and Gay and Lesbian Studies. In W. Pinar (Ed.), *Queer Theory in Education.* NJ: Lawrence Erlbaum.

University of Maryland College. Park President's Commission on Lesbian, Gay and Bisexual Issues. http://www.inform.umd.edu/PCLGBI/

U.S. Census 2000
www.hrc.org

U.S. Department of Education
http://www.ed.gov/offices/OPE/

Waldo, C. (1998). Out on Campus: Sexual Orientation and Academic Climate in a University Context. *American Journal of Community Psychology, 10*(5), 745–774.

Ward, A. (1998). Advising Student Organizations: Opportunities for Student Development. In R. Sanlo (Ed.), *Working with LGBT College Students: A Handbook for Faculty and Administrators*. Westport, CT: Greenwood Press, 339–347.

Weiss, K. R. (1998, June 20). Mixing Commencement and Culture. *Los Angeles Times*, A1, 21.

Zemsky, B. (1996). GLBT Program Offices: A Room of Our Own. In B. Zimmerman & T. McNaron (Eds.), *The New Lesbian Studies: Into the Twenty-First Century*. NY: Feminist Press at the City University of New York, 208–214.

Zimmerman-Oster, K., & Burkhardt, J. C. (1999). *Executive Summary. Leadership in the Making: Impact and Insights from Leadership Development Programs in U.S. Colleges and Universities*. Battle Creek, MI: W. K. Kellogg Foundation, 17.

Index

About the Editors and Contributors

Patricia Alford-Keating is a psychologist at the UCLA Student Psychological Services Center. Pat is the founder and director of the UCLA LGBT Mentoring Program. She and her partner Shannon have been at the forefront of legalizing marriage for same sex couples.

Brett Beemyn is the LGBT Center Director at Ohio State University and editor of *Creating a Place for Ourselves* (1997) and other texts in LGBT Studies, including two works on the experiences of bisexual men.

Christine Browning has worked as a psychologist at university counseling centers throughout her career and works currently at the University of California, Irvine. She has been active in American Psychological Association governance, including President of the APA Society for the Psychological Study of Lesbian, Gay, and Bisexual Issues (Division 44).

Therese Eyermann is an Executive Assistant in the Chancellor's Office at UCLA. She was formerly Coordinator for Program Evaluation and Research at UCLA's Office of Residential Life. Her research interests are in the area of higher education policy as it relates to financial aid and in issues of equity and access.

Steven J. Leider's volunteer work in the LGBT Campus Resource Center began when he arrived on the UCLA campus in 1996 and eventually lead to his being hired there as a full-time career employee.

Sue Rankin is a Senior Diversity Planning Analyst and Coordinator of Lesbian, Gay, Bisexual, and Transgender Equity at Pennsylvania State University. Before moving into her current position, she served for 17 years as the Head Coach for Women's Softball and Lecturer in Kinesiology at Penn State. She has presented and written several papers on the impact of heterosexism in the academy and in inter-collegiate athletics. In addition, she has presented workshops on cultural diversity and heterosexism for several companies (AT&T, IBM, and Xerox). Her research focuses on the assessment of institutional climate and providing program planners and policymakers with recommended strategies to improve the campus climate for under-represented groups. Much of this work focuses specifically on the lesbian, gay, bisexual, and transgender community. In addition, she writes and speaks on the subculture of intercollegiate athletics and the politics of homophobia in sports. She examines the conditions that exist in intercollegiate athletics to silence and marginalize LGBT coaches and athletes. She also serves as the co-chair of the Statewide Pennsylvania Rights Coalition, a network of individuals and organizations across the Pennsylvania Commonwealth committed to securing and defending full civil rights for lesbian, gay, bisexual, and transgender (LGBT) individuals.

Ronni Sanlo is the Director of the UCLA Lesbian Gay Bisexual Transgender (LGBT) Campus Resource Center and teaches in the UCLA Graduate School of Education. Her research area is sexual orientation issues in education. Before joining the staff at UCLA, she was the LGBT Center director at the University of Michigan. She is a frequent presenter and consultant in the area of LGBT issues and services in higher education, the founding chair of the National Consortium of Directors of LGBT Resources in Higher Education, and the past chair of the Gay Lesbian Bisexual Transgender Issues Network for the National Association of Student Personnel Administrators (NASPA). Her books, *Working with Lesbian, Gay, Bisexual, and Transgender College Students: A Handbook for Faculty and Administrators* and *Unheard Voices: The Effects of Silence on Lesbian and Gay Educators,* are published by Greenwood Press.

Robert Schoenberg has been the Director of the Lesbian Gay Bisexual Transgender Center at the University of Pennsylvania, one of the most advanced programs of its kind in the nation, since its founding in 1982. He was the second chair of the National Consortium of Directors of LGBTResources in Higher Education. He edited the collection *Homosexuality and Social Work* published by Haworth Press. In 1989, he was named Social Worker of the Year by the Philadelphia Division of the National Association of Social Workers. A community activist for many years, he served on Philadelphia's first mayoral Commission on Sexual Minorities; was Chair of the Board of Directors of the Eromin Center, which provided counseling services to sexual and gender minorities; and was a founder and first Board President of ActionAIDS, now Pennsylvania's largest HIV service organization. He has twice coordinated the campus track at the National Gay and Lesbian Task Force's Creating Change conference, has frequently made presentations and led workshops at national meetings, and has served as a consultant to several institutions of higher education.

Patricia Walsh is the Director of the University of California, Irvine LGBT Center and is the first director of such a center in the University of California system. She is also a founding member of the National Consortium of Directors of LGBT Resources in Higher Education.

Jonathan Winters is an out, gay, HIV+ man who works at the University of California, Berkeley. As an activist in progressive social movements since childhood, he founded ACT UP East Bay and was a co-chair of the local Host Committee for the National Gay and Lesbian Task Force's 1999 Creating Change Conference. He is a former co-chair and current secretary of the University of California Lesbian Gay Bisexual Transgender Intersex Association.